D0097691

The Scientist as Consultant

BUILDING NEW
CAREER OPPORTUNITIES

The Scientist as Consultant

BUILDING NEW CAREER OPPORTUNITIES

CARL J. SINDERMANN
and
THOMAS K. SAWYER

PLENUM TRADE • NEW YORK AND LONDON

Library of Congress Cataloging-in-Publication Data

Sindermann, Carl J.
    The scientist as consultant : building new career opportunities /
Carl J. Sindermann and Thomas K. Sawyer.
        p.   cm.
    Includes bibliographical references and index.
    ISBN 0-306-45637-0
    1. Science consultants. 2. Science--Vocational guidance.
I. Sawyer, Thomas K. II. Title.
Q147.S562   1997
502'.3--dc21   97-22444
                                                                   CIP

ISBN 0-306-45637-0

© 1997 Carl J. Sindermann and Thomas K. Sawyer
Plenum Press is a Division of Plenum Publishing Corporation
233 Spring Street, New York, N.Y. 10013-1578
http://www.plenum.com

10 9 8 7 6 5 4 3 2 1

Printed in the United States of America

Preface

We are in the midst of a revolution—one characterized by an enormous increase in technology and its applications, and especially by the emergence of almost instantaneous transfer and worldwide availability of information. One concomitant of that revolution has been unequaled expansion of opportunities for consulting by scientists skilled in acquiring, analyzing, and packaging highly technical data and offering advice on science-based problems and issues.

Scientific consulting, like many other forms of consulting, is a dynamic field of economic activity for professionals. It is populated by highly trained individuals who combine their technical expertise and good business practices to provide a service to clients in the form of science-based information and advice not generally available from other sources. This book tries to capture the essence of the scientific consultant and to sketch in some particulars about the field, such as organizing and managing a consulting group, professional ethics, objectivity in data collection and analysis, balanced interpretations of data, marketing strategies for technical skills, performing as an expert witness in legal proceedings, international consulting, and many other aspects.

Scientists usually find employment in one of three

principal consumer categories—academia, government, and industry—although the boundaries of these categories can at times be fuzzy. Consultants are, of course, a subset of the industrial group, although many academic professionals augment their university incomes by doing part-time consulting work. For clarity we note here that the term "consultant" as used in this book (except where otherwise stated) refers to the scientist who is engaged, full or part time, in paid consulting as a *job*, not as a *hobby*—although the book will show how to build a hobby into a part- or full-time profession.

Consultants, as distinguished from scientists employed in industrial research and development organizations, are often individual enterpreneurs rather than salaried employees, and make their own choices as to the kind of work they will accept. Here again, though, distinctions become just a little blurred when we include those consultants who get much or all of their incomes from annual retainer fees paid by large companies rather than from individual project contracts. Are they consultants, or are they simply industry employees without benefit packages? Distinctions can be further clouded by the inclusion of salaried professional employees of large consulting organizations. Are they consultants, or are they only industry employees with benefit packages?

This book is based on three tiers of background information: (1) that which the coauthors have brought to it, based on experiences and observations made during long professional careers, (2) that derived from responses of more than one hundred professional scientific consultants to a detailed questionnaire (a copy of the standard form that we developed is provided in Appendix 1), and (3) that supplied to us during interviews with a selected group of successful scientific consultants. The questionnaire responses have been important in developing a statistical database for the book, but the interviews have been our best sources of information. We must acknowledge the help of those scientists who responded to the questionnaire, and especially those who discussed at length many routine and unique aspects of their work as consultants. We should point out that the italicized vignettes in the book are based on real events, but the names are fictitious and some of the details have been changed to ensure the anonymity of the individuals.

Despite some mention of the downside of scientific consulting, we have been impressed with how often the successful consultants have affirmed their satisfaction and even their pleasure with the career they have chosen. Discussions with those consultants have served to clarify the existence and nature of a discrete kind of employment for scientists, and one worthy of book-length exploration.

Many of the successful scientific consultants admit that their primary occupation is business—but a form of business that depends heavily on professional credibility. The best scientific consultants thus are an amalgam of technical competence and business acumen. These are the professionals best equipped to participate in the revolution.

We thank our editor at Plenum Press, Linda Greenspan Regan, for her initial insight about the potential utility of a book on scientific consulting and for her continuing support, enthusiasm, and editorial contributions during its development. We also thank Mrs. Dorothy Sawyer, president of Rescon Associates, Inc., for her active participation in critical phases of this project.

We acknowledge and affirm that scientists (and scientists who are consultants) may be of either gender, but we employ the pronouns "his" and "he" instead of the awkward and somewhat disruptive "his or her" and "he or she" throughout this book—however unsatisfying this usage may be to some readers.

Contents

Contents

Contents

Introduction
SCIENTIFIC CONSULTANTS—
ON THEIR NATURE

The role of scientists in today's world has been greatly enhanced by the explosive growth of the new technology that they have helped to create. Those of us who fit the category of television-watching newspaper-reading average citizens would probably admit to a love/hate relationship with those scientists; we love the comforts and conveniences made possible through advanced technology and scientific research, but we tend to be uneasy because so much of the technical base of our existence is just beyond (or far beyond) the limits of our easy grasp and full perception. More and more we come to depend on a special class of skilled scientists to interpret environmental and health issues, to provide technical contributions to industrial decision making, and to assist government agencies in assembling and evaluating data for regulatory uses. Members of this special (some might even say elite) class of scientists are called "consultants."

Our mental image of a scientist is frequently that of an academic professional, working almost nonstop in a university laboratory, surfacing only often enough to attend conferences and to hold classes for future scientists—or that of a government researcher, doing project-oriented work while surrounded by a sea of paperwork—or that of an industrial researcher, working in a managerially dominated but well-paying development laboratory. These are not incorrect perceptions, but they do tend to ignore or overlook a unique breed of professionals, namely, those who form and head consulting groups. They are the *scientific entrepreneurs*, who market and sell technical and scientific expertise and advice for a price. They may have come to their present position through industry, government, or university research. They are fundamentally marketing and sales people, as much of their time and energy has to be spent in the acquisition of new contracts. They must, however, simultaneously maintain professional competence and credibility in their own technical specialties.

Scientific consulting can be categorized as both "high profit" and "high risk" for competent professionals. A 1985 publication about consulting and consultants[1] listed 56 consulting specialties in the United States, from "Accounting" to "Travel," and it is likely that many others could have been added (such as "Editorial Services for Writers"). What is important to us here is that in a survey of these groups conducted in 1985, *scientific consultants reported the highest median daily billing rates and the highest median annual income of any category that was included*— surpassing other high-income consulting specialties such as investments, health care, finance, and engineering. How can this be? Was the sampling adequate? Was the truth being told? Scientists are notorious for being consistently at the low end of professional pay scales (when viewed against groups such as physicians, lawyers, and business managers). Have scientists finally found, in a consulting practice, a way to get a fair return on their investment in technical training? If so, are they still finding great satisfaction in their careers? We may be able to offer some insights about these questions in later chapters.

There is, of course, a negative side. New consulting groups are formed every year, but the mortality rate is very high, usually because of too low initial financing, inadequate business procedures, or inability to acquire sufficient contracts. With new firms, the successful completion of an initial contract is a major step toward survival, if not well-being. After that, though, the flow of contracts needs to be continuous, as should be the maintenance of quality in contract performances.

It may be worthwhile, as part of this introductory material, to give a more detailed answer to a basic question: "What is a scientific consultant?" We've wrestled with a good definition, but the subject is so diverse that the best recourse seems to be to list the things that a scientific consultant *does*. So, in response to the question we offer this list:

- One who provides, for a fee, scientific data and/or scientific analyses
- One who provides, for a fee, advice and opinions on matters with scientific content, based on his previous training and experience, and on available information
- One who provides, for a fee, evaluations of the scientific merit of specific proposals, or of the probable scientific effects of such proposals
- One who provides, for a fee, recommendations concerning a proposed action, based on scientific examination
- One who contributes, for a fee, the scientific credibility associated with a reputation in a specific professional subdiscipline

The obvious constant in all of these descriptors of a scientific consultant is "for a fee." The scientific consultant is clearly an *entrepreneur*, selling his expertise, experience, and judgment for a stated price. In this respect he is

unlike most of those scientists who are *employed* full time
by academic institutions, government agencies, or industries to provide scientific services, or who offer free services on a voluntary basis. But maybe it is wrong to
overemphasize the financial aspect of consulting too
early in this book. That aspect is obviously not unimpor-
tant, and we will return to it later, but there are other
considerations—professional reward systems and motivations—that should be touched on lightly in this introductory material (and revisited in detail in later chapters).

Many scientists are remarkably inadequate as businesspeople—and this is understandable, as they usually
want to get on with professional activities (research and
teaching) without investing too much time and thought
in the nuts and bolts of financial matters. These scientists
appreciate an adequate salary (an increasing rarity in
academic science) and are willing to do what is required
for grant applications, but beyond that they want to be
free to do the science that they were trained to do.

The scientific consultant does not fit this character-
ization. He can be equally as competent and credible
professionally as the academic cohorts just described, but
in addition has a dimension that can be identified as
"entrepreneurial" or "business sense." People in this category want to be more in control of the kinds of technical
activities that they engage in, and of the financial returns
on those activities. They tend to be more realistic about
the role of science in today's increasingly technological
society, and often make significant contributions to data
analysis and interpretation.

The motivations of these "entrepreneurial scientists"
are complex. Once beyond the financial component, the
driving forces in a consulting career become varied in the
extreme. Some scientists apply to consulting work the expertise and credibility acquired earlier in academic or

government positions; some find great satisfaction in analyses and syntheses drawn from large data sets; some find challenges in interacting with industry executives and even (ugh!) lawyers; and some provide critical data to environmental agencies and public interest groups. Scientific consultants differ from other kinds of consultants only in the nature of their expertise.

After all of this maneuvering, if we are forced to make a one-sentence response to the question "What is a scientific consultant?" our answer would be something like this: "The scientific consultant is a technically trained entrepreneur who makes available for a stated price his expertise, data, data analyses, evaluations, and recommendations relevant to a client's needs."

We have just roughed out an elaborate if vaguely dissatisfying description of a scientific consultant, but we should probably also present our understanding of the nature of the "science" that we allude to throughout this book. We like the list of characteristics of science that was enunciated more than three decades ago.[2] Principal elements include the following:

- Its terms and descriptions are unambiguous and understandable.
- Its procedures and results are entered into the public domain promptly and in adequate detail to permit reasonable attempts at replication by colleagues.
- Its conclusions are based on data that are accurate and unbiased.
- Its hypotheses depend for validity on adequate reproduction of experimental findings by other investigators.
- Its findings form part of a larger system of verified information leading in turn to a theoretical struc-

ture for increased understanding of the physical universe.

It will become evident later in this book that the kind of science practiced by the consultant is *not* that of the academician, but its core, as described above, does not change—with the possible exception of the sticky matter of timely public disclosure (which we will also address later).

This book is an examination of the phenomenon of scientists functioning as consultants. It attempts to describe the successful scientific consultant and his professional activities. Structurally, the book is partitioned into three major sections. The first contains chapters providing a broad perspective on scientific consulting as a career, the second reviews specific operational considerations for scientific consultants, and the third examines an array of special topics in scientific consulting. Part One— the broad view—has chapters on "The Prospective Scientific Consultant," "Early Phases in the Evolution of a Scientific Consultant," "Distinguishing Characteristics of Successful Scientific Consultants," and "The Transition from Solo Practitioner to Business Executive." Part Two— the nitty-gritty areas of consulting—considers "Organizing a Scientific Consulting Group," "Managing a Scientific Consulting Organization," "Ethics for Scientific Consultants," "Marketing and Selling Scientific Expertise," "Completing the Consulting Assignment," and "Maintaining Professional Competence." Part Three—a potpourri of special topics in consulting—delves into "The Legal Side of Scientific Consulting Practice," "The Downside of Scientific Consulting," "Possible Escape Routes, if Consulting Should Not Work Out," "Megaconsulting Organizations," "International Consulting," "Junior Professional Members of Scientific Consulting Organizations," "University Faculty Members as Scientific Consultants,"

"Retirees as Scientific Consultants," and "The Future of Scientific Consulting."

We think this book will be very useful to those contemplating a career in scientific consulting, and to those who are already committed to it. Parts of it may even be instructive for those who must interact with scientific consultants, as it offers a small window on a demanding but rewarding occupation.

PART ONE

A Broad Perspective on Scientific Consulting as a Career

The first part of the book consists of four chapters:

- Chapter One: The Prospective Scientific Consultant
- Chapter Two: Early Phases in the Evolution of a Scientific Consultant
- Chapter Three: Distinguishing Characteristics of Successful Scientific Consultants
- Chapter Four: The Transition from Solo Practitioner to Business Executive

We've tried in this part to sketch the principal steps in the emergence and development of a scientific consultant, beginning in graduate school and moving erratically and variably through a progression that includes maturation as a scientist as well as acquisition of skills as a businessperson. The text serves to emphasize the diversity of goals, from a lifelong solo practitioner to an executive of a large consulting corporation. It also provides our analysis of the factors that characterize a successful consultant, regardless of the simplicity or complexity of the organization.

ONE

The Prospective Scientific Consultant

motivation for a career shift to scientific consulting • periods in the life span of a scientist when consulting is especially attractive as a career option • resolving uncertainties about becoming a consultant

D emand for the services of scientific consultants will undoubtedly increase in the coming decades, and compensation for technical expertise should likewise increase. It behooves us, therefore, to pay some attention early in this book to three fundamental questions about the continued supply of such professionals:

1. Why do scientists become consultants?
2. When do scientists become consultants?
3. What are the uncertainties that prospective scientific consultants face?

We have assembled some brief responses to these questions, developed from the perspective of addressing the concerns of professionals exploring what is for many of them an entirely new kind of career in science.

WHY DO SCIENTISTS BECOME CONSULTANTS?

After reading some of the manuals and how-to books on consulting published by others, then scrutinizing the responses to our questionnaire, and conducting interviews with scientific consultants, we are left with mixed feelings about consulting as a career of choice for most scientists. Consulting seems so, well, "commercial," with little apparent time to do any science, except to acquire some piece of data to satisfy the needs of a client. It also seems like a high-stress occupation, characterized by an endless search for the next contract, so as to stay alive financially and to run a balanced operation.

Trying to organize our thoughts on this important question of career choices favoring consulting, we have resorted to a pro/con table, listing favorable and unfavorable points side by side (Table One).

Like most objective pro/con tables, this one leads only to a subjective decision—which in the case of the individual scientist must depend on what kind of professional he is. Some scientists truly enjoy research and teaching; others require a structured environment in which to do their work, free from worldly distractions. These types should stay far away from consulting. The more business-oriented or entrepreneurial scientists interested in high incomes, even at the expense of firsthand involvement in doing science, are the ones who should become consultants. Not all or even most of these suc-

Table One
Pros and Cons of Consulting as a Career for Scientists

Pro	Con
Consulting offers an avenue for scientists with some degree of business acumen to capitalize on training and experience—possibly with financial returns far beyond the potential in government or academia	Most scientists have little or no business sense, and do not prosper in a commercial environment. Furthermore, any advantage in annual income can be very variable, depending on the state of the economy and the current demand in any specialty area
Consulting permits a greater flexibility in choosing the kinds of projects that will be accepted—hence the kinds of science that will be practiced	Any temporary shortage of new contracts may make the consultant uneasy enough to accept contracts that are on the periphery of his expertise,or that are routine without any creative component
Consulting frees the scientist from the time commitments of university teaching or the bureaucratic demands of paperwork of government research	Consultant's time can be totally occupied with marketing and selling, or with routine data analyses, or with managing an organization, leaving nothing for the actual practice of science
Consulting offers the midcareer or preretirement scientist an opportunity for a major change in focus, without leaving science completely	Midcareer or retiring scientists may make a change to consulting, only to find that they don't enjoy it and are poorly equipped for it. Any return to a previous position may be difficult or impossible
Joining a consulting company offers entry-level bachelor's degree people an alternative choice for employment in science	Consulting companies offer entry-level jobs to bachelor's degree people, but their duties are often routine, repetitious, or subprofessional, with little opportunity for advancement and minimal job security.

ceed, however, and if they do it is usually as business-people and not as scientists.

In our attempts thus far in this chapter to facilitate the pro/con decision making process favoring or rejecting a career change to consulting, we have still not addressed the two negative descriptors most commonly applied to scientific consulting: "commercializing science" and "high-stress occupation." The charge of commercializing science is to us the more serious—because it is true! Consultants (along with their data, their conclusions, their advice, and their reputations) are for hire—often to people who have their own selfish plans for the use of those commodities. To some observers this seems like a subversion of the noble purposes of science; to others it may appear to be a reasonable attempt to insert some science-based thinking and data into an otherwise subjective adversarial process. This does not imply ethical lapses to satisfy clients' needs. Prostitution is not a part of the commercialization process, nor need it be, as scientific advice and recommendations are based on objective information. The other charge—that of a high-stress occupation—is easier to deal with. Consulting *is* stressful, but then so is any job that pushes people with ambition and competence to the limits of their abilities. Moreover, anyone employed as a scientist these days is likely to be stressed by the prospect of downsizing.

We have introduced, at this suitably early point in the book, the question "Why do scientists become consultants?" We have provided a scrap of analysis here with our pro/con table, and we promise that the question will resurface in later chapters.

Before moving on to the other principal questions about prospective consultants, we should insert here a summary of relevant results from our questionnaire. More than half of our respondents had been consultants for at least a decade, and most had specific career goals in mind before joining the ranks. The most common reasons given for becoming consultants were:

- Freedom to work as an independent professional
- Opportunities for professional growth
- Greater likelihood of achieving career goals
- Opportunities to maximize qualifications and expertise
- Financial well-being

Probably the most frequently expressed career objective was the acquisition of job freedom and the opportunity to use creative abilities—all contributing in a major way to job satisfaction.

"Why" questions always seem to lead to open-ended replies, and to responses that do not always fit easily into neat pigeonholes. Consultants cluster in the creative part of the spectrum of scientific abilities, so it is not surprising that their replies to standard questions would be diverse. We think, though, that in this matter of career motivation, reality has been approximated, and we can move confidently to the second major question: "When do scientists become consultants?"

WHEN DO SCIENTISTS
BECOME CONSULTANTS?

Scientists are fortunate in having chosen an occupation that permits them to have exceptional mobility. Technical expertise is often highly transportable from one to another of the three principal science user groups: academia, government, and industry (Table Two). This unusual flexibility, even during periods like the present one when jobs in science seem to be in short supply, allows a decision in favor of consulting to be made at any point in a professional career (Figure One). Examination of the job

Table Two
Career Categories of Scientists

Type of employment	Initial selective factors	Critical elements
Academic	Interest and ability to interact with students Interest in basic research Some freedom of choice in selecting research projects	Willingness to compete aggressively for research grants Willingness to participate in institutional social and political activities Willingness to balance research and teaching commitments
Government	Interest in participation in long-term goal-oriented research Importance of a high level of job security Importance of the availability of technical support	Interest in large-scale programs concerned with science-related issues Willingness to use a significant part of duty hours for paperwork and other bureaucratic nonsense
Industrial	Interest in research and development narrowly oriented toward new products Interest in patents as research goals	Availability of state-of-the-art equipment Availability of advanced training programs Willingness to accept restrictions on publications and to have research findings become proprietary information belonging to the employer

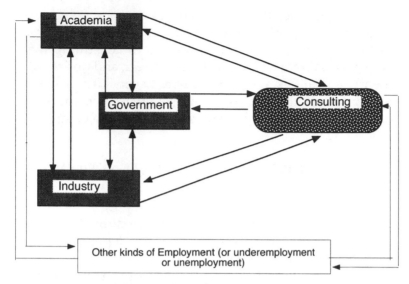

One. Pathways of career changes for scientists.

histories of enough scientific consultants indicates three periods when such decisions are most often made:

1. A direct move from graduate school to a consulting job, often in a trainee role with a large consulting organization
2. A midcareer move to consulting from academia, government, or industry
3. A major career change after retirement, based on expertise acquired in preretirement years

Each of these transition points leading to consulting careers has favorable and unfavorable components that require detailed exploration before the definitive step is taken. This does not imply that any decision is irrevocable, although some midcareer changes are difficult to reverse without loss in scientific status and productivity.

Accepting for the moment that a decision favoring a career in consulting has been made, and that the three major entry points into the universe of consulting that were listed above (early career, midcareer, and postretirement) are realities, we propose here to consider each one in depth, looking particularly for the reasons mentioned earlier for or against the choices made (Table One).

A DIRECT MOVE FROM GRADUATE SCHOOL TO A CONSULTING JOB

For many new scientists, emancipation from the strictures of graduate school or from dependency on postdoctoral appointments can be euphoric. The time has come finally when research projects can be planned and carried out without the required approval of other more senior people, and when escape from the extreme poverty of graduate school existence is at hand. Why shouldn't something resembling euphoria be permitted—at least briefly?

Some new scientists have, however, been so traumatized for so long by absence of a living wage during graduate and postgraduate days that their overriding early objective is to find an entry-level job that will enable use of their training, and will let them begin paying off loans and living like human beings. To these early professionals especially, the salaries and programs of selected consulting organizations can look very attractive, even though the more astute will recognize that a stringent sorting out process will take place resulting in the early disappearance of many in the recruited cohort group. The same astute ones will also accept, with some aplomb, the likelihood of mass dismissals or furloughs or "downsizing" whenever ongoing contracts terminate. These perceptive individuals will not be too chagrined to find that some entry-level duties are at a technician rather than a professional level.

On the sunny side, recruits to a large consulting organization will have an insider's opportunity to study the reasons for that group's success (or lack of it) with a view to applying the winning techniques when it is time to form an independent consulting company. Junior membership in an ongoing firm can provide other learning experiences as well: how to prepare successful contract proposals, how to interact with government functionaries at all levels, how to manage a scientific group, how to participate in presentations and hearings, how to prepare final contract reports, and so on, and all vital to future success.

A MIDCAREER MOVE TO CONSULTING FROM ACADEMIA, GOVERNMENT, OR INDUSTRY

Science is, for most of us, a deeply satisfying occupation. The challenges and joys (yes, joys) of discoveries or new syntheses, or of concept development, are very real. Sometimes, though, the institutional infrastructure of science—whether it be created by universities, government laboratories and bureaucracies, or industrial research groups—can become onerous and restrictive. University salaries never seem adequate, the research grant environment is increasingly competitive, and faculty committee assignments occupy too many hours of the workweek. Government science, federal or state, suffers from endless bureaucratic demands and arbitrary shifts in program emphasis and funding at the whims of legislators or politician-bureaucrats. Industrial science can be confining because of its overriding product orientation and restrictions on publications.

Whatever the precipitating event, midcareer job changes are common among scientists—maybe more so than among many counterpart professional groups. Certainly a good portion of this high mobility derives from availability of alternatives, of which consulting is a very attractive one. Success in consulting depends to a great extent, as will be emphasized throughout this book, on *credibility* that is developed gradually over years of performance, and on *networks* that are developed through long-term interactions with colleagues at professional and personal levels. Fortunately, these critical attributes can be readily transported by the midcareer scientist from several types of positions—academic, government, or otherwise—to consulting.

One very critical decision facing a midcareer science professional contemplating a career change into consulting is whether to establish a solo practice or to join (if only temporarily) someone else's business. There are good reasons for moving in either direction. Joining an ongoing practice is undoubtedly less stressful, as all or most of the start-up problems have been solved, or else the company would not exist. Working for a successful consultancy can be regarded as an advanced apprenticeship—an opportunity to participate in production systems that are effective (e.g., data collection and analysis, marketing, cost control, report preparation, client interactions). Such employment also provides the opportunity to evaluate aspects of the practice that are less successful and to form opinions about alternative approaches. Additionally, being part of a large consulting organization can provide insights about human resources management—good or bad—and about the kinds of personal relationships that make such organizations function well. There are subsidiary reasons for joining someone else's consulting firm. Certainly the contacts with clients and prospective clients—government and private—and the exposure to techniques of getting new business can be important when one makes the move to become an independent practitioner (although we are not in any way suggesting that clients be stolen when that time comes). Additionally, the full realization that scientific consulting *is* a business can be a valuable insight, especially for professionals who have worked previously in an academic environment.

There are, of course, compelling reasons for a decision by a midcareer professional to begin an independent consultancy, rather than to work for someone else. This is the only real test of just how effective and successful a scientifically trained would-be entrepreneur can be in the somewhat alien universe of business. It is not a decision to be made by those with marginal motivation; they probably have a proper niche in the organizational hierarchy of someone else's consultancy. It *is* a decision for those with high motivation to succeed, and a willingness to adapt to totally new environments and methodologies, dominated by a business-oriented perception of science and the world.

A MAJOR CAREER CHANGE AFTER RETIREMENT

Probably the greatest influx of scientists into the ranks of consultants occurs at the time of retirement—voluntary or involuntary—from other types of professional employment. This is an entirely logical career progression, building as it does on the experience, credibility, and contacts acquired up to that point, and buttressed at least partially by pensions or other financial residues from previous work. Consulting under such circumstances can be genuinely pleasurable—without the do-or-die, sink-or-swim financial stresses, and with the opportunity to continue practicing science in areas of individual choice.

It has been our observation that many scientists don't really want to retire, if it means giving up activities that they enjoy. Consulting offers a means of staying alive professionally—of staving off obsolescence—by doing paid research and/or advising in areas of personal expertise. An important fringe benefit is that such employment can prevent decline, through lack of use, in technical capabilities that have been acquired during an entire career. Such a decline in that hard-won expertise is a demon that haunts most scientists.

It has also been our observation that retirement planning by many technical people is predicated on the expectation that they *will* become consultants; that they will become masters of their professional futures by selective acquisition of contracts that make the greatest use of a lifetime of experiences in specialty areas of science. Some expect, too, that they will become involved in areas related to, but not the same as, those that characterized previous employment. This can transform the consulting experience into a personal growth activity, rather than just a retracing of steps already taken. And then there is the matter of money; retirement incomes are rarely, if ever, adequate enough to finance all of the things still to be done in this life. Consulting fees help.

And so we have, thus far in this chapter, tried to respond to the "why" and "when" questions about scientific consulting. Any prospective consultant will still have many other uncertainties that should be addressed, and we have gathered some of them for consideration in the following section.

WHAT ARE SOME OF THE PRINCIPAL CONCERNS OF PROSPECTIVE SCIENTIFIC CONSULTANTS?

Scientists who have made a career transition to consulting often remember the preceding period as one of marked instability and uncertainty. Many significant problems and questions had to be considered and some sort of tentative course of action planned—often to be modified the next day. Retrospective examination and a little soul-searching by some of our interviewees allowed us to assemble a core list of concerns very much on the minds of scientists who were on the verge of electing a career in consulting—concerns that undoubtedly face any professional contemplating a career change of such magnitude. Some of the tougher questions were:

- Where do I get financing, and how much do I need?
- What kind of product will I provide, and do I have the necessary expertise?
- Will I be able to maintain scientific competence?
- Do I have the right temperament to be a consultant?
- Can I run a business successfully?
- Where will I find clients?
- Can I interact effectively and comfortably with clients?

In the long hours of sleepless nights these major problems come crowding in, demanding attention and reasoned evaluation. As a possible contribution to the long-term human quest for peace of mind, we offer some assistance in replying to each of these questions—with information drawn principally from responses to our questionnaire.

WHERE DO I GET FINANCING,
AND HOW MUCH DO I NEED?

Start-up budget projections for a solo consultancy should anticipate at least one year of only minor business income, and probably one or two years beyond that before a break-even point is reached. Survival funding for that predictably lean period should come from personal savings, bank loans, family contributions, or (in the case of retirees) annuities, stocks, pensions, and the like. Unless the proposed consulting services are equipment intensive, start-up expenses for a home-based venture should not be overwhelming, if office equipment, word processing, personal services, and computer costs are kept at absolutely minimal levels.

Of course, one temporary solution to funding problems is to begin consulting on an intermittent or part-time basis, following the well-tested advice always given to freelancers in writing, illustrating, photography, and countless other initially underpaid entrepreneurial occupations: "Keep your day job" (at least until income from consulting offers some hope of providing a subsistence level of existence). Advantages, other than financial, exist when early immersion in consulting is intermittent or part time; probably the most valuable is a low-risk opportunity to "test the waters" for suitability of that occupation on a full-time basis—a test that should also examine the potential for a *pleasurable* as well as a *profitable* career.

WHAT KIND OF PRODUCT WILL I PROVIDE,
AND DO I HAVE THE NECESSARY EXPERTISE?

The consultant's principal stock in trade is *information*—valid, factually based, current, well packaged, and suitably interpreted. Data sources can help shape the nature of the emerging practice, depending on the relative amounts of technical information that are acquired *de novo*, specifically for a contract, and the amounts that are available from published sources. Some consultants emphasize hands-on physical data acquisition to resolve clients' problems, whereas others offer advice and recommendations based almost entirely on available information from outside sources, and on their own experience. Any decision about which direction to orient the practice should be based on the preferences of the individual consultant. Some like active involvement in research-type data collection and analysis, and others are more excited by syntheses and interpretation of data from multiple sources. The right decision can be important to the *pleasure* to be derived from the work—and pleasure should be one reward, as it should be in any scientific effort.

The level of expertise needed for successful completion of any contract is always a factor to be considered in making proposals. Probably the best advice for a new practitioner is to accept work that is challenging, that stretches the limits of available knowledge, and that is creative—but not that which is so far beyond existing personal capabilities and knowledge that it could lead to anxiety, frustration, and failure.

WILL I BE ABLE TO MAINTAIN SCIENTIFIC COMPETENCE?

Being simultaneously a scientist and a businessperson can be a daunting way of life. A strong sense of purpose and a serious commitment to both aspects of scientific consulting are required. Often the scientific component, which is the foundation of the business, can all too easily be slighted in favor of the mundane day-to-day time-consuming requirements of running a commercial enterprise. The problem is not intractable, though, and many consultants have been able to bridge the twin pillars supporting a successful practice: science and business.

Elements that enable success include (1) a resolve to remain alive as a scientist, regardless of other pressures, (2) acceptance of the inevitability that some aspects of technical competence will be affected negatively by those pressures, and (3) realization that the consultant's role in interpreting and applying scientific information to practical problems is an important one—maybe an indispensable one—in today's onrushing technology-based society. There can be comfort too in recognizing that the specter of loss of competency haunts every scientist; there is never adequate time to keep up with developments in a narrow specialty area or in broader but peripheral areas, even for academic scientists.

DO I HAVE THE RIGHT TEMPERAMENT TO BE A CONSULTANT?

This seemingly innocuous question gets us close to the essence of successful scientific consulting. The selective processes that produce technically trained professionals do not favor candidates with high levels of business acumen or intense interest in the details of business practice. The mental characteristics of scientists tend to emphasize creativity, abstract problem solving, appreciation for rigor of proof, validity of data analyses, and a host of other attributes that have little relationship with the world of commerce. It is true, though, that the selective processes that produce scientists do not *exclude* those individuals possessing both characteristics useful in science and characteristics that will be advantageous in a business venture (interest in applications of technical information, abilities in effective communications, enthusiasm for personal contacts with people in many categories, fascination with the financial aspects of living, inherent leadership qualities, and organizing capabilities).

Individuals with a combination of attributes—technical training and appreciation for aspects of business practices—are the ones who do best as consultants. Some of the favorable elements can result from or can be enhanced by training and cultural pressures, but others seem to be innate. The incipient consultant will do well to make a careful assessment of how he views and can interact with the often disparate worlds of science and business.

CAN I RUN A BUSINESS SUCCESSFULLY?

We will reiterate throughout the book that *scientific consulting is a business*—with the clear message that scientists who would be consultants must be, simultaneously, technical specialists and businesspeople. Fortunately, for those suited temperamentally to exist in a commercial environment, there is much about business practices that can be learned from books, seminars, workshops, and college courses. Help is also available (at a price) from accountants and lawyers, when necessary. As to the "successfully" part of the question, much more than business training is required. This is the zone where scientific competence and business practices intersect, and where success is fashioned from elements of each universe.

From our background studies for this book we have developed a short list of maxims about the successful scientific consulting business (in addition to the one italicized in the first sentence of this section). They are:

1. Scientists, because of the usual absence of any attention to business and finance in their technical training, must fill in those gaps in their backgrounds if they are to enjoy commercial success as consultants.
2. Scientists who would succeed in the consulting business must not shrink from investing adequate time in the essential business functions of their practices.
3. A successful scientific consulting business depends fundamentally on the technical competence and credibility of the founder, enhanced and supported by a necessary overlay of effective business policies and practices.
4. A successful scientific consulting business can function at any organizational level, from solo practitioner to megaconsulting corporation, but, at any of those levels, business methodology must be the servant and not the master of the science produced.

This book is replete with other maxims, admonitions, cautions, suggestions, and advice. The short list above is only introductory, but we believe in every item.

WHERE WILL I FIND CLIENTS?

Anyone seriously considering a career in scientific consulting should already have in mind a tentative list of prospective clients. These will be individuals or organizations that may have need for a particular expertise. Prospects may emerge as a result of networking with colleagues in academia, government, or industry. Word-of-mouth advertising can be effective too. Many leads are accidental or fortuitous, but they should be pursued aggressively once a decision to consult has been made. Early contracts, regardless of size, are crucial to survival, for, if carried out professionally and excellently, they can lead to referrals that will constitute the bulk of future business— and they help to establish the consultancy as a viable enterprise. Direct marketing methods—brochures, advertising, and phone solicitation—can be useful too, but referrals from pleased clients, or repeat business from those clients, are the most reliable sources of continuing business, according to the results of our research.

Indirect marketing—activities such as speaking engagements, technical paper presentation, or scientific society participation—can be a source of leads as well, but these tend to be slower to develop and difficult to quantify. It seems, from the information we have, that *professionalism*—demonstrated expertise and credibility combined with outstanding contract performance and efficient business practices—will help ensure a flow of clients, new or old, solicited or unsolicited, that constitutes the lifeblood of a consultancy.

CAN I INTERACT EFFECTIVELY AND COMFORTABLY WITH CLIENTS?

Courses dealing with communication skills and effective interpersonal relationships are not normally part of today's intensive technical education. One of the unfortunate consequences of these deficiencies is that many scientifically trained people, when they elect to become consultants, must function initially as *amateurs* in these areas that can contribute to success. This condition should not persist, as innate capabilities can be augmented by college courses in subject matter areas such as public speaking, psychology, and business management (taken in the evening, after a hard day at the office). Experience is, of course, an additional source of knowledge, but by itself it is an inefficient and often difficult route to follow, and one often marked with failures.

Successful interactions with clients depend on a plethora of variables—speaking a common language (as opposed to technical jargon), appropriate body language, adequate preparation for presentations, straightforward discussion of financial terms, clear indications of professionalism, adequate comprehension and visualization of the problem at hand, appreciation for the client's stature and accomplishments, mutual exchange of information— all of which can enrich what should be an effective and pleasant business relationship. Practice and observation can improve performances, once defects have been identified, but each encounter between consultant and client must be considered as a separate learning experience.

This section on concerns, worries, and uncertainties of prospective scientific consultants has indicated some of the questions that are certain to be in the minds of those poised for the leap. They reflect real doubts about the projected dramatic career shift—and understandably so, for consulting is a perceived outlier as an occupational choice for scientists, as compared with research and/or teaching. We have provided here some glib responses to especially urgent questions—responses that will receive appropriate elaboration somewhere in the chapters that follow.

•   •   •

A decision by any scientist to abandon the familiar career goals of research and teaching in favor of participating in a frankly commercial venture (consulting) is not one to be made frivolously. We have structured this chapter around responses to a series of questions, general and specific, that may help resolve some of the uncertainties that must accompany a decision of such magnitude. The questions are:

- Why do scientists become consultants?
- When do scientists become consultants?
- What are the principal concerns of prospective consultants?

Our responses are based on information from question-naires and interviews; we think they can be useful to the professional contemplating a career change to consulting.

TWO

Early Phases in
the Evolution of
a Scientific Consultant

graduate training of new consultants: mentors
and indoctrination • intermittent and part-time
consulting as entry routes to full-time
practice • factors involved in a decision to
consult on a full-time basis • the critical first
year of a solo consultancy • early appraisal
of success or failure in consulting

This chapter continues our exploration of the early
life histories of scientific consultants. We are now
ready to move beyond the doubts and uncertainties of Chapter One and closer to some decision-making
activities before and after full-time consulting has become
a career choice. We will examine some aspects of the
graduate training of consultants, and then tout part-time
consulting as a favored entry to full-time practice. Once
the part-timer has taken the bait and made a decision to
go full time, we will follow him through that always

33

difficult but sometimes rewarding first year, and then, with the new practitioner in mind, we will propose an early assessment of success or failure, and recommend timely responses to the results of that assessment in terms of subsequent career orientation.

THE NEOPHYTE

Most scientists are trained, nurtured, and mentored by academically oriented faculty members of research universities. It is, therefore, not at all surprising that graduate students are frequently molded and transformed into replicates or at least close copies of their major professors—which implies that the students' perception of science is an academic one, complete with a firm belief in research and teaching as the logical career objectives of all scientifically trained professionals.

Only rarely, and almost incidentally, are graduate students made aware of career opportunities in science that emphasize the *applications* of knowledge, rather than its acquisition and transmission. Those students fortunate enough to be told about alternate occupational pathways are usually so informed by:

- A mentor or faculty member who carries on a part-time consulting practice, and may employ certain graduate or undergraduate students as part-time aides or laborers
- An adjunct faculty member who is a full-time employee of an industrial R&D laboratory, but who teaches one or more specialized courses on a released time basis, and who may facilitate employment of certain graduate students as interns or seasonal assistants

- An adjunct faculty member who is a full-time employee of a federal or state agency with a research and/or regulatory mission, but who offers a university course on a released time basis, and may facilitate employment of certain graduate students as assistants in seasonal field projects
- A successful full-time scientific consultant who, by choice, elects to teach a graduate course in his technical specialty area, and who may employ students as aides for contract field investigations, or who, through consulting networks, may find in other consulting organizations part-time or seasonal jobs for students

Whatever the route of exposure, association as an undergraduate or graduate student with individuals who *apply* scientific information to real-world problems can be a mind-expanding experience—one that might change forever that student's perspective on the true boundaries of science and on the kinds of science that he may wish to pursue in the future. We are sure that many good consultants have been conceived in this way.

But the full story of this early indoctrination has some wormholes in it, as might be anticipated. One potential problem with too-early exposure, as a graduate student, to applied science, as practiced by the mentor who is also a consultant, is that the theoretical and fundamental aspects of basic scientific training (usually referred to as "academic science") may be relegated to the background—to the category of "nice to know, but not too relevant to today's competitive world." This should not be allowed to happen. The sweep and grandeur of academic science must not be compressed or jostled by tendencies to emphasize only utilitarian values of any discipline. Fortunately, most university departments have sufficient depth to ensure student exposure to a wide range of faculty members—most of whom will have a broad perspective on, and approach to, the science that they practice and teach.

Another potential problem with too-early exposure to applied science is a tendency by some new professionals to plunge into consulting too soon, before an adequate base of expertise has been built up, before a reputation has been established in a specialty area, and before visibility in the scientific community has been achieved. The almost universal advice from practicing consultants whom we have queried is, "Acquire a foundation of knowledge and experience in a scientific subdiscipline *before* becoming a consultant."

Of course, the job and financial situation of each new scientist is unique, and is difficult to generalize about, but if circumstances allow, entry into consulting from other professional employment should be *gradual*, through a series of nonbinding steps. For the university faculty member—probably an assistant professor—the method of choice could be a search for and acceptance of *intermittent* consulting assignments in areas related to his research interests. An alternative might be to act as coinvestigator or subcontractor on a colleague's consulting contract. These initial projects should be deliberately spaced so that periodic evaluations could be made at any time. Such a trial period can serve many purposes:

- Most importantly, part-time consulting permits assessment by the junior professional (or any professional, for that matter) of the desirability of consulting as a personal career objective.
- Part-time or intermittent consulting does not, at least at the outset, become so demanding of time and focus as to inhibit development of research projects in more fundamental areas of a specialty.

- Part-time consulting permits the gradual building of expertise in the *business* of consulting (e.g., proposal and report preparation, fee setting, client relations), to occur simultaneously with maturation of the individual as a scientist and accretion of credibility in a specialty.
- Part-time consulting ensures development of a very important list of clients and prospective clients, and an active network of colleagues who also consult—as a bank account for any future more extensive commitment to consulting as a career.
- Part-time consulting affords an insider's view of the careers and lifestyles of full-time consultants, and makes it easier to get advice and opinions from them about consulting as an occupation.
- Part-time consulting affords opportunity for side-by-side comparisons of academic versus applied science, permitting the practitioner to evaluate realistically the *personal satisfactions* derived from both kinds of career emphasis (and those personal satisfactions can be significant in the long term).

A reasonably similar sequence of gradual steps consisting of intermittent consulting projects could be feasible for scientists in industrial research, although the strictures may be more severe than in academia. To some, this would be a form of "moonlighting," so the projects should deal with nonproprietary topics; they should not involve company time or equipment; and they should probably be authorized in advance (depending on company policies about outside work). Of course, in industrial research, and to a lesser extent in academic research, there is always the delicate question of divided loyalties—principal employer versus private entrepreneurial venture.[3] Fortunately, most employers of scientists have encountered these situations previously, and have developed policies to clarify their positions. Regardless of stated policies, though, outside employment can be viewed by some managers and executives as indicating lack of commitment to the full-time job.

THE PLUNGE INTO FULL-TIME CONSULTING

The kind of intermittent consulting recommended in the previous section is a good safe prelude to the giant step—a decision to try full-time consulting, probably as the sole proprietor of a new venture. A solo practice is the most common consulting choice, although other entry routes are available, such as becoming a junior partner in someone else's practice, or becoming a project scientist in a megaconsulting corporation.

One or more precipitating events—some positive and some negative—may force, or at least suggest strongly, that the time to become a full-time consultant is at hand. A sampling of motivating factors would include:

- Good indications that results of intermittent contract studies have been well received by early clients
- Recognition that the list of clients and prospective clients has grown steadily during the trial period of intermittent consulting
- A partnership proposal from a friend who is a consultant
- An offer of a position from a megaconsulting firm
- Downsizing and the resulting disappearance of an industrial research job
- Nonrenewal of a university contract
- Delay in promotion or denial of tenure

- New and onerous faculty committee assignments
- Inability to acquire adequate research grant support

Confidence in the correctness of a move into full-time consulting must be high (even though some lingering doubts may always remain). That confidence can be buoyed by the belief that certain key elements are in order before final commitment:

- The potential for a more than adequate income has been assessed realistically, and a market exists for the consultant's expertise.
- The likelihood of an initial period of lean times has been explored, and is acceptable to the scientist *and* to his family.
- The potential for internal satisfactions as a professional has been evaluated properly.
- Attainable goals have been set in matters of maintaining technical competence, participating in the affairs of science, and personal interactions with colleagues.

The moment for action is finally at hand, and it is time to release the trapeze (always with the comforting realization that a safety net—retreat to the university or to industrial research—exists, even though reentry may be somewhat painful).

THE CRITICAL FIRST YEAR

The solo practitioner can be seen, figuratively, standing out there somewhere on the boundary separating an informed technical community from a vastly larger but scientifically illiterate populace—some of whose members need and are willing to pay for information for their own uses. The individual consultant has little visible support (except perhaps an intermittent secretary and a partly furnished home office), but has many critical but invisible resources: background and experience in a technical specialty, support from networks of peers and other colleagues, access to the scientific literature, access to computerized information sources, and contacts with government and private funding sources. The challenge for the practitioner—and it can be a daunting one—is to make possible the transfer of relevant information and advice from the scientific community to the user groups, and to do so in an efficient businesslike manner. That is the essence of scientific consulting, but the essence often gets lost in details, and this chapter is about those details, especially as they crowd the existence of a new consultant during the first year of his commitment to full-time practice.

So many things must be done, and done well, during that busy but exhilarating entry year. Here is just a sampling:

- A place of business must be established. The home office is a first option, because it is inexpensive and it provides a tax write-off. Despite some obvious disadvantages (such as lack of privacy and inadequate storage space) we recommend a home office initially, assuming that the technical activities of the consultancy are not equipment intensive.
- A major effort must be made to obtain signed contracts for projects, large or small, that can produce the initial income of the venture, and, if completed in exemplary fashion, can begin to shape the reputation of the enterprise.
- A major effort must also be made to develop and then expand a list of potential clients. The list can include referrals from professional friends and colleagues, leads from published sources, leads

from networking sources, or positive responses from marketing activities.

- A significant effort should be made to market the expertise and capabilities of the consultancy, especially those specialties that are unique or uncommon. Marketing can be either direct (through personal contacts or interviews with potential customers, phone solicitation, media advertising, or general distribution of a distinctive and informative brochure) or indirect (by presenting invited talks to service clubs, presenting technical papers at local or regional scientific meetings, networking with colleagues, or contacting business leaders in person).

- Technical work specified in existing and new contracts must receive principal attention, to ensure that it is done excellently and completed on time, with results incorporated into superb final reports.

- Networking with colleagues, competitors, prospective clients, and contacts within known funding organizations should be a significant part of every workday.

- Some minor effort should be made to read a few journals, attend an occasional seminar, or go to a regional scientific meeting—recognizing that these activities will usually be preempted by business demands.

Remember that all of these time-consuming business activities must be carried out by *one person*—the solo consultant—who *is* the company, and who will be responsible for the daily nitty-gritty functions like preparing mailings, answering the telephone, buying office equipment and supplies, traveling to meet with potential clients, and many other routine chores.

Remember, too, that this is a *science-based consultancy*,

which requires that the science be current—a very difficult requirement, even assuming that the practitioner began with a high level of competence and has made sporadic efforts to maintain it.

Remember, also, that the consultancy is planned to be a *profit-making venture*. To this end, expenses must be kept at minimal levels, especially during the initial period of existence, and fees must be set at a level that includes a reasonable profit.

Remember, finally, that the consultancy exists to produce a form of scientific information that is useful to clients—and that anything else must be subsidiary to that role.

AN EARLY APPRAISAL
OF SUCCESS OR FAILURE

Notwithstanding that the average professional career spans three to four decades, the *course* of that career is often fixed during the first decade, even though explorations of alternatives in the practice of science can be made at any time up to and including retirement (as pointed out in Chapter One). Scientists may be intelligent, creative, and dedicated people, but often, as an occupational group, they are conservative or even ultraconservative about making personal decisions that affect their future development as professionals. Commitment to consulting represents, for many technically trained people, a major decision point in their lives, but not one that is immutable. We therefore propose in this discussion that an early appraisal of success (or failure) should follow a one-year trial period as a full-time consultant, and results of that evaluation should be critical to any decisions about a next career step.

Elements that should be part of an early assessment of success as a full-time consultant include:

- Financial reward level, measured in terms of existing and projected contracts
- Personal sense of accomplishment, satisfaction, and pleasure
- Progress as a businessperson
- Status as a scientist: publications, meetings attended, and oral presentations made
- Personal interactions: client relationships
- Referrals: abundance thereof

If the objective one-year assessment proves to be positive, then the choice of full-time consulting was probably a good one, and consulting could become a lifetime occupation. The new consultant should not be satisfied with quick success, though, for much remains to be discovered and accomplished. An important lesson to be learned early is that exceptional work must be done—always—as competence, vigorously applied, is what all prospective clients are searching for.

If the objective assessment, on the other hand, adds up weakly or poorly, the new consultant should do something else—go back to research and/or teaching, take a postdoctoral appointment, teach in a community college—but should not keep doing a professional job at *any* level of mediocrity. Technical training is too valuable for that, but it can also be a transient and rapidly eroding asset if not put to intensive use. Maybe the new consultant's aptitudes for business are weak; maybe his specialty is not currently in demand; maybe marketing has not been aggressive enough; maybe entrenched competition is too strong—so many "maybes" but only one reality, namely, consulting may not be the best choice of a career for every scientist, and the time to recognize this should be sooner rather than later. One year, to some observers, may seem too short as a test period; if so, then a later deadline could be set—but never more than three years to reach profitability and a satisfactory professional comfort level for the practitioner.

●　　　●　　　●

Early phases in the evolution of a scientific consultant—the neophyte, the part-timer, and the beginning full-time practitioner—encompass a period of rapid change and growth in a professional career. Early interest in applied science may be created in graduate school, and may lead to intermittent consulting projects carried out in the early years of an academic or industrial research career—when a reputation as a scientist is being developed. At an appropriate point in the life history of a scientist interested in consulting, a major career change to full-time practice may be made. Critical actions and events during the first year of that total commitment— positive and negative—can help to shape that individual's entire future. A reasonable view of that future can usually be seen by the end of the first year of full-time consulting; this is a good time for decisions about the kind of science that offers the greatest individual satisfaction.

THREE

Distinguishing Characteristics of Successful Scientific Consultants

the success triumvirate: technical proficiency,
interpersonal skills, and business acumen •
the general reward system of scientific
consulting • case histories of successful
scientific consultants • credibility as a
success factor

Successful scientific consultants, as individual entrepreneurs, must achieve and exhibit a workable mix
of three sets of characteristics: one related to technical proficiency, another to interpersonal skills, and a third
to business practices. Of the three, technical proficiency is
undoubtedly most important, but it cannot prosper without the more mundane supporting categories of good
interpersonal skills and efficient business practices. To
begin an exploration of these categories that contain the

ingredients of success, we have chosen gross dissection of each, followed by microscopic examination of their component parts.

TECHNICAL PROFICIENCY

There can be no question that credibility and competence are the foundations of any consulting venture. The scientific consultant can make a unique contribution to the resolution of problems or disputes by providing interpretations of technical data, as well as professional opinions on the value of the data. Most of the worth of that contribution depends on the consultant's credibility as a scientist, and his competence in the relevant specialty area(s). These are qualities that can only be acquired by training and long experience, punctuated by brilliant insights and deductions, and accompanied by skillful presentations of findings. *This* is what credibility is all about, and it is a scarce commodity. Credibility, once acquired, tends to persist as a constant over the years, provided that technical competence is maintained—which is not an easy task for consultants.

CRITICAL INTERPERSONAL SKILLS

Taking technical proficiency as a necessary given, the second category—interpersonal skills—contains elements that contribute significantly to the success of a consulting venture. We have identified three of these elements: (1) skill at professional networking, (2) excellent negotiating abilities, and (3) effective personal relationships. Each requires some initial investigation.

SKILL AT PROFESSIONAL NETWORKING

The old and incorrect perception of the scientist as a laboratory-bound asocial loner has just about disappeared—replaced by the more realistic image of an aggressive team player who interacts constantly with associates, attends professional meetings, and travels frequently to confer with colleagues and present seminars. This socially adept scientist talks to many people, and in the process develops complex communication webs, some of which persist for long periods of time. These communication networks can be of particular significance to scientific consultants, helping them to keep up with the literature and with new techniques. Frequently a casual conversation with a colleague at one of the interstices of the networking web can lead to a joint project proposal or to information about future funding sources or potential clients. Sometimes, too, the network can be the best source of information about competitors, and even about their relative effectiveness. The network is also a constant source of information about failures, poor contract performances, or other aspects of the downside of consulting life. For the perceptive participant, these observations can provide wisdom about one's own practices.

But the successful consultant has a deeper understanding of networking than that presented by the idealized model just described. He knows that networking by scientific consultants is not the relatively straightforward give-and-take process that characterizes the professional interactions of academic or even government research scientists. Exchanges are subject to many of the same strictures that limit professional communications of industrial research scientists, and new limits are imposed. Some realities of networking for scientific consultants are the following:

- Networking can be a highly *selective* process; not everyone is welcome to the net, and many applicants are actively excluded.
- Networking contains no element of altruism; it operates on the principle of *quid pro quo*, with a rigid system in which credits and debits are carefully tallied.
- *Trade secrets* are excluded from networking as it is practiced by consultants. On the restricted list would be such topics as how to get international contracts, new sources of funding, or names of productive contacts in government agencies— anything that might give a competitive advantage to a "colleague."
- Discussions of proprietary information are verboten—even at the very real risk of incurring the disfavor of others in the scientific community.

Networking with colleagues by scientific consultants can be compared to negotiating a thicket of fruit-bearing thornbushes. Sensitivities and minor traumas abound, although unexpected advantages may accrue during the trip.

EXCELLENT NEGOTIATING ABILITIES

The technical consultant has a special role to play in resolving disputes that include the interpretation of scientific data. Because of training and/or experience, the consultant can be expected to provide an unbiased technical opinion based on analysis of available information, and to provide it in a form that is fully intelligible to the client. Quite often the consultant makes the sole scientific input to the resolution of a problem; the consultant *is* the science advisor, and is expected to suggest ways to mitigate damage or potential damage (in the special case of environmental disputes), and to present optional courses of action in any kind of dispute.

But negotiating can be important to success in a much broader sense than that of a technical advisor helping to resolve a problem. It permeates the entire consulting practice. Negotiations with clients can affect fees, details of contract specifications, delivery dates, nature of the final report, and any follow-up activities; negotiations with other consultants who act as subcontractors can help to determine price, areas of responsibility, extent of staff involvement, and scheduling of work; negotiations with representatives of regulatory agencies can identify and reduce any confrontational aspects, and lead to rational compromises.

We are convinced that negotiating skills are critical to viable consultancies—probably more so than for most other businesses—because of the greater flexibility of the consulting practice, and because so much depends on intangibles, such as mutually agreed on objectives, assumption of ethical conduct, technical competence, and professional credibility. The range of items subject to negotiation is remarkably broad; this can act to increase rewards for the skilled practitioner.

EFFECTIVE PERSONAL RELATIONSHIPS

We introduced the concept of networking in the first part of this section, indicating that it is an indispensable characteristic of successful consultants. What was not covered then, and should be now, is *how* interactions with other people—colleagues, competitors, or clients—can be all-important to success. One of the real joys of a scientific career is frequent contacts with bright, vocal, and informed peers and colleagues. Consultants get this in abundance. They also interact with intelligent perceptive members of other groups—clients, potential clients, lawyers, representatives of advocacy groups, and government bureaucrats. Effectiveness in most of these interpersonal encounters is usually a blend of experience, applied psychology, technical competence, and positive self-image. To some consultants, maintaining good customer relations is the key ingredient of successful practice, even ranking in importance above technical skills.

Liberal quantities of the two principal attributes—technical proficiency and interpersonal skills—are commonly found in successful scientific consultancies, but they are not enough. They must be accompanied by elements that we have lumped together in the third and final category, correct business practices.

CORRECT BUSINESS PRACTICES

Consulting is a highly specialized business, so some further practical criteria of success turn out to be not too different from those that characterize other kinds of businesses and businesspeople. Included in the litany should be (1) development and maintenance of efficient and effective business practices and attitudes, (2) marketing skills, (3) high level of abilities in human resources management, (4) exceptional personal presentation (appearance and communication skills), and (5) effective time management. Each of these should be examined briefly at this point in the narrative and reviewed in greater detail in later chapters.

EFFICIENT AND EFFECTIVE
BUSINESS PRACTICES

Consulting is a business, and to be successful it must be approached and managed as such. Acceptance of this dictum requires some (and often much) reorientation in thinking and acting by scientific consultants. Practices and procedures common to most businesses—all of the elements discussed in introductory community college business management courses—need to be applied. Included would be topics such as cost accounting, choice of organizational structure, tax advantages and disadvantages, prompt billing procedures, meeting deadlines for contract proposals, and submitting reports when due. If other staff people are hired, a host of additional human resources considerations appear—benefit packages, supervision, motivation, evaluation, promotion, termination—all items that must be handled effectively by a postmetamorphic scientific consultant. Of course, the individual entrepreneur is not subject to some of these added burdens, but even the smallest consulting group needs periodic advice from a good professional accountant (and possibly a management consultant too).

PROFICIENCY IN MARKETING

Consulting organizations differ from many businesses in that their product or service is information, usually in the form of a report or data set with interpretation. As with more tangible products of other businesses, quality is critical to marketing. Marketing efforts of successful consulting groups often focus on demonstrated excellence in previous contract performance. In the case of individual entrepreneurs, specialized or unique knowledge and techniques often form the basis for repeat business.

All of this is not to imply that aggressive marketing, in the form of queries, responses to requests for proposals, or even unsolicited proposals, should not be a part of any sales strategy. Contract awards are usually based on a blend of proven competence and a correct correspondence chain from initial query to definitive proposal.

HIGH LEVEL OF ABILITIES IN HUMAN RESOURCES MANAGEMENT

Most consultancies are not big enough to afford a full-time human resources specialist. This usually means that the owner-director (or one of the principals) must handle personnel problems, large and small. The way in which he carries out the added assignment—with whatever skill or native ability he has—can do much to influence the kind of work environment that will characterize the company. Critical aspects of the job are hiring, counseling, and firing. None of these functions is included anywhere in the graduate curriculum of most scientists. Fortunately, if the new responsibilities show signs of persistence, specialized human resources courses are available at most community colleges or schools of business management.

Probably more important than formal courses, though, are the attitudes and policies of the owner-director. A sincerely caring and egalitarian business philosophy diffuses quickly to senior staff members, especially if the expectation of such an operating policy is reemphasized periodically. A reality to be considered, though, is that consulting groups do have a high ratio of professionals to nonprofessionals, and some professionals do expect special perks or freedoms not available to the rest of the staff.

Uncorrected, the presence of too many distinctions between professionals and nonprofessionals can affect productivity, encourage turnover, and reduce the expected pleasures of consulting work.

EXCEPTIONAL PERSONAL PRESENTATION

The award of a contract to a scientific consultant is and should be based on the client's expectation of competence, ensuring that the proposed work will be done efficiently and well. This seems almost axiomatic, but there are so many nuances and minor factors that contribute to a go or no-go decision by a client—some of them extraneous or subjective, but not to be dismissed too easily. The impression that the consultant makes on a prospective client with little things like how he is dressed as a businessperson, whether he seems knowledgeable in the area of the proposal, whether he seems relaxed or ill at ease, what kind of eye contact is made—all are registered as background to the decision to hire one consultant and not another.

EFFECTIVE TIME MANAGEMENT

A concept that is familiar to all people who have ever taken a business management course but seems unfamiliar to most scientists is time management—organizing work habits to make the best use of every minute of the workday. The guiding principle, for scientific consultants, seems simple enough: maximize the return on billable time and make certain that every possible hour is billable. This principle is perfectly obvious to lawyers and physicians, but it seems to elude many technically trained specialists. The deficiency is probably an unfortunate consequence of that very scientific training, which often seems less time-driven than most other professions.

Whatever its origin, inability or unwillingness to manage time effectively can be one sure pathway to failure for a scientific consultant. Among the many behavioral changes that a new consultant must make is to recognize the deficiency in his training, and to develop a rigorous replacement program of time control. Some important ingredients of the program would include developing and maintaining a strict written hourly schedule of projected activities, confining telephone use to specified hours through use of answering devices, being sure that time spent in travel is fully accountable, and making use of every lunch period for client contact or networking with colleagues.

Successful consultants take time control techniques to even higher levels, making full use of electronic communications (e-mail and Internet), and allocating specific but carefully restricted portions of the workweek to non-billable activities (e.g., journal reading, new marketing approaches, refresher training). Initial attempts at rigorous time control may seem foreign to new consultants who come from previous jobs in academia, but if pursued aggressively these measures can become routine after a difficult break-in period, and can be essential to success.

This description of characteristics of successful scientific consultants—superior competence and credibility, skill at networking, excellent negotiating abilities, effective interpersonal relationships, efficient business practices, proficiency in marketing, high level of abilities in human resources management, exceptional personal presentation, and effective time management—can provide an initial insight into how successful consulting businesses are created and fostered. It should be obvious, though, that such an ideal combination of virtues would be unusual in the real world, and would be more in the nature of a long-term goal, to be achieved some day, but not tomorrow. Examining these attributes of successful ventures can serve another purpose: as a model for organizing and managing consulting groups—to be considered in Chapters Five and Six.

THE GENERAL REWARD SYSTEM OF SCIENTIFIC CONSULTING

Success in scientific consulting is so important, but so elusive as a discussion topic, that we have chosen to take four different approaches to it. You have just read the first: a listing and brief description of the outstanding characteristics of successful practitioners and practices. Our second approach is to consider the general reward system of scientific consulting, and how it is viewed by successful practitioners.

We have found in our background research that successful scientific consultants are usually quite willing to discuss their perceptions of what constitutes success and how it can be achieved. The topic is often intertwined (in their thinking) with what we call the "general reward system" of technical consulting, and because that system serves as a primary motivator for success, it needs to be scrutinized carefully.

In trying to identify and encompass the elements of the reward system of consulting, as perceived by its practitioners, we quickly began to recognize key words being used by them repeatedly in questionnaires and interviews. Most frequently encountered by us were:

- Financial advantages, open-ended

- Freedom of choice in selecting projects
- Flexibility in hours worked
- Independence in making decisions
- Relationships with competent aggressive colleagues
- Absence of structured supervisory levels
- Problem solving in the real world
- Applying scientific information to issues of significance
- Meeting challenges presented by each new client
- Providing meaningful advice to clients, and finding it to be useful to them
- Internal personal satisfactions from superior performance of contract responsibilities
- Professional growth through necessary involvement in new technical areas
- Expansion of skills in interpersonal relationships
- Acquisition of competence in interactions with the legal universe
- Opportunity to straddle more than one kind of science practice (e.g., consulting and teaching)
- Greater control over professional destiny

In scanning this list of frequent responses to our questionnaires about elements of the reward system that are important to scientific consultants, it is apparent that rewards are both professional and personal. As might be expected, the weight of an individual component of the system can vary greatly, depending on the background, attitudes, and experiences of the practitioner.

This, then, is our perspective on the second approach to capturing the essence of success in scientific consulting—consideration of the general reward system that has evolved. We are now ready for a third approach: discussion of case histories of scientific consultants who, in our opinion, are successful in their chosen occupations.

CASE HISTORIES OF SUCCESSFUL SCIENTIFIC CONSULTANTS

An ancient and somewhat shopworn tale chronicles the reactions of three blind men to their first tactile experience with an elephant. The first, touching the trunk, described the beast as much like a fire hose; the second, feeling the leg, described the animal as much like a tree; and the third, grasping the tail, found the elephant to be remarkably snakelike. Each, of course, was right and wrong, and so it is for our attempts to identify the ideal (successful) scientific consultant. Which one of the following descriptions would you select?

1. The ideal scientific consultant is one with high native business savvy who has acquired technical credibility in someone else's research organization (university, government, or industry), and then has transported this business savvy and professional credibility to a new joint entrepreneurial venture with two other colleagues. The business is starting small but it is adequately capitalized and has a business plan aimed at growth.

2. The ideal scientific consultant is one who came ten years ago to an entry-level job with a large successful consulting company. She had a bachelor's degree, high intelligence, business sense, good writing skills, and a lot of energy. She was a quick learner and a survivor, and eventually a good supervisor. After several years she returned to graduate school in a specialty relevant to the company's area of emphasis, on a released time basis. She then rejoined the company full time in a midlevel managerial position. After a few years she transferred all of her experience and training to a new entrepreneurial venture of her own.

3. The ideal scientific consultant is one who ascended during a long career to the upper managerial–executive ranks of a science-oriented federal agency, where he was involved in regional and national planning, and in implementing large field programs. His work assignments included interactions with foreign countries and international organizations, in advisory capacities. He liked what he did, but the federal salary cap seemed too restrictive. He also became more and more disenchanted with bureaucratic strictures and political budget manipulations. He left the government on short notice and, with several colleagues from universities, formed an international consulting company that specializes in providing advice to intergovernmental commissions, United Nations agencies, and Third World countries.

4. The ideal scientific consultant is a university professor with an international reputation in one of the emerging subdisciplines of high-tech science. He has published a series of so-called "seminal" papers in his area of specialization, and is in demand at society meetings and international symposia. Much of his research has potential industrial applications, and he has a continuing retainer contract with one of the larger multinational chemical companies. He prefers to remain an academic, however, as he finds the mix of research and graduate teaching best suits his personal and career goals.

To choose our ideal scientific consultant from these options would not be possible. They are all successful, by anyone's criteria, but they are also unique in what they do and how they do it.

Here, then, in this section on case histories, we have continued an attempt to encircle the elements of success in scientific consulting—following earlier approaches that delineated the outstanding characteristics of successful consultants, and then considered the general reward system for successful practitioners. It is now time for our fourth and final approach to a clearer perception of what succeeding in this specialized consulting business implies. For this, we propose a more detailed examination of the all-important concept of credibility in science and scientific consulting as a key to success.

CREDIBILITY AS A SUCCESS FACTOR IN SCIENTIFIC CONSULTING

Defining success in scientific consulting has proved to be difficult enough with the approaches already used in this chapter, but we have one more intangible to add to the formula, namely, credibility as a scientist and as a scientific consultant. In our opinion, credibility as a scientist is essential to long-term success as a consultant. Our descriptors for a credible *scientist* are the following:

- One who has earned a place among peers by acquiring advanced degrees from reputable universities
- One who has conducted original research and has published the findings from that research in peer-reviewed journals
- One who has given evidence of broader thinking in his specialty area through development of syntheses, concepts, or principles
- One who participates in the activities of professional societies in his area of specialization

- One who subscribes to a code of ethical practices in the conduct of science
- One who interacts frequently and effectively with peers and other colleagues
- One who expresses reasoned opinions on issues that affect the practice and future of science
- One who exhibits a high degree of professionalism in all kinds of public forums
- One who has achieved recognition from peers as a significant participant in the development of a specialty area within a discipline

Scientific credibility can be translated into successful consulting practice in several ways. Most important, it is a critical attribute that every prospective client will be concerned about and will include in decision making about contract awards. Additionally, it is an important consideration in any legal proceedings in which a consultant appears as an expert witness. It is also an important marketing factor for any consulting organization. Distinguishing characteristics of a credible *scientific consultant* include the following:

- One who has achieved recognition among peers for expertise in a specialty within a scientific discipline
- One who is capable of translating technical information into language understandable to nonscientists
- One who has a history of successful completion of contract responsibilities, without cost overruns or client complaints
- One who achieves reasonable organizational financial stability
- One who interacts effectively with the public, with industry representatives, with government bureaucrats, and with politicians

- One who is carefully and consistently ethical in all interactions with clients and competitors
- One who publishes occasionally on material relevant to science, to consulting practice, or to business in general
- One who interacts freely and comfortably with colleagues and competitors, and is an important member of professional networks

When the credible scientist and the credible scientific consultant are embodied in the same person, this is usually the formula for success, especially for solo practitioners.

Technical credibility of the company's key staff members can be augmented by the organization's credibility as an ethical consulting firm—an attribute that can be acquired and fostered by correct business practices. A consultancy that consistently meets or exceeds contract specifications acquires credibility. One that produces excellent and usable final reports also acquires credibility, as does one that works effectively (sometimes even cooperatively) with other consultants, or one that is noted for good human resources management and fairness in contract negotiations.

Credibility can serve one other less obvious purpose. Senior consultants, because of their real-world orientations combined with their technical backgrounds, can often act as catalysts, bringing together people with disparate viewpoints and perspectives on a particular issue or problem. Consider the land use area, in which the development of agricultural land is in dispute. Here developers, politicians, regulators, and environmentalists might be convinced by a consultant with adequate credibility to meet and explore issues and options, before resorting to legal actions. Or consider disagreements over shoreline modification, where a consultant with an impeccable reputation—a person well known in political, regulatory, and scientific circles—could assume a catalytic role as leader of a continuing advisory group, to ensure a modicum of rationality in the decision making process.

Most of us know or have heard of such individuals, who are capable of "bringing it all together"—or energizing people with widely divergent attitudes to reach a common understanding on a troublesome issue. This is a function that a consultant with appropriate credentials can assume. If the job is carried out with great skill, such a "group dynamics facilitator" (who may also be a scientific consultant) can find a rewarding new aspect to an already satisfying career.

> A superb example of a consultant who fits our concept of a catalyst is Dr. L. E. Crawford, who was first a research biologist, then a laboratory director, then a university professor, and then a research consortium president. He acquired credibility as a scientist early in his career, and as a state research laboratory director he learned about politicians and how to survive and prosper in an intensely political environment. His university appointment brought close contacts with academic scientists, and his consortium tenure offered opportunities to carry his natural abilities in leading group interactions to truly professional levels. With all of this as background, he began a postretirement career as a consultant—in a very special kind of consulting that emphasized attempts to blend interests of politicians, natural resources experts, public interest organizations, and government agencies. One of his greatest successes was the formation and implementation of a multistate aquatic pollution abatement program, with major federal funding, and with full participation from state politicians, state natural resources agencies, universities, and federal agencies. The program, now in its tenth year, has been recognized as a national model for cooperative environmental action. Although many scientists, bureaucrats, politicians, and concerned citizens

contributed significantly to the positive results obtained, Dr. Crawford was, in most people's view, the key—the catalyst.

Admittedly, the kind of consulting that we have been discussing here, represented by scientists like Dr. Crawford, is elitist and not accessible to every practitioner. But it does exist as an example of the various career paths that become available to scientific consultants with special abilities and interests.

●   ●   ●

Here, then, are four approaches to understanding the nature of success in scientific consulting: (1) a listing of outstanding characteristics of successful practitioners, (2) an examination of the reward system for successful consultants, (3) case histories of successful consultancies, and (4) an investigation of the role of credibility in successful consulting. Because consulting firms vary so much in size, objectives, and operations, it is not easy to assemble a short list of overriding principles, but we'll try:

- Success can only result from intimate association of good science and effective business practices.
- Success is measured by a reward system consisting of tangible and intangible benefits—any one of which may have variable significance to practitioners.
- Success frequently depends on unique characteristics of the principal practitioner(s).
- Success requires the existence of credibility—scientific and organizational.

We leave this topic of success in consulting with some vague unease—an uncertainty that all of the ingredients have been added and have blended adequately. Maybe that feeling is not uncommon when dealing with intangibles such as "success." We do know, however, that there are many successful scientific consultants, and we are convinced that they have certain characteristics by which they may be recognized.

FOUR

The Transition from
Solo Practitioner
to Business Executive

is growth of a consultancy inevitable?   •   if so,
why do some ventures remain small?   •   a
generalized progression of steps leading to the
emergence of a large consulting organization

W e began outlining the evolution of a scientific
consultant in Chapter One, examining questions such as "Why (and when) do scientists
become consultants?" and "What are the uncertainties
that prospective consultants face?" Then in Chapter Two
we picked out the future consultants from a lineup of
graduate students whose mentors were often part-time
consultants as well as full-time university faculty members. We gave them, after they received their Ph.D.'s,
further training as part-time consultants while simultaneously establishing reputations in a scientific disci-

pline, and we then traced them through the first difficult year following a decision to become full-time consultants. In Chapter Three we provided a long list of criteria by which new consultants could measure their success (or lack of it).

Most of the discussion in those chapters focused on the development and emergence of an *individual practitioner*—the sole proprietor of a small consultancy. And now, in this chapter, we'll complete this introductory material on the generalized evolutionary history of a scientific consultant, recognizing that, at any stage in the lengthy process we have described, changes may be made in the script, so that the outcome may be quite different from that originally envisioned. But our script at this point calls for growth of the consulting venture through an orderly sequence of steps, and the metamorphosis of the consultant from an insecure scientist to a business executive.

SOLE PROPRIETORSHIP AS A CAREER OBJECTIVE

We can't begin this discussion of a transition from solo practitioner to business executive, though, without inserting a large caveat: A significant percentage of consultants would *reject* any such "orderly transition," preferring to remain as individual entrepreneurs or sole proprietors of circumscribed practices that are both manageable and enjoyable, and permit them to be scientists in fact and not just in someone else's perception. Professionals with this attitude and philosophy about consulting, in our opinion, perform much of the day-to-day technical work and most of the client interactions that take place. They may function as contractors on limited projects, or as subcontractors to other consultants on bigger projects, but the size of their practice is, by their choice, strictly limited. They may elect to expand the business slightly by moving, over time, from a "solo practice" (consisting of one professional with no permanent staff) to a "sole proprietorship" (consisting of no more staff members—professional or subprofessional—than can be managed and directed efficiently by the proprietor), but never going beyond that point.

We were curious, during the background research for this book, about the possible reasons for an insistence by many consultants on remaining small—so we asked. Some of the responses were predictable, but others were not. A sampling included the following:

- "I plan to continue to be a scientist as well as a businessman; this would not be possible if the practice got too large."
- "I expect to develop a close working relationship with every client; this would be impossible if the operation expanded."
- "I enjoy fieldwork as well as office tasks; this would not be feasible in a large organization."
- "I can't enjoy a job that requires a lot of travel; a small business allows me to be in control of my own schedule."
- "Large organizations require an unreasonable commitment of time to almost interminable meetings, conferences, conference calls, and planning sessions. I don't want those activities to dominate my business day."
- "To ensure the level of quality in contract performance that I insist on, I feel it necessary to be involved in every phase of the work."
- "I admit to being a perfectionist, and therefore maybe a little difficult to work for."
- "My financial goal in consulting is to make a very

comfortable living with some measure of security, but amassing great wealth and power is not part of the goal."

- "My background is in science and my greatest pleasures are derived from scientific activities. Don't ever try to convert me into an executive."

These, then, are the inveterate "solo practitioners," the "sole proprietors," and the "individual entrepreneurs." But growth is such an ingrained part of U.S. industry that tendencies for expansion exist in many business ventures, including scientific consulting.

ROUTES TO EXPANSION OF THE CONSULTING VENTURE

Some solo practitioners, regardless of good intentions, eventually find their form of business too restrictive; others see a solo consultancy as a temporary state, to be modified as soon as it is financially possible. Some routes to expansion used by individual entrepreneurs are:

- The solo practitioner tires quickly of doing daily office tasks (like answering the telephone) and initiates a growth pattern by employing a part-time but permanent secretary and then a part-time permanent assistant to do routine data management tasks (thus becoming a "sole proprietor" rather than a "solo practitioner"—using our definitions).
- The sole proprietor acquires a number of contracts, each of which demands more attention than one person can provide. A junior professional is hired to assist the proprietor with such tasks as field collections of data, proposal writing, and report preparation.
- The sole proprietor identifies, during his market-

ing efforts, a significant pool of prospective clients not exploitable without additional professional help. Contracts are signed based on the availability of part-time university faculty members, with their students as assistants.

- Problems with scheduling part-time or intermittent professional help from university sources suggest the hiring of one or more full-time professional staff members, with some experience and with expertise complementary to that of the proprietor-founder. A search begins and acceptable people are hired.

- The new professional staff members quickly identify a shortage of subprofessional technician-level and other support staff members; additional staff is hired, including a computer jock and an accountant.

- A close professional friend of the founder, who is also a successful consultant, proposes a partnership that will greatly broaden the areas of expertise of the combined consultancy and spread the administrative responsibilities. The partnership is formed.

- The partners find that overlapping projects require management time that they no longer have, as they are usually in travel status, developing new sources of funding and meeting with former, current, or prospective clients. Some professional staff members with managerial skills and interests devote more and more of their time to project management and project coordination, creating new *de facto* supervisory levels within the growing organization.

- As more and larger contracts are awarded to the consulting *corporation*, an increasing percentage of project funding supports an array of subcontractors—usually smaller sole proprietor companies. This requires that much of the in-house professional staff's time is spent managing, coordinating, and evaluating subcontractors' work, and preparing massive integrated contract reports.

- The partners, whenever they happen to be in town, devote their time to policy development, long-range planning, and signing final contract reports, as financial management has been largely delegated to a senior administrative staff member who is also a CPA. Science intrudes on the workday of the partners—now properly labeled executives—only when problems develop with technical aspects of a large contract, or with technical performance of a subcontractor.

All of these possible steps may have almost infinite variations (for example, a partner is not necessarily a crucial actor in the drama), but the progression toward a bigger and more complex organization is real for many successful ventures. Exceptions are those ventures formed by the staunchly individualistic entrepreneurs discussed earlier, who draw lines in the sand—and who may go on to be successful by their own criteria.

●   ●   ●

With this chapter, our initial probe into the life and times of the scientific consultant is complete. We have explored, very briefly, the evolution of a specialized professional, and we are now ready for a more intensive investigation of a consulting career, with details and opinions that we hope can provide guidance for those who envision a career in applied science. Let the games begin!

PART TWO

Specific Operational Considerations for Scientific Consultants

This, the second part of the book, consists of the following chapters:

- Chapter Five: Organizing a Scientific Consulting Group
- Chapter Six: Managing a Scientific Consulting Organization
- Chapter Seven: Ethics for Scientific Consultants
- Chapter Eight: Marketing and Selling Scientific Expertise
- Chapter Nine: Completing the Consulting Assignment
- Chapter Ten: Maintaining Professional Competence

This part contains much of the substance of our advice about a suite of activities critical to the well-being of any consultant or consultancy. The chapters may tend in places to be a little dogmatic or even dictatorial, but the ingredients of success in consulting are lurking here, and need to be exposed in as much detail as possible, and as forcefully as possible.

FIVE

Organizing a Scientific Consulting Group

the size and complexity of a consulting
company • kinds of science-based consulting
organizations • organizing for success:
flexibility, stability, interchangeability of functions,
open communications, hierarchical clarity, high
professional expectations, favorable work
climate, and shared responsibilities for success
or failure • some basic early steps: preparing
a business plan and deciding about the legal
structure of the venture

O rganizing a scientific consultancy can be a daunting kind of activity for a scientist, immersing him
into areas undreamed of in graduate school—
especially business-oriented matters for which a technical
education provides zero preparation. Fortunately, good
advice about how to start is available, from a library
bookshelf of how-to books like this one, from short-term
workshops at a nearby Holiday Inn, or from colleagues
already involved in a consulting business.

Somewhere early in the preliminary planning phases
the matter of size must be addressed. By far the great

majority of scientific consultants function as *individual entrepreneurs*, possibly assisted by a part-time typist or a part-time technician if field or laboratory support is needed for some projects. The individual scientist *is* the business, and he is responsible for every first and last aspect of it: marketing, proposal preparation, data collection and analysis, report preparation, client conferences, problem resolution—on and on until far into the night at times. Many scientific consultants *prefer* to operate alone, and may even resist allowing the business to grow in volume beyond the point where they can be on top of every aspect of it. These are often scientists with great expertise in a narrow subdiscipline, who can provide information valuable only to a limited number of clients, or those scientists with great credibility in broad science-related policy areas concerned with international trade, who may be paid to advise government agencies or multinational companies.

Organizing a consulting "group" of just one professional plus part-time help is not too onerous, provided the professional has reasonable business sense and seeks early advice from a good accountant (and maybe from a management consultant too). The scientific consultant at this level is essentially running a small business, often from a home office, selling expertise, data analysis, and advice. The operation may be full or part time, depending on the financial needs and personal preferences of the principal and on the market for his services. University faculty members make up a substantial proportion of the part-time individual scientific consultants, and many academic institutions have explicit policy statements about the amount of time that their paid faculty may spend in consulting.

Independent consultants often start their business venture by investing their personal savings, by applying for small business loans, or by seeking venture capital from investors. One highly successful diagnostic laboratory was established by several senior microbiologists who had specialized in rare and unusual microbial diseases. They started in a small leased building with funds provided by a few venture investors. Soon after establishing the company, and with successful advertising and networking, they became nationally recognized for quality services. In addition to providing consulting services, the business was contracted to propose and publish up-to-date standardized laboratory methods that were required by federal and state agencies. The company's success was so great that other investors provided funds for the construction of expanded laboratories and offices—some leased by other noncompeting technical groups.

Start-up costs may vary according to the geographical location of the business, equipment required, staffing, and costs for leased space when rented facilities are required. Such costs are of less concern when the new consultant begins a business in a home office with plans for future expansion. Initial or "start-up" costs may qualify as income tax deductions amortized over a period of years; this benefit should be verified by an accountant as IRS regulations may change from day to day. It is a very safe practice to proceed slowly, paying careful attention to terms and conditions defined in the articles of incorporation (if any), which spell out exactly how the company is legally allowed to operate. If the company is to be successful as determined by its cash reserve, some profit should be forthcoming within a year—two or three at most. During this initial period, it is likely that profits will be realized only after a cash reserve has been established to take care of taxes, office equipment, travel, supplies, and the like. It is essential that the company operate on either a cash or accrual basis—terms best explained by an accountant. Also, there are some requirements that when a contract is obtained for an amount of $10,000 or more, estimated taxes must be paid whether or not the consultant has actually been paid. The amount due is considered income whether or not it has been received (this requirement should be verified by an accountant). There are many examples such as these that emphasize the importance of retaining the services of a qualified accountant who specializes in business or corporate taxes.

Bookkeeping is another business requirement that confronts the individual consultant—whether or not it is carried out by the individual, a family member, or a part-time employee. In many new businesses numerous small expenses may seem insignificant at the time but may represent a significant dollar value when totaled at the end of the year. Purchases such as postage stamps, pencils, paper, a quick lunch while on the road—all represent expenses that erode profits, unless they are itemized as income tax deductions. Careful record keeping is essential to be able to respond to questions that may arise from a tax return audit by the IRS.

With any increase in size beyond the individual entrepreneur level of consulting, though, the world becomes more complicated, and organizational skills have to be added to the technical expertise that forms the base of the venture. Additions to the staff may be in response to larger contracts, or to acquisition of retainer contracts that require commitment of specific amounts of time on a regular or irregular basis. The first new hires are often bachelor's degree-level people with computer or other technical training—people who will, for very modest pay and no security, do much of the background work and data collection that may be a large part of contract performance. The founder of the organization may, up to a critical saturation point, still stay on top of daily activities and client interactions, but beyond that point the appearance of other professionals can be predicted. These new associates will probably have skills that augment those of the principal, to broaden the range of technical areas in which proposals can be offered. The new relationship may be variously defined as that of a partner or a department head, or a data manager, or a field operations supervisor responsible for specific areas of contract performance. Concurrent with these staff additions (or possibly preceding them) the services of an administrator, or at least an administrative assistant with growth potential, will become necessary to ensure that finance and procurement receive continuing attention. Data entry and word processing staff round out the nuclear group of this consulting *organization*, as it must now be classified.

Whatever the chosen structure of the new organization, its precise nature should be fully documented *in writing* in a partnership agreement, in a charter, in a memo of understanding, or in articles of incorporation. Handshakes or oral agreements are totally inadequate as they will surely lead to misunderstandings and disputes in the future. Similarly, new staff members at any level should expect to receive, soon after they are recruited, a detailed written job description—tailored specifically for the position and not just boilerplate. These and other documents should emphasize that this is a *professional* group, and that its business will be conducted accordingly.

The success of this new scientific consulting venture will be shaped by the presence and abundance of many ingredients—technical expertise, credibility of the senior staff, aggressive marketing, good contract performance— but the components of the mixture must be *organized for success* in the sense that *the organizational structure must contribute to rather than impede operations*. Elements of this include flexibility rather than rigidity, interchangeability of functions among midlevel staff, abundant channels of communication, clearly understood hierarchy among senior and midlevel staff, insistence on professionalism in every aspect of job activity, relaxed but productive work climate, and shared responsibility for excellent contract performance as well as failures that may occur. The objective is *to create a money-making scientific microcosm inter-*

*active with the scientific community as well as with other
economic and government bodies.*

But the administrative officer-business manager who
has been hired recently by this emerging consulting organization probably has quite a different perspective on the
organization that exists. Because of a business or accounting background, he may be wondering about cash flow—
or about marketing and sales strategies that are essential
to survival and well-being. Other thoughts may be about
the legal structure of the venture now that it has out-
grown the one-person entrepreneurial phase. Will it persist as an individually owned small business? What elements should be included in its charter? Should it be
incorporated, and, if so, at what point in its development?
Still other thoughts concern the kinds of financial and
legal services that the organization will need, and when
and at what cost.

These are aspects of the business that seem far removed from its original reason for being, but they can
affect the viability of the venture in what is becoming a
highly competitive marketplace for scientific information
and advice.

Once a consulting organization starts down the route
of increasing size and complexity of operations, there are
vistas ahead that are awesome and almost totally foreign
to many of us in science. The superconsulting or umbrella
consulting corporation is a wonderful example of the
ultimate logical step, in which mammoth contracts are
acquired but most of the work is actually performed by
smaller consulting groups through subcontracts. The consulting giant skims off a surprisingly generous overhead
to maintain an in-house cadre of midlevel scientifically
trained bureaucrats who prepare proposals, monitor subcontract performance, and draft final contract reports to
be signed by executives of the corporation. The extent of
the grasp of such superconsulting firms is impressive.
Corporate headquarters may be populated with com-

puter specialists, grant preparation and report experts, analysts of various technical persuasions, legislative analysts, marketing specialists, and public relations staff, as well as the occupants of executive suites. Furthermore, company operations may extend to branch offices and laboratories in various locations in this country and elsewhere in the world.

These massive consulting empires have close networking ties with national and international agencies that typically award large block grants and contracts rather than dealing directly with smaller consulting groups. The U.S. Environmental Protection Agency and the U.S. Army Corps of Engineers are outstanding practitioners of this method of doing business at a national level, and the U.S. Agency for International Development is noted for the same practices internationally.

Here, then, are some of the horizons available to the individual scientist contemplating a career in consulting. He can function in the quiet confines of a home office, dispensing expertise and advice in small doses at small prices, or he can soar with the big boys at Battelle, Dynamac, Versar—either as a subcontractor or as a competitor. Each level of organization has satisfactions and disadvantages—all of which must be evaluated by the individual professional before charging on.

PRINCIPAL ACTIVITY-BASED CATEGORIES OF CONSULTING ORGANIZATIONS

One of the many early decisions that must be made in organizing a consulting group is that of positioning its capabilities to be able to deliver specific kinds of services and products. For example, if services are to be principally advisory—based on experience, credibility, and status as experts in the area of consultation—then the organizational structure created would be quite different from that of a consultancy emphasizing operations (field surveys and data analysis). Although variability is great, we can distinguish five principal kinds of activity-based consultancies (with the usual overlaps):

1. *Evaluation/appraisal/advisory consulting.* This kind of consulting is based on remote fact-finding and analysis of data acquired by others, to supply advice to a client. (An example might be an economic feasibility study of a proposed closed system aquaculture facility.)

2. *Research/survey consulting.* This kind of consulting emphasizes on-site hands-on research and data collection. Information acquired is provided to the client for staff analysis and interpretation. (An example would be collecting and testing water samples for microbial and chemical contaminants, with data supplied directly to the client.)

3. *A combination of types 1 and 2.* This kind of consulting uses an amalgam of new data and those collected by others, as the basis for analysis and interpretation, with conclusions and advice to be supplied to the client. (For example, the evaluation of a potential aquaculture site would include on-site data collection and literature search for other data, before advice is given to the client.)

4. *Remedial or second-opinion consulting.* This is a difficult kind of consulting in which a consultant replaces one who has not met contract specifications or client expectations. The client may have been expecting findings that were not part of the original consultant's report (and may prove not to be part of a follow-up report either). Remedial consulting frequently leads to adversarial actions and

associated unpleasantries that are best avoided, especially by a new consultant.

5. *Science management consulting.* This is a kind of consulting in which a funding source (governmental or industrial) provides money to the consultant to manage a large project. The actual work is performed by subcontractor consultants, but the project *management* is in the hands of the primary consultant. One example would be a large international contract awarded by the World Health Organization to a megaconsultant firm that would subcontract much of the work, do some of it in-house, and manage the entire project. A hypothetical contract might be to structure a program to reduce the abundance of a specific disease vector in a central African country. Or a federal agency, such as the U.S. Environmental Protection Agency, might award a project management contract to handle the entire review and selection process for research grants in a specific area. A hypothetical contract could call for developing expert panels in a number of subdisciplines, screening nominees, outlining procedures, and carrying on tests and then actual selections of grant proposals for funding.

BASIC EARLY STEPS

Organizing a scientific consulting group is obviously a major career undertaking—one that indicates a personal commitment to the use of science in the solution of real-life problems. This chapter, thus far, has included discussion of the sizes and kinds of consultancies, and some important aspects of organizing for success. Our next step is to consider several early and basic activities that should be undertaken during those exciting stressful formative days. We offer four:

1. Developing a detailed business plan
2. Deciding about the legal structure of the business
3. Developing a formal organizational structure, with lines of authority
4. Preparing an employee handbook (beginning with the operating philosophy of the founder/owner)

This list seems too short, somehow, but then we have already examined other forms of advice and other admonitions earlier in this chapter.

DEVELOPING A DETAILED BUSINESS PLAN

With so many crucial decisions to be made, any new consulting venture must have a detailed written business plan, to be completed, evaluated, probed, revised, and made available in final polished form (in multiple copies) well before any business actually takes place. *Such a plan is an absolute necessity.* Any scientist contemplating the formation of a consulting enterprise should, ideally, aim for a year (year 0) of part-time planning before start-up—time to attend seminars for consultants, to talk at great length with consultants of all kinds and ages, to assess current financial status, and (most importantly) to prepare a formal business plan.

The plan has been described succinctly as "a blueprint for organizing, marketing, managing, and financing a proposed venture."[4] It is needed "to address such questions as business location, products or services to be provided, potential market, regulatory requirements, sources of start-up capital, and a profitability timetable." Some general guidelines for preparing the plan are:

- The business plan is a conceptual and structural design for the venture.
- It must be the product of much thought and realistic assessments of the likelihood for success.
- It must include consideration of every aspect of the proposed business.
- It must include a projection for at least the first three years of operation, with an annual goal for income and growth.
- It should be reviewed and updated annually.

The plan may be structured in many ways, and elaborate outlines of sample plans have been published.[5] Whatever the structure selected, key elements that should appear in every plan are:

- Objectives of the venture
- Market evaluation
- Kinds of people who will become clients
- Kinds of services to be provided and *not* provided
- Financing of the company, including realistic forecasts of income and expenses
- The structure of the company—short and long term (sole proprietorship, partnership, corporation)
- Staffing, and the functions of each staff member
- How leads for new business will be developed, and by whom
- How a unique company image will be developed—strategies and philosophy (includes brief policy statements on such strategies as marketing, sales, client services, communications, fee setting, billing and collections, and others)
- *A code of business practices*—determining fees, patent rights, hiring staff, interactions with IRS, initial funding needs and sources

- *A statement of ethics* that will form part of the operating policies of the venture

We have summarized in Table Three the temporal sequences of events in a sample business plan.

An integral element of the business plan must be affirmation of *a commitment to serving clients*. The company policy statement should emphasize the importance of clients to the survival and well-being of the consultancy. Such a policy can be reflected in responsiveness of the entire organization to client needs, cooperation and regularly scheduled contacts with client staff, careful control of proprietary information, and timely completion of assignments.

DECIDING ABOUT THE LEGAL STRUCTURE OF THE BUSINESS

The individual entrepreneur can function quite effectively as a consultant with a minimum of formality, beyond having some business cards and stationery printed. He may elect to confer with an accountant about minimal bookkeeping procedures necessary for tax purposes, and may even choose to pay a management consultant for some preliminary advice. Beyond this minimal level, though, the structure of a consulting company quickly becomes more complex, and more demanding of informed advice and assistance. Some organizational entities beyond that of sole proprietor include:

The Partnership

It is quite common for two or more professionals to form a partnership that makes use of their combined talents and expertise. Such combinations work best when each participant is fully acquainted, well in advance, with

Table Three
A Business Plan for a Scientific Consultancy

Year	Organizational steps needed (manpower, etc.)	Marketing activities	Financial steps including sales projections	Human resource needs	Contract performance activities
Year 0 (prior to start-up)	Make decision about initial size: solo, partnership, etc. Make decisions about goals and operating principles of the venture. Make decisions about the kinds of services to be provided.	Make decisions about the markets to be targeted: government, industry, subcontracts, etc. Prepare market evaluations for each client category—size, trends, competition.	Develop initial financial plan, including anticipated profit and loss, cash flow projections, and break-even analysis. Determine source(s) and size of start-up funding—and determine availability of funds.	Seek one-time or part-time advisory services in accounting, legal and business management. Make decisions about minimal functional staff size, and the nature of specialities needed.	Affirm the criteria of excellence and service in all phases of contract performance. Develop operations plans and protocols for all phases of contract work—specifying how the job will be done. Include every step from sales to final report.

(continued)

Table Three (*Continued*)

Year	Organizational steps needed (manpower, etc.)	Marketing activities	Financial steps including sales projections	Human resource needs	Contract performance activities
Year 0 (*continued*)		Assemble lists of potential clients. Make preliminary contacts with prospective clients.	Determine initial size of overhead expenses, and method of billing (hourly rate, cost-plus, etc.)	Investigate sources of intermittent or part-time support services.	Develop several levels of complexity in contract forms and specifications.
	Develop a code of ethics that will govern the business practices of the venture.	Seek discussions with scientific consultants who are conducting successful businesses.	Purchase equipment and supplies with great conservatism.	Avoid making any commitments about partnerships.	Emphasize significance of constant communication with clients and develop strategies to ensure that this will happen.
	Develop an event diagram that includes every major step in the first 3 years of the new venture.	Prepare a distinctive company brochure, emphasizing capabilities and services.	Pay a good accountant for advice about finances of a small business.		

| Year 1 (start-up year) | Prepare legal document (with advice from a good lawyer), describing the nature and organization of the venture. | Make modifications in target client market. Emphasize activities to expand lists of potential clients. | Examine initial contracts as tests of billing rates. Institute overhead control measures. | Evaluate, during performance of initial contracts, early decisions about staff size and composition. | Carry out initial contracts in an exemplary manner—even if at the expense of some profits. |
| | Reexamine original organizational steps:
• size and structure of the consultancy
• objectives and operating principles
• kinds of services to be supplied
• kinds of clients to be accepted | Advertise. Intensive networking is high-priority activity. Initiate and publicize a unique public image. | Additional sources of funding may be necessary at this point. Set annual goal for net income. Scrutinize cash flow very carefully, and compare with projections. | Recruit only the best, and be certain that each staff member understands the functions and responsibilities of his position. | Institute a system of quality control—which can be especially critical in periods of rapid expansion. |

(continued)

Table Three   (Continued)

Year	Organizational steps needed (manpower, etc.)	Marketing activities	Financial steps including sales projections	Human resource needs	Contract performance activities
Year 1 (continued)	• code of ethics • specialities Prepare a detailed company policy statement emphasizing the cornerstones of excellence and service to clients.	Analyze competititor's strengths and weaknesses, with the objective of increasing market share.		Hire part-time or intermittent support staff initially. Use professional support assistance on a limited intermittent retainer basis.	Develop a team approach to contract work. Be certain that any proposal work can be accomplished with the expertise that is available.
Year 2 (start-up plus 1 . . . moving toward profitability)	Review original decisions about key staff and the structure of the venture—still solo or partners?	Expand list of potential clients and client categories. Develop methods of referral and follow-up marketing. Begin emphasis on indirect marketing methods,	Profitability should be achieved (or at least be in sight) during this operating year. If not, then a full and honest review of all	Management of professional and support staff must be given adequate attention by founder(s). Create and improve work environment	Communication with clients and prospective clients must have high and continuous priority.

Year 2 (continued)	Decide, based on experience, what the optimal staff size should be, and what kinds of expertise are necessary. Reexamine the support staff requirements. Examine the advantages and disadvantages of incorporation.	especially through academic contacts. Develop innovative marketing approaches as a method of increasing market share for existing services. Consider expanding the areas in which services can be provided—then market them vigorously.	business practices will be required, possibly aided by advice from a management consultant. Set annual goal for net income. Reexamine fee structure of the consultancy. Pay close attention to billing practices and methods of collection.	conducive to recruitment and retention of good professionals. If the practice is expanding, recruiting the right kind of professionals is a critical activity. Pressure to expand support staff by hiring permanent workers should be carefully controlled.	An expectation of excellence should be part of every contract performance. Explore the desirability of greater emphasis on subcontracts with compatible colleagues. Explore the concept of joint projects with compatible colleagues on a continuing basis.
Year 3 (start-up plus 2) . . . Profitability should have been achieved by now.	Growth of the venture may suggest a change in structure from solo or partner to corporation; legal assistance will be required.	Emphasize repeat and referral business—by ensuring effective communications and consistently excellent contract performance.	Reexamine fee structure and billing practices. Is a fee increase indicated?	As the staff increases in size, greater attention must be devoted by the principal(s) to personnel matters.	Improve quality control and work evaluation procedures.

(continued)

Table Three *(Continued)*

Year	Organizational steps needed (manpower, etc.)	Marketing activities	Financial steps including sales projections	Human resource needs	Contract performance activities
Year 3 *(continued)*	Incorporation may lead to rapid growth, with the addition of new areas of professional expertise. Explore flexible kinds of temporary work arrangements for some projects. Determine the best mix of in-house and subcontract work.	Build indirect marketing methods. Improve networking activities. Examine feasibility and desirability of international consulting as a possible expansion route for the company. Principals of the venture should be visible in the scientific and the business community.	Work toward an appropriate mix of short-term and long-term projects to ensure an adequate level of financial stability. Set annual goal for net income. Evaluate the entire history of the consultancy in terms of progress in achieving projected level of profits.	A reasonably stable table of organization should be in place. A favorable work environment must be maintained. Retention of key professionals should have continuing high priority, so incentives to achieve this goal must be effective.	Begin assessment of extent to which recommendations are used or implemented by clients. Maintain strict limits on nonbillable staff hours. Use the amount of repeat and referral business as a good criterion of effective contract performance.

the capabilities, limitations, and foibles of all other participants. Once this criterion is met satisfactorily, and the
proposed terms of the partnership are discussed and
agreed on, then the services of a lawyer become obligatory—to prepare a draft legal statement of the responsibilities of each participant. After multiple revisions by
all partners, the draft metamorphoses into the structural
and functional foundation of the consultancy. The legal
nature of the partnership must be defined with exquisite
clarity, for various kinds of responsibilities (such as those
characteristic of limited partnerships) exist. Other critical
aspects include assignment of managerial authority, ap-
portionment of profits, terms of initial investments, and
exit procedures as required. In addition to a lawyer, the
partnership will require financial services—in-house or
by contract—with an extent of involvement dependent
on the level of business generated by the venture.

The Small Consulting Company

Ventures in this category can be defined here as entities that employ a limited number of professionals in
addition to the principal(s) (sole proprietorship or partnership). Such companies constitute orderly expansion
phases of consultancies that can be planned from the
outset. The business plan, if developed with sufficient
detail, should provide guidelines for any future system-
atic growth. Included would be decisions about the kinds
of hired expertise that would best complement or augment that of the founder(s); the kinds of support staff
needed, and the timing of their recruitment; the definition
and assignment of principal marketing roles; and the
provision of adequate facilities for an expanding group. It
is at this operating level that managerial and personnel
issues assume much greater significance than was the
case with the original start-up group.

Joint Ventures

It is not unusual, and sometimes advantageous, for two or more small consultancies to develop and carry out mutually complementary joint ventures, either for a single project or as part of a long-term relationship. For example, consultants in geology, soil chemistry, and meteorology might combine their talents in soliciting contracts concerning land use practices. Such a combination of capabilities, with equal responsibilities, must, of course, be carefully documented to avoid any misunderstandings. Specific problem areas can include the degree of autonomy in any long-term agreement, how profits are to be divided, and the responsibilities for client interaction.

Subcontracting

Subcontracting can be a way of life for many consultants. Smaller firms may elect to remain small by subcontracting for specific talents or expertise with other consultants, thereby avoiding commitment to a larger permanent staff of their own and enabling lower overhead. This route seems eminently sensible in a business area often characterized by extreme fluctuations in availability of contract funding. Subcontracting can be reversible, of course. Consultants may, in any project, be either the principal contractor or a subcontractor. This seems, superficially, to be a delightful state of affairs, but, of course, there may be problems. Some of these include the possibility that the right consultant for a given subcontract may not be readily available, or that the subcontractor may emerge as a competitor in any future work. Additional problems could be in the lack of compatibility and/or competence of the subcontractor.[6]

Organizing   93

The Corporation

A normal organizational sequence, as consultancies
expand, is to move from a sole proprietorship to a partnership to a corporation. The progression is by no means
arbitrary, though; it depends mostly on the relative tax
advantages of each kind of structure, and on the degree of
financial risk that is acceptable to the principal(s). Incorporation transfers fiscal responsibility from the princi-
pal(s) to a new financial and legal entity—the corporation. A decision about whether to incorporate or not can
be deferred for some reasonable time (or for a lifetime in
the case of a sole proprietorship).

The advantages of incorporating are:

- The corporation is an important vehicle for attract-
  ing investment by outsiders, through stock offerings.
- Financial responsibility is limited to the amount of
  *tock held by the individual.
- Potential life span of the corporation is unlimi-
  ted—unlike that of the sole proprietorship or partnership
- Ownership can be transferred with relative ease
  from one person to another.

The disadvantages of incorporating are:

- Costs of incorporation (obtaining a charter, legal
  fees) may be high in some states (sometimes in
  excess of $3000).
- Taxation may be higher and more varied with a
  corporate form of business (although some of the
  tax disadvantages may be mitigated by formation
  of a so-called S corporation, which is taxed by the
  IRS as a partnership instead of a corporation).
- The amount of paperwork required can be extensive, and will usually require legal assistance.

From our observations, smaller consultancies may or may not be incorporated, whereas larger consultancies are usually incorporated. Advice on options for a new consulting venture should be sought from an accountant and a lawyer, as recommended earlier in this chapter.

DEVELOPING A FORMAL TABLE OF ORGANIZATION

It is a truism that, for certain people, a diagram can be much more meaningful than pages of text. An early and elaborate table of organization can help to satisfy members of that special group, and can be instructive to others as well. The diagram should clarify every specific line of authority in the company, and it should evolve just as rapidly as those lines change. The diagram has limitations, of course. It cannot include every instance of partially shared responsibility, and it rarely portrays the shadowlike patterns of informal authority that characterize the day-to-day operations of most organizations. Nor can it make visible the *extent* to which designated authority is to be exercised—a critical consideration when supervising professionals. Despite these limitations, a readily available and current staffing diagram indicates a comforting level of order within the organization, and reassures each employee that he exists, and occupies a specific niche in the hierarchy.

PREPARING AN EMPLOYEE HANDBOOK

An early start on a set of guidelines for all employees may seem like a peripheral sort of activity in a new venture that may be struggling daily for mere survival. We are convinced, though, that everyone in the growing company will appreciate information about such items as the purpose of the organization, office procedures to be followed, channels of communication, shared responsibilities, and a host of other nuts-and-bolts aspects of employment. The guidelines may begin as a series of separate memos or statements distributed in multiple copies. They proliferate, of course, and are eventually stapled together, provided with a cover bearing the company logo, and titled "Employee Handbook." In every organization, regardless of size, there will be a person, searching for order and logic in the universe, who will volunteer to assemble such a document, and to see it through repeated revisions.

Regardless of the degree of informality involved in its creation, every employee handbook must have, as an introductory section, a statement by the founder/owner of the purpose and operating philosophy of the venture. Preparation of such a statement is a responsibility that shouldn't be shirked or ignored or delegated, as it sets the tone for the future and creates a yardstick with which performance can be measured. Subsequent sections can be more mundane: a history of the company, personnel practices and guarantees, communications, grievance procedures, performance evaluations—all as extensions or elaborations of the operating policies stated by the founder in the introductory section of the document.

ORGANIZING FOR SUCCESS

Earlier in this chapter we mentioned some elements of an organizational structure that would contribute to success rather than impede it. We think this concept is important enough to go back to those elements— flexibility, stability, interchangeability of functions, open communications, hierarchical clarity, high professional

expectations, favorable work climate, and shared responsibilities for success or failure—and to discuss each one
in detail:

FLEXIBILITY

Creation of a science-based company with a high
ratio of professionals to nonprofessionals (technicians,
aides) provides an excellent opportunity to explore organizational structures with wide choices of options. The
goals are productivity and excellence. Their achievement
can be enhanced by approaches such as rotating temporary teams to carry out specific projects, broad availability
of temporary leadership positions, and group development of proposals and technical methodology for problem solving. The advantage of a liberal attitude toward
structural flexibility is that it allows experimentation and
it encourages implementing structures that succeed and
discarding those that don't.

STABILITY

We began this section on "Organizing for Success"
with a brief discussion of flexibility, and that seemed
logical, but the availability of options should not be
construed as leading to uncertainty, disorder, or chaos.
Structural flexibility must, for optimum results, be accompanied by funding stability (or a situation that approximates that desired status as closely as is possible within
the consulting universe). Organizational steps that can
foster stability include early and consistent emphasis on
achieving and maintaining a predetermined mix of short-
and long-term projects, development of networks that
provide entry at several levels to government agencies

that employ consultants and to megaconsulting companies, provisions for a constant flow of proposals to
prospective clients, restraint in expanding the permanent
staff to meet short-term demands, and a continuing search
for long-term retainer agreements. In the early organizational phases of a consultancy, the availability of adequate
start-up capital can provide a temporary sense of stability,
but such funds are finite, and must be replaced as soon as
possible by earned income.

INTERCHANGEABILITY OF FUNCTIONS

Consultancies larger than a single individual are normally populated with midlevel or senior professionals
who have particular skills. This is a proper state of affairs,
but people tend to remain in niches unless the organizational structure permits and even encourages diversifica-
tion. There are limits, of course, as specialists are hired to
do what they have specialized in, but there are peripheral
areas of expertise—such as computer dexterity, super-
visory/management skills, writing proficiency, analytic
techniques, and modeling—that should be accessible to
all during an extended period of employment with the
same firm. This constitutes a form of professional growth
that many midlevel scientists welcome. Temporary experience in managerial roles is especially attractive to many
scientists, even though their major assignment may be
(and may continue to be) a technical one.

OPEN COMMUNICATIONS

One of the most common complaints from the
workplace—almost any workplace—is inadequate communication. Large production organizations worry con-

stantly about the problem, but it persists. Consultancies of modest size should not suffer from it, but they do—and there is little excuse to be found, except for the favorite one that the principals in the company are always on the road looking for new business. This means that regularly scheduled staff meetings, or project conferences, or performance evaluations must be aborted, delayed, or conducted by someone in an acting capacity—all highly unsatisfactory to the employees. Communication, up and down and person to person, should be a high-priority organizational *imperative*, not be cast aside lightly under pressure from other commitments. It might be expected that groups of professionals would naturally interact more freely than nonprofessionals, but we see no evidence that this is so—without some prodding from the leadership of the organization, or by having formal or even semiformal mechanisms for constant communication in place. There is room for innovation here, far beyond the weekly staff meeting, the company newsletter, or the occasional idea-generating session.

HIERARCHICAL CLARITY

The structural experimentation that we advocated earlier does have one defect that must be considered, namely, a potential for uncertainty about lines of authority. This is probably most important for midlevel staff, but has to be of concern to all employees. A printed current table of organization must exist, and must be updated every time a change occurs. Each person must know who his supervisor is. This is especially critical in those companies that utilize temporary project teams, formed to meet specific objectives and then disbanded. The extent of authority given to a temporary team leader can be a source of disagreements, so it must be clearly circumscribed, preferably in writing. The usual procedure is to detach team members from their operating divisions or departments, and assign them for a stated period to a project team leader—but only for activities directly related to project objectives. Responsibility for other aspects of employment would continue to reside with the permanent supervisor. Stating this principle is easy, but implementing it can be a source of uncertainties about turf borders, and resentments about perceived abuses.

A clearly designated hierarchy is important for senior staff members too. There must be no misunderstanding about the managerial chain of command, and about who reports to whom in what areas of responsibility. Scientific consultancies differ from many others in that the upper levels are inhabited by people with great technical competence and not just by those with managerial skills. This dual path to power—scientific and managerial—can lead to conflicts, if guidelines about spheres of authority and responsibility are inadequate.

HIGH PROFESSIONAL EXPECTATIONS

Science-based consultancies depend for success ultimately on the technical quality of their products and services. Quality can be measured by many criteria, but a significant part of the evaluation process hinges on assessing the competence and credibility of the technical staff. Recruitment and retention of good professionals must, therefore, be a major goal in organizing and developing a consulting group. The goal can be met in part by fostering an *expectation of excellence* from every employee in every project assignment. Scientists, like the members of any professional group, form a Poisson distribution of individual capabilities and productivity, occupying a bell-shaped curve ranging from outstanding to excellent to good, then through various levels of mediocrity, terminating with the abysmally unproductive. Of course, scientific organizations, regardless of their nature, want their recruits and their permanent staff to come from and to remain on the extreme left-hand limb of that curve, where ability and productivity are highest.

Expecting excellence is, of course, only one of the organizational ingredients that result in *achieving* excellence. Other ingredients include (but are certainly not limited to) the provision by management of a physical environment conducive to the practice of good science, opportunities for professional growth, adequate support staff, sensitive human resources policies, effective communications, and interactive management policies. Beyond the measurable ingredients, though, there must be a spirit, an attitude, an ideal, a managerial philosophy, that affirms to every member of the organization that "good science is practiced here, and compromises with that principle will not be tolerated."

FAVORABLE WORK CLIMATE

Recruiting and retaining good professionals can be affected by many variables—not the least of which is the creation and maintenance of a pleasant and productive work climate. That climate, as envisioned here, includes the physical environment, managerial policies and actions, attitudes of colleagues within the organization, stability of support (funding), kind and extent of staff social interactions, and opportunities for exchanges with the larger scientific community outside the organization.

Organizing for success in consulting should include careful consideration of ways to promote a favorable work climate, recognizing the gap that may exist between the ideal and the reality. Professionals expect to be treated

like professionals; they perform best when they are ensconced in an environment conducive to the practice of
good science, and they tend to remain longest where the
intellectual climate is most suited to their expectations
and needs.

SHARED RESPONSIBILITIES FOR
SUCCESS OR FAILURE

Scientific consultancies, along with many other kinds
of industrial organizations, are committed more and more
to a relatively new work ethic—that of *joint employee–
management responsibility for productivity and quality*. The
concept surfaces in unexpected places, such as in the
small independent work group approach to auto assem-
bly. It is easier to understand in consulting firms, where
future contracts (hence future jobs) clearly depend on
outstanding performance on existing projects, and delivery of excellent science-based services is a professional
investment in the future as well. Scientists, whether they
are consultants or not, expect to be scrutinized and
judged by their peers and colleagues on the value of their
technical contributions. They thus become personally responsible for the quality of those contributions, whether
they are produced in the commercial environment of a
consultancy or not. The consulting scientist serves two
masters—management and science—both expecting excellence, but for somewhat different reasons.

Another workplace concept, of less recent vintage
than that of shared responsibilities, that has been explored by scientific consulting organizations, and seems
worthy of widespread adoption, is *participatory management*. Operating within this concept, management and
decision making become group activities, by group
leaders or their representatives. Examples of this ap-

proach, in formal or informal patterns, can be found in many consulting companies of modest size, beyond that of the individual entrepreneur. Advisory roles in managerial decision making have long been expected of senior professional staff members, individually or in committees, but their participation can extend far beyond that level, to operational, evaluative, and planning functions. After all, consulting companies are peopled by professionals who provide science-based services, so it is not unreasonable for them to expect major participation in decisions that affect their careers. In all of this participation, though, none of the professionals who are involved should ignore the reality that the founder still has ultimate authority in all matters that affect the future of the enterprise.

So here then, in this section on "Organizing for Success" we have given our perceptions of nonstructural and structural elements that can be important in organizing a consulting venture. It is too easy, in thinking about organizing, to overemphasize physical aspects such as staff size and tables of organization, and to be inattentive to less tangible factors related to structure that can affect success or failure. This is not intended to minimize any of the early nuts-and-bolts steps, considered in the previous section, that are required to organize a consulting venture.

•   •   •

This chapter describes some aspects of the growth stages in a scientific consultancy, beginning with an individual entrepreneur or an entrepreneurial partnership of compatible professionals. An assumption is made—and it may not be true in every case—that growth is a desirable and necessary objective. In opposition to this assumption would be the many members of the consulting community who are and who prefer to remain solo operators.

For those consultancies whose visions of the future do assume that growth is good, the key message from us is that increases in size and complexity of operations must be *planned*, and must be *structured for success*. Some important elements that we see in such a structure are flexibility, stability, interchangeability of functions, open communications, hierarchical clarity, high professional expectations, favorable work climate, and shared responsibilities for success or failure.

Most of the elements that can contribute to a successful consulting operation need to be carefully thought through, and then committed to a formal document called a "Business Plan"—a combination bible and constitution that should form the conceptual and operational foundation for the venture. With this in hand, the risky, sometimes discouraging, but always exciting foray into scientific consulting can begin.

SIX

Managing a Scientific Consulting Organization

scientists are special people and not just "staff
members" or "personnel" • some inevitable
guidelines for managing technical
consultancies • evolution of administrative
functions within a consulting practice •
financial and human resources management in
scientific consulting organizations • some
recent developments in management
techniques that may be useful to managers
of consultancies

P rinciples of business management, as discussed in
every college-level course with that catalog name,
present good initial guidelines for managing the
business of scientific consulting. The components, with
some variations, can be found in the usual course syl-
labus: financial control, communications, hierarchy of reporting responsibilities, human resources, production
control, public relations, and so forth. These textbook
approaches to good management are useful as a foundation for everyday business practices, but the scientific

consulting organization has unique attributes that require more elaborate procedures and strategies.

Foremost is the reality that most of the staff consists of technically trained professionals, often with specialties that are critical to the success of the organization. Early in this discussion we should try to find some reasonable answer to the question "Who is a professional?" A half-century ago, a crisp definition of a professional was proposed as "one who maintains a loyalty to a code of ethics that transcends his or her loyalty to the rest of the organization."[7] We like that description, and find it still relevant, even in today's climate of disappearing value systems— as exemplified by a more recent, too inclusive, and obscure definition of a professional as "one who creates, processes, and distributes as his or her primary job."[8] A middle ground, retaining some degree of exclusivity, describes professionals as "employees with specialized or technical education who utilize that knowledge in performing their regular work."[9] For purposes of the present book, we have developed our own somewhat restrictive definition of a professional—thinking particularly of the scientific consultant—as "a person who possesses one or more earned degrees beyond the baccalaureate, and who uses his or her training and subsequent experience in performing the duties of a paid occupation." This new definition, unfortunately, reduces the focus on ethics that characterized the earlier one, but is probably more useful in the modern world.

However we may choose to define professionals, most of us should be willing to concede that scientific consulting is densely populated with them and that managing them requires approaches that differ from those that may be effective with nonprofessionals. Generalizations can be misleading, but most professionals have a very positive self-image, and expect that managers in the organization will be highly qualified, nonintrusive in most technical matters, but sources of stimulating and rewarding work assignments. Professionals make only a few basic demands of their managers: a relatively free work environment, satisfaction of status and ego needs, and recognition of good work.[9] Those of us who have been part of science management would probably add quickly that *some* professionals go on to make many other demands—but these three seem to constitute the core.

People with technical backgrounds tend to be highly individualistic, and may not take kindly to typical business management techniques—in fact, they may resent attempts to apply those techniques. Many—probably most—professionals prefer flexibility in work schedules and dislike unnecessary paperwork. Some do not prosper with too much close supervision, and a majority would prefer to participate extensively in project planning as well as in its implementation. They expect membership in team efforts, but also expect that their personal contributions will be recognized and rewarded, professionally and monetarily.

This brings us to another somewhat unique attribute of the staff of scientific consulting groups, namely, the pay scale. Salaries for highly trained professional members of consulting groups must be competitive with those of counterpart positions in industrial research and development, in academia, and in government agencies. Therefore, to attract and keep the kind of scientific staff that can produce consistently excellent contract performances, wages must be more than adequate, as must fringe benefits. Additionally, job security—the assurance of relative continuity of employment and freedom from repeated layoffs—is an important, though more universal consideration. Consulting groups depend on a constant flow of contracts, and in well-managed organizations, maintenance of the flow is an extremely critical management function, in part to prevent discontinuities in employment that can encourage departure of the best people.

A related managerial responsibility, and one that has somewhat unique aspects for consulting groups, is *the creation and sustenance of a pleasant and productive work environment*. Members of the group are professionals, so they should assume, correctly, that their workplaces—offices and laboratories—will be representative of their positions and expertise. Laboratories should be equipped with state-of-the-art instrumentation, and technician-level support staff should exist. Makeshift facilities in urban industrial zones have difficulty in competing with rural campuslike settings in retention of good scientists, although some professionals may prefer the cultural pluses that urban centers offer.

Once the proper work environment has been assured, managers of scientific consulting groups have a major but ill-defined responsibility *to keep the spirit of challenge and growth alive in the group*. Scientists at every professional level can detect instantly the presence or absence of this spirit, and will respond to its existence with enthusiasm, energy, and accomplishment. Often the managerial role here is to hire and retain excellent scientists, and to put them in charge of flexible task-oriented teams of mid- and entry-level staff members for the duration of each project.

Another management responsibility, again not unique to scientific consulting groups, but important to them, is to *encourage professional growth and development* of staff members. Included would be liberal policies concerning released time for further academic training, short-term courses in specialized techniques, support for meeting travel, and even sabbaticals. Often the more senior, and even some of the midlevel members of scientific groups are offered adjunct faculty appointments at nearby academic institutions; this should be encouraged by management as it allows those staff members with a lingering yearning for the academic life to participate without defecting from the company.

So here then is a sampling of some unique and not-so-unique attributes of scientific consulting organizations that are deserving of managerial attention: (1) staff members may be highly individualistic, and this should be accepted, (2) salaries should be higher than those in counterpart professional groups, (3) a pleasant and productive work environment is important, (4) a spirit of challenge and growth should prevail, and (5) professional development should be fostered.

Superimposed on these somewhat idealistic managerial responsibilities are others that are more mundane but no less vital to the well-being of the enterprise. Of these, *financial management* is absolutely crucial. We have already emphasized the importance of maintaining a constant flow of contracts, as this permits continuity in the employment of essential staff members. Financial management ramifies in many directions beyond this key responsibility. Planning for future contract proposals, decisions about the breadth and depth of support staff, expansion of facilities, and upgrading of instrumentation all require managerial actions.

THE EVOLUTION OF ADMINISTRATIVE FUNCTIONS WITHIN A CONSULTING COMPANY

As a consulting venture begins, then expands and matures, the administrative activities of the founder tend to evolve through four phases: solo practitioner, project manager, project coordinator, and executive, as illustrated

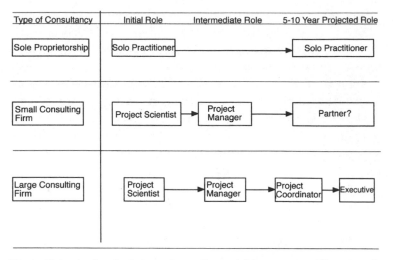

Type of Consultancy	Initial Role	Intermediate Role	5-10 Year Projected Role
Sole Proprietorship	Solo Practitioner ────────────────→		Solo Practitioner
Small Consulting Firm	Project Scientist →	Project Manager →	Partner?
Large Consulting Firm	Project Scientist →	Project Manager →	Project Coordinator → Executive

Two. Principal administrative roles within a scientific consultancy.

in Figure Two. In the earliest *entrepreneurial stage*, the founder *is* the business, and must be a "jack-of-all-trades"—especially as an information gatherer, a salesman, and a document processor. He maintains the office, solicits business, acts as resident expert, does the work associated with contracts, writes the proposals and reports, and oversees the finances.[10] This stressful stage can be concluded quickly (at least by some consultancies) through acquisition of one or more partners and/or additional professional staff, assistants, and support people once profitability is achieved at the lower staffing level. The administrative responsibilities still remain principally with the founder, but most aspects of *project management* are assumed by other professionals. They begin to supervise project staff, ensure that the work is done and the product meets contract requirements, monitor work flow, and maintain project documentation. As projects begin to multiply and overlap in time, the administrative ranks expand to include a new level, the *project coordinator*, who supervises project managers, integrates project needs, controls work flow, and deploys company resources. Beyond the multiple project stage, the founder (or his successor) is usually no longer involved directly in project work, but acts as *executive head* of the entire consultancy. He develops plans and strategies, sets goals and policies, provides leadership, maintains the financial health of the organization, takes the risks, provides the credibility, and gets the rewards.

This is a normal sequence in the evolution of a large consultancy, but it is not necessarily typical of all consultancies. Some remain determinedly small at the insistence of the founder, some enter joint relationships with other small consultancies to handle larger contracts, some grow to intermediate size and deliberately restrict further growth in the interests of maintaining quality, and some expand continuously to become national or multinational businesses—the megaconsulting corporations to be described in Chapter Fourteen.

FINANCIAL MANAGEMENT: DETERMINING THE COST OF CONSULTING SERVICES

Pricing of consulting services is one of those critical management responsibilities that many professionals would prefer to have disappear—but it doesn't, and must be confronted. Fees for consultants should be realistic, and based on some specific calculations—not plucked from the air the first time the issue is raised by a client. Whether contracts are fixed-price or open-ended, it is the determination of *daily rate* that shapes the rest of the calculations. The total cost for services is often presented as a daily rate, which consists of three elements: (1) daily labor rate (as fixed, after careful thought, by the consultant), (2) overhead (as determined by the consultant, but often hovering around 90% of the daily labor rate), and (3) profit (as fixed arbitrarily by the consultant, but often around 20–25% of the sum of items 1 and 2). This method of calculating fees does not include direct expenses such as travel, which would be included separately in the total bill. Fortunately, a book on contracts and fee-setting for consultants is available.[11] Even with this help, though, fee-setting is still a very sticky matter—too high and potential clients are turned off; too low and potential clients are suspicious about quality. Then too, there are always those potential clients who want to negotiate a lower fee. The recommendation from several qualified sources is, "Once the daily rate has been fixed by you as a consultant, do not reduce it in order to ensure receiving a contract. The proposed amount of work to be done may be negotiable, but not the daily rate."

Probably the best advice about financial management in scientific consultancies is to invest as soon as it is economically feasible in the services of a communicative and very bright accountant—at least on a part-time basis during the start-up, and eventually as a full-time member of the management team. One important admonition about your accountant, though. Seek and listen carefully to advice from that person, but never put him in a decision making role. Availability of financial expertise is critical to the success of the consulting venture, but only as a source of specialized information and a unique perspective (cash flow). Operational control of a science-based company must *always* be vested in a person with a scientific background, regardless of other favorable characteristics possessed by nonscientist staff members. Deci-

sions that involve the future of the business will ultimately affect the quality of the scientific product, and
should be made by a scientist.

But beyond the too facile instruction to "Hire a good
accountant" there are many, many facets of financial management that require attention if the consultancy is to
prosper. Setting fees is certainly a crucial managerial
function, but it must be accompanied by other income-
producing activities such as proposal writing, constant
searches for new clients, public relations, contract preparation and negotiation, prompt billing and report preparation.

HUMAN RESOURCES MANAGEMENT: PEOPLE IN CONSULTANCIES

Nonfinancial matters can at times become overriding, and of these, *human resources management* (formerly
personnel management) issues and policies usually occupy a great chunk of managerial time.[12] This is only
proper, as people, with all their foibles and idiosyncrasies,
produce the information required for effective contract
performance. Human resources problems requiring management actions are almost endless, and are gluttonous
consumers of time. Examples include the following: What
will the technical hierarchy be, and how permanent
should it be? What should be the nature and routes of
public contacts? Who should participate in marketing,
and in what way? How are replacement professionals
and other new hires selected? How is the work performance of scientists to be evaluated? What is a reasonable
termination policy for poor performers? How should
psychological abnormalities be dealt with in the workplace? Understand now that these and many other human resources problems confront the scientist-manager,

who is also trying to maintain position as a professional and as a team leader, trying to run a business that shows a profit, and trying to feel good about his career choice as a consultant.

If any conclusion can be reached from all this, it may be that solo entrepreneurs who remain so, and resist all temptations to add staff, may in the end have the best solution, from the perspective of stress control. Of course, others would disagree strongly. To them, that solution reduces all of the excitement of creating a successful science-based business organization, and eliminates many of the satisfactions of applying scientific concepts and data to the resolution of significant real-world controversies.

Another and probably more realistic solution available to the hard-pressed founder-manager of an expanding consulting company is to hire (when the business can support it) a part-time human resources specialist to act as an adviser and to interact with staff members in ways that are entirely at the discretion of the manager. The role could expand as the business does, and the right specialist could, in time, become part of the management team.

MANAGEMENT OF PROFESSIONALS: A BROADER PERSPECTIVE

Earlier in this chapter we mentioned briefly a few approaches to managing professionals in a large consulting organization. More should be said; much has been written about how to manage professionals.[9,12,13] Emphasis in these publications has been placed on communication, leadership style, motivation, and status enhancement in the management of professionals.

- *Communications* with staff members should always be clear, constructive, and positive and supportive of individual contributions.
- *Leadership styles* of heads of organizations, or managers of their subunits, have been categorized most frequently as autocratic, bureaucratic, laissez-faire, or democratic. As might be expected intuitively, a limited form of democratic leadership is considered most effective in managing groups of professionals (this would include consulting organizations).
- *Motivation* of scientists in business organizations can be influenced by peer opinion and evaluation, personal satisfaction for a job well done, and opportunity to participate in organizational goal setting.
- *Status* can be a strong influence on professional behavior, and is shaped by the importance and difficulty of the work and the abilities of the employee.

Many scientists within industrial organizations believe that status can be achieved only by becoming managers. Furthermore, status has countless nuances that may be expressed in the ways in which professionals employed in consultancies interact:

- Professionals with doctorates tend to look down on those with lesser degrees—especially if they are managers—as second-class citizens with inferior status.
- Any perceived attempts by nondoctorate or inept managers to interfere with the freedom of professionals to use their skills as they see fit in work assignments will be opposed strongly.

- The invisible but very important line that separates professional from nonprofessional employees must be respected by managers.[9]

These, then, are four critical foci for managerial attention in modest to more than modest scientific consultancies—communication, leadership, motivation, and status. Deficiency in any one factor can affect the quality of contract performance and, indirectly, the survival potential of the manager and the firm.

RECENT DEVELOPMENTS IN MANAGERIAL METHODOLOGY RELEVANT TO SCIENTIFIC CONSULTANCIES

Consulting on scientific matters is a growth industry, with every potential for expanding as technology becomes increasingly complex and remote from easy comprehension by nonscientists. The management of those expanding consultancies is also becoming more demanding—to the point where the M.B.A. degree should logically accompany the Ph.D. science degree as background for the professional who moves into a key managerial role.

In doing the research for this book, we have discerned four emerging practices and developments that may be of interest and utility to hard-pressed managers of consulting firms:

1. A larger role for female scientists in consulting
2. Specialized managerial training for scientific consultants
3. "Coaches" for scientific managers

4. Published and unpublished sources of information for managers of scientific consultancies

A LARGER ROLE FOR FEMALE SCIENTISTS
IN CONSULTING

One of us (C.S.) a few years ago had the temerity to
coauthor a book about female scientists.[14] Of the many
points not made in that document, one was the virtual
exclusion, until recently, of female scientists from upper
management roles in consulting companies. This could
have been yet another example of the existence of a so-
called "glass ceiling" separating women from the choicest
jobs in corporations, academia, and the professions—a
concept that is gradually receding in all of those occupations. The barrier hasn't evaporated entirely, though; a
recent article on women in business[15] indicated that women
still make up only 5% of senior managers (although, interestingly, 85% of the female executives who were queried
detected some progress for women in moving into senior
management positions). One of the conclusions in the
book that concerned female scientists in universities reflected this same trend, namely, that whereas women
were approaching equality with men at introductory and
intermediate academic levels, they were disproportion-
ately scarce at the senior faculty levels.

In our research for the present book on scientific
consultants we (as men) very sensibly avoided the entire
gender problem, except to observe anecdotally that men
certainly continue to predominate as heads of consulting
organizations. We observed, also anecdotally, that occasionally—but only occasionally—a female scientist does
head the company, although many junior and some
intermediate-level positions are occupied by women. We
think that this continuing imbalance may be the conse-

quence of two realities: the lingering presence of the glass ceiling, and the history of scientific consulting, which, until the mid-1970s, was largely concerned with engineering problems. Women have been consistently underrepresented, and still are, in all engineering fields.

SPECIALIZED MANAGERIAL TRAINING FOR SCIENTIFIC CONSULTANTS

Scientists, whether male or female, typically move into supervisory or managerial roles with little or no preparation for their new responsibilities. Many who are so chosen avoid or delay or even refuse training that is absolutely required—preferring to bumble along learning (they hope) by their mistakes, depending on intuition or common sense to rescue them from managerial crises. The intelligent ones, however, take advantage of the many forms of training that are now available: business management and psychology courses at nearby colleges or universities, intensive short courses or seminars (one day or a weekend) focused on management techniques relevant to consulting organizations, or retreats designed to refocus scientists entering the business world.

We suggest these approaches to managerial training for scientific consultants too glibly. Short courses or intensive seminars for consultants are not readily available, they are expensive, and instruction is dominated by a very small number of practitioners who have become seminar organizers. Fortunately, several of these experts have also written books that contain most of the seminar material, except that information about *managing* consulting firms usually makes up only a small part of the total text material, and discussions directly relevant to *scientific* consultancies (as compared, for example, to those relevant to business management consultancies) are similarly limited. We think there is a real opportunity here for scientists who are already managing consulting companies successfully, and who enjoy public speaking, to investigate the rapidly expanding field of "how-to" seminar presentations, and to put together a test one-day seminar titled "Managing Scientific Consulting Organizations." We predict that the response will be very positive, and may lead the exceptional and motivated scientific consultant into an entirely new career area and an additional source of funds.

"COACHES" FOR SCIENTIFIC MANAGERS

There is an alternative approach to training managers of scientific consultancies that should receive much greater attention—as it has recently in other business circles.[16] This method can be loosely described as "coaching" or "short-term mentoring," and it is particularly applicable to managers of established and/or expanding consultancies. The core of the approach is a specified period (usually one month to one year) of continuing one-on-one interactions between a manager and a paid "coach" (probably self-identified as a human resources consultant). This technique is especially useful in improving the job performances of managers with serious deficiencies or blind spots (and most scientist-managers would readily admit to some of those). Coaches usually have strong psychology and business management backgrounds, and their work has been described as therapy masquerading as coaching. We think that the best coaches for managers of scientific consultancies should have added elements in their backgrounds—training as a scientist and sensitivity to the unique demands of managing a science-based business. Individuals with this dauntingly complex mix of expertise are not abundant, but they do exist, and they can be splendid sources of advice for consulting companies who can afford them.

PUBLISHED AND UNPUBLISHED SOURCES OF INFORMATION FOR MANAGERS OF SCIENTIFIC CONSULTANCIES

The outpouring of books on business management topics has been remarkable. Walk the aisles of a chain bookstore, visit a secondhand book sale, or browse through the appropriate sections of most large public libraries. Shelf after shelf of business management-oriented volumes offer wisdom for those with time to read, and are an endless source of advice on administrative/management techniques. Most of the general literature on business management contains information that can be applied directly to consulting organizations—which are, after all, only a specialized type of business. Unfortunately, the sheer quantity of titles to choose from often makes the task of selection a difficult one. The more specialized publications on consulting as a business take up only limited shelf space, but even here, their numbers exceed intuitive expectations. Books on consulting should be read carefully, from the perspective of applicability to day-to-day needs in the real world.

A relatively new source of information is available now through computer-based electronic communications. After appropriate fees are paid, the entire planet is accessible through the Internet and the World Wide Web. Of particular importance to scientific consultants is regularly updated information about *government programs and contracts*, domestic and foreign. Probably of equal value are suggestions and tips from other scientists and other consultants about possible clients and projects. We will have more to say about these emerging communication methods in Chapter Nineteen on future trends.

•   •   •

Managing a scientific consulting company has much in common with directing a government research laboratory or leading an industrial research group. The commonalities are: the need for good, relevant, sustained science-based production and the need to recruit and retain the best possible professional staff people to ensure maintenance of that productivity. Managers of consulting organizations must satisfy those primary needs in addition to coping successfully with all of the usual demands of running a profitable business. The best managers somehow carry out all of these functions well, and are flexible enough to modify their approaches and behavior to correct deficiencies if they appear.

SEVEN

Ethics for
Scientific Consultants

---

a code of ethics for scientists • an expansion
of that code for scientific
consultants • business ethics

T here has been much discussion and some publicity,
especially during the past decade, about ethical
practices in science, and about individual viola-
tions of a "code of ethics" that has the dictionary definition of "the system or code of morals of a particular
person, religion, group, or profession." Public scrutiny
has focused (at times gleefully) on cases of professional
malfeasance among academic and industry scientists in
particular. One positive effect of the media attention has
been to make it clear to the public that most professionals

123

and professional organizations adhere to codes of ethical practices that have been formulated, debated, accepted, and published. Scientific consultants find themselves in the somewhat unique position of being expected to subscribe, in their professional behavior, to *three* interacting codes of ethical practices: that related to *science per se*, that related to *scientific consulting* as a science-based business, and that related to *business practices* in general, whatever their form. The body of rules that describes each of these codes of practice can be visualized as a circle (or at least as an irregularly circular and easily punctured membrane) encompassing acceptable ethical behavior. Acceptability is strongest at the center of the enclosure, but is never universal, and decreases rapidly to zero as the margins of the circle are reached (Figure Three).

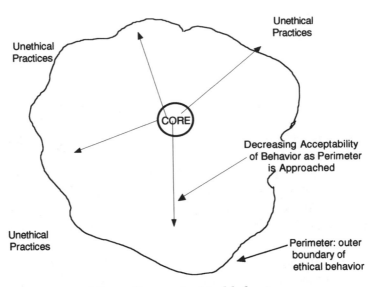

Three. Zones of ethical behavior.

ETHICS FOR SCIENTISTS

An example fitting this illustration, drawn from a code of ethical practices for scientists, would find admonitions such as these, with almost universal acceptance, near the core:

- Design and conduct investigations in conformity with accepted scientific methods.
- Report in full, on a timely basis, the results of investigations, basing conclusions solely on objective interpretations of available data.
- Do not publish or disclose data provided by others without their express permission.
- Give proper credit for ideas, data, and conclusions of others.

Other dicta, with lower levels of acceptance among scientists, would be closer to the periphery of the circle:

- Prevent release or publication of preliminary or misleading reports of results obtained.
- Resist temptations to utilize news media as first outlets for significant scientific information, in advance of disclosure to peers through normal publication channels.
- Challenge unethical conduct of other scientists, using professional journals and scientific meetings as proper forums for debate.

In the increasing darkness outside the circle would be those practices deemed by a majority of scientists to be marginally or clearly unethical. A few of these, adapted just for illustration from an earlier publication,[17] include the following progressively unethical abuses of data:

- Extrapolating—developing curves based on too few data points, or predicting future trends based on unsupported assumptions about the degree of variability in factors measured

- Massaging—performing extensive transformations or other maneuvers to make inconclusive data appear to be conclusive
- Smoothing—discarding data points too far removed from expected or mean values
- Slanting—deliberately emphasizing and selecting certain trends in the data, ignoring or discarding others that do not fit the desired or preconceived pattern
- Premature disclosure—reporting, discussing, or citing work of others that is unpublished or in press, without their stated permission
- Scientific ectoparasitism—deliberately exploiting or developing ideas or proposals of others, made available in oral or other unpublished form for review or comment
- Fudging—creating data points to augment incomplete data sets or observations
- Manufacturing—creating entire data sets *de novo*, without benefit of experimentation or observations
- Plagiarism—outright lifting of data or text from the published work of others without permission from or credit to original sources

Scientific ethics and its boundaries would be interesting topics for extended debate, but not here. We are more concerned in this chapter with other ethical borders—those of the scientific consultant and those of the businessperson—and how they all intersect with and overlap those of science.

The scientific consultant, enshrouded by his circle of acceptable ethical behavior as a scientist, is also being nudged on either side by consultant ethics and business

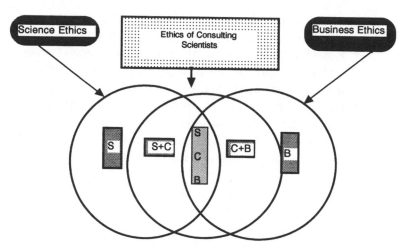

Four. Overlapping codes of ethics for scientists, scientific consultants, and businesspeople.

ethics (Figure Four). The existence of these overlapping codes of practice imposes additional guidelines, well beyond those familiar to academic or government scientists.

ETHICS FOR CONSULTING SCIENTISTS

The scientific consultant, already carrying the baggage of scientific ethics just described, which is common to all professional colleagues, must also assume the added burden of *consultant* ethics. These new ethical considerations involve situations where science and business practices intersect and overlap—and their admonitions are at least as numerous as those of science. Here are a few:

- Offer scientific advice only in areas in which background and/or experience provide(s) professional

competence, and promise only those results that
you can reasonably expect to produce.
- Resist pressures to support decisions based on social, economic, or political considerations by warp-
ing conclusions based on scientific evidence.
- Respect the terms of any agreement concerning
proprietary information, but avoid entering into
agreements that may lead to prolonged suppres-
sion of significant new information.
- Encourage, by whatever means available, payment of adequate compensation to professionals
for professional services.
- Discourage, by whatever means available, the employment of professionals in subprofessional jobs,
except as temporary expedients.
- Discourage, by whatever means available, the employment of subprofessionals in professional scientific positions.
- Encourage the professional development of scientists for whom one has supervisory or management responsibility.
- Ensure that your clients will receive proper respect, and objective technical information and advice.
- Refuse to participate in any project that is illegal,
may be illegal, or even feels as though it might be
illegal.
- Complete assignments according to contract stipulations.
- Try to make excellence a major criterion for every
aspect of work performance, especially in project
planning, use of current techniques, quality control, and timely reporting.

Despite these high-sounding guidelines, a basic limiting fact of life for consultants is that, *in areas of contro-*

versy, if they do not develop data and reach conclusions favorable to the client, they will very likely lose that client. This reality can lead to the kinds of marginal ethical practices that some consultants have been accused of. Public perceptions of such practices, whether justified or not, include the following:

- Data are developed that will lead most directly to validation of the client's position.
- Data are interpreted in such a way as to support the client's position.
- Data are gleaned from public agencies for free, then packaged and sold to the client at a high price.
- Data developed by consulting firms are often not published, or are not otherwise available to the larger scientific community.
- Consulting groups with a record of producing data and conclusions favorable to clients persist and prosper, whereas others disappear.

Ethical scientific consultants will insist vigorously that these negative perceptions are not true for their operations, but, if pressed, they may acknowledge the existence of a tiny percentage of practitioners who are hungry enough to resort to such marginal activities.

The most perplexing ethical problem for scientific consultants would seem to be maintaining an objective unbiased approach in developing conclusions and interpretations of data that may or may not conflict with the preconceptions or wishes of a client. To many observers who lack scientific training, the problem approaches the insoluble. Acceptance of a consulting fee would to them seem tantamount to assumption of an *advocacy position* in favor of the funding source—and yet this stance should be ethically unacceptable to any scientist, whose concern must be for truth, unfettered by the practical and often selfish desires of a client.

It needs to be said, however, that most consulting projects are not in areas of controversy. Many scientific consultants provide scientifically supportable conclusions and recommendations on a variety of noncontroversial issues that lead to industry decisions. Many provide much-needed and balanced perspectives on complex long-range problems, and do it well. All of these activities constitute legitimate and valuable uses of scientific data and expertise.

The list of ethical considerations for scientific consultants could be lengthened indefinitely, depending on the authority making the pronouncements. Here are several more that have been proposed:[5]

- Consultants should avoid involvement in areas of potential competitive conflict, in which contracts are accepted from two client organizations that are competing with each other.
- Consultants should be scrupulously honest in all dealings with clients, especially in areas of expenses, billing, stated technical capabilities, and objective advice.
- Consultants must respect the confidentiality of the client relationship, unless it becomes apparent during the project that public health and safety are being endangered.
- Consultants should not undertake research or survey work with the purpose of gathering proprietary information for a client without disclosing whom he represents.
- Consultants should not hire away any staff members of a client organization.

The other side of the ethical story—ethics for *clients* of consultants—includes timely payments, honesty about objectives of the consultation, respect for the consultant's time, and provision of in-house support to the consultant that was promised in the contract.[5]

BUSINESS ETHICS

If the ethics of science and those of consultants are not complex enough, there is a *third* area that must be considered by every scientific consultant: the ethics of business itself. A first response to this statement may be hard barking laughter, followed by the assurance that business knows no ethics, that the rule of the marketplace is to kill or be killed, and that any survival method is permissible. We like to take a softer stance, preferring to think that the scientist as a businessperson should subscribe to rules of conduct that are accepted by many other legitimate businesspeople. We will even mention a few of these rules, even though our naiveté will be thereby fully exposed:

- Business enterprises should respect the dignity of every human being, and should conduct their operations in a manner that demonstrates this respect.
- Business enterprises have a right to expect adequate profits, but do not have the right to charge excessive prices far beyond the value of their services or products.
- Business enterprises should be expected to be honest with their customers and should not deliberately cheat them or lie to them.
- Business enterprises should pay legitimate bills on a timely basis.
- Business enterprises should create and maintain a productive and pleasant atmosphere within the organization.

- Employees of business enterprises should have reason to trust management decisions to be fair, honest, and equitable.

The ethical scientific consultant is thereby firmly enclosed by three codes of ethical practice—those of science, those of consulting, and those of business—as illustrated in Figure Four. He should always be found stubbornly ensconced in the narrow zone where the three ethical circles overlap (zone SCB in the figure). To reach this zone, a scientific consultant should review the guidelines published by professional organizations, and then develop a personal code of ethics—early in a career—that will serve as a guide for the consultancy. There might be limited room for later evolution of such a code, provided that changes do not include *major compromises* with earlier positions.[18] In the long term, ethical attitudes and practices are intensely personal matters. Each scientist, whether a consultant or not, must select a professional position somewhere between the saints and charlatans (but preferably closer to the former than the latter).

•   •   •

We should probably give greater attention to consulting ethics in this book, as it is a topic of concern to every practitioner. Despite stories told thirdhand and muttered implications of professional wrongdoing, we remain convinced that *most scientific consultants are carefully, unobtrusively, but persistently ethical in the conduct of their practices.* Misunderstandings can arise, of course, particularly about actions taken out near the ethical boundaries that we identified earlier in the chapter. The boundaries may be poorly defined in the view of some professionals, or the *perception* of their precise location may vary with the individual consultant. In our opinion, uneasiness about ethics appears most frequently when conclusions and/or interpretations of data are questioned. This is quite distinct from the rare examples of fraud or deliberate abuses of data—examples that always seem to attract the greatest media attention.

EIGHT

Marketing and Selling Scientific Expertise

---

direct marketing methods and their
utility • value of indirect marketing
methods • referral marketing • selling
consultant services from preliminary meeting to
contract signing • government as a client—
marketing directed toward public agencies

S uccess in the business of consulting depends to a great extent on two interrelated sets of activities: (1) *marketing* (promoting) consulting services and (2) *selling* those services. To many consultants these are two integrated components of a single package that can result in success or failure of a venture, but for purposes of discussion here we can treat them separately.

The kind of marketing that consultants must do has been defined as "all the activities that are designed to establish the image and reputation of the consultant and to make the market aware of the availability of his or her

135

services," whereas selling, as a separate yet integrated effort, includes "all activities that cause an interested prospect to engage the services of the consultant."[1]

DIRECT AND INDIRECT MARKETING METHODS

Marketing methods, which are really ways of making potential customers aware of the company's existence and qualifications, can be quickly subdivided into those that are *direct*, such as direct mail solicitations, responses to requests for proposals (RFPs), or targeted media advertising; and those that are *indirect*, such as presenting talks to service or professional organizations, networking, or publishing in popular or scientific magazines.

Direct marketing methods can be assessed for effectiveness by the number of prospects that are stimulated by direct mail solicitations or local and regional advertising. Internet announcements can also be effective if they are cast appropriately. Responding to RFPs can also be a source of contracts if the right funding agencies have the company name on their mailing lists. Every consultancy will develop its own approaches to direct marketing, but here are a few suggestions:

- Develop a very professional brochure, with excellent graphics and hard-hitting informative text, and then disseminate it widely.
- Develop a mailing list of potential customers and make periodic or occasional mailings that may even evolve into a newsletter. Don't depend on someone else's list, but build your own through networking contacts.

- Develop responses to RFPs from government agencies—a difficult art form that will be considered gingerly very late in this chapter.

Indirect marketing methods, to some consultants, are more effective in acquiring new business than the direct, but results are, of course, less quantifiable and take longer to achieve. Tangible results from most of the indirect methods of marketing are at first harder to recognize, but over the long term they can be important ingredients of success. Indirect marketing, in the case of the individual entrepreneur or the executive head of a larger organization, can be viewed as building personal and company credibility, reputation, and visibility—resulting in his emergence as an "authority figure" in the specialty area of the consultancy. Some indirect techniques that contribute to image enhancement include:

- Participating in annual meetings of professional societies, including paper presentations, poster presentations, office seeking, and committee membership. In each of these activities, do not just be present, but be present and *make some kind of positive impact.*

We witnessed not too long ago a specific example of how a technical presentation at a scientific meeting by the head of a small consulting company led rather quickly to a new contract. Normally, meetings, symposia, or workshops are useful mechanisms for advertising or networking, as they are a means of highlighting the name of the consultancy and its area of expertise, but rarely do they lead directly and immediately (as they did in this case) to a financial payoff.

The consultant presented a talk on the value of certain sewage-associated microorganisms as indicators of the direction of flow of sewage wastes from a point source.

As sewage enters the coastal zone there is a concern as to what direction wastes will disperse—seaward, to the north, back to shore, and so forth. In this instance the consultant was queried at length after the presentation by an engineer employed by an international megaconsultant group, and soon after the meeting was offered a subcontract to use the methodology in an ongoing project in a foreign country. The consultant was able to clearly demonstrate the usefulness of biological indicators, in addition to hydrographic and oceanographic measurements, in determining the direction that sewage would disperse when a discharge system was put in place.

Results from the first project then led to her inclusion, by further subcontracts, in multidisciplinary projects elsewhere in the world, and the rapid expansion of her horizons as a consultant. Her specialized knowledge made an excellent fit with the engineering and chemical aspects of large environmental projects—and it all developed from an encounter at a professional meeting.

- Publishing in scientific journals and science-oriented magazines, and even contributing articles to popular periodicals, Sunday supplements, newspapers, and trade magazines.

One of our favorite stories about successful indirect approaches to marketing involves the efforts of Dr. Daniel Brewster, a journeyman-level international consultant in the rapidly expanding area of world aquaculture. Despite a heavy travel schedule to service current clients, he found time to write and publish, in a leading technical magazine, an excellent review of the status of food production from aquatic sources in a number of developing countries, and the role assumed by the United States in the progress being made in technology transfer, facility construction, and market development. The article was authoritative and readable, and it received favorable comments from other scientists and aquaculture business representatives.

Although it is difficult to assign direct cause-and-effect consequences to a single publication, Dr. Brewster's practice prospered thereafter to the point where he added three partners to the enterprise. He had the article translated into the languages of several countries with interests in economic growth through aquaculture production, and included it with all of his company mailings. Probes and invitations indicating a desire for consulting services came from financial interests in a number of foreign countries; some of these eventually developed into contracts. Dr. Brewster is a firm believer in the importance of indirect marketing, and has since published other articles in trade and popular magazines, as his specialized approach to a critical aspect of successful consulting practice.

- Joining some of the numerous lecture circuits, especially those maintained by organizations such as Rotary, Kiwanis, or Lions—*if* you are a capable speaker, and *if* your specialties would lend themselves to interesting presentations. Such organizations are usually desperate for good informative talks by professionals. Exceptional performance at the local level can lead to invitations to make presentations at regional- and national-level meetings of those groups.
- Being alert for opportunities to get newspaper or television coverage of your activities. If these public relations activities are pursued consistently, with the utmost professionalism, they can lead to contracts. Of possible media interest could be examples of pro bono work with citizens groups, or biographical sketches of outstanding staff members who may have made a significant finding or contribution.
- Conducting, preferably jointly with other professionals, workshops or seminars in selected areas of scientific consulting (e.g., environmental, medi-

cal). This could easily lead to opportunities to teach courses at local colleges or universities. Adjunct academic appointments confer status, and enhance personal and company visibility as well. Course materials can then be incorporated into books—which confer even more status and credibility.

- Networking—constantly and aggressively—developing and maintaining contacts with large numbers of potential clients and with other scientific consultants.
- Finding or manufacturing reasons to call, fax, go to lunch with, or otherwise interact with people in both categories as often as possible.
- Developing an informal newsletter for scientific consultants.
- Organizing a special session or symposium on specific aspects of scientific consulting as part of an annual professional society meeting.
- Proposing a regional or national organization of scientific consultants with meetings concurrently with those of the principal society (societies) in the subdiscipline(s) represented by the consulting group.

One important addition to this discussion of marketing consulting services, applicable whether the prospective client is a government bureaucrat or a business executive, concerns an activity described as "referral marketing"—receiving business from "clients to whom you have been recommended by past, prospective, or existing clients . . . or follow-up business from existing clients."[11] This may be the best and most cost-effective source of new business, but the process is not passive; referral marketing requires its own effort, including provision of consistently excellent service, continued communication with former clients, and indications to clients, colleagues, and even competitors that their recommendations are appreciated. Referral marketing has as its foundation a record of outstanding contract performances and professionalism in all aspects of client interactions.

A part of the referral marketing effort must be devoted to dispelling fears that often make those qualified to offer a recommendation reluctant to do so. They would not like to be proven wrong in their evaluation, thus damaging their own status unnecessarily; they may not want to participate in the risk-taking that would be required. The best way to allay those fears is to demonstrate consistently exceptional performance.

Turning now to the *selling side of consulting*, we confront the nitty-gritty part of the business that is sometimes repugnant to scientists with long-term academic or government backgrounds and experiences—those who do not want to be cast as "salespeople." This is, however, an activity where success or failure of the enterprise can be determined. The *preliminary meeting* is unquestionably the most critical point in the actual selling process leading to a contract. All of the direct and indirect marketing approaches—advertising, mail solicitations, referrals, establishing credibility and visibility, networking, and many others—have led to this first face-to-face interaction between prospective client and scientific consultant. What takes place from here on depends on the proper integration of client needs and consultant capabilities, leavened by the nature of the interpersonal rapport that may develop between the two principals. Some excellent guidelines for conducting the initial meeting have been reviewed recently.[11] Key points for sales presentations leading to closure and contract signing include individualizing the sales message, allowing the prospective client time to enter the conversation, communicating to the prospective client the next step in the process, and even practicing (in private) possible closures leading to contract signing.

Other authors have tried to dissect the process of selling consulting services, recognizing that there is an element of innate sales ability in most of us (but probably less of it in scientists). One of the best attempts[5] visualized the sales process in five key steps: initial contact with the prospective client, screening of the potential client, initial meeting with the prospective client, development and presentation of a proposal for work to be accomplished, and follow-up meeting leading to contract preparation and signature.

We have attempted to integrate the entire sequence of consulting activities—marketing, selling, and performance—in a reasonably simple almost circular diagram (Figure Five). Moving around the wheel of fortune illustrated in the figure, way stations and critical junction points can be recognized. All are important, but three on the left side of the diagram need further description here, in this discussion of marketing and selling: (1) the preliminary meeting, (2) the proposal, and (3) the contract.

1. *The preliminary meeting.* The preliminary meeting with a prospective client marks the logical consequence of successful earlier marketing efforts and the beginning of the selling phase. Its outcome can be determined quickly. Some authors think that the assignment can be won or lost in the first few minutes of the initial consultant–prospective client meeting, and that the remainder of the dialogue can then be focused on the prospective client's problem and its possible resolution, aided by the expertise of the consultant.[10] Those first few minutes, though, can be extremely stressful ones for both parties, as they try to establish a working

Marketing and Selling Scientific Expertise   143

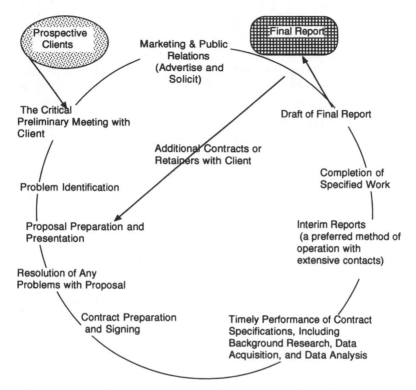

Five. Principal steps in the consulting process (based in part on discussions in Shenson[1] and Greenbaum[5]).

relationship. The prospective client may be unsure about the consultant's competence, and is concerned because a substantial amount of money is involved. The consultant may need the assignment desperately to pay bills, and may not see at first how the prospect's problem should be addressed. With enough discussion, though, the psychological power games and the interpersonal traps can be overcome, especially if the consultant is experienced in this crucial phase of selling his expertise. Some of the keys to success are questions about the would-be client's interests and business—all part of a structured interview approach based in part on whatever preliminary information the consultant may have been able to acquire before the meeting. Somewhere in the dis cussion, the matter of consulting fees will be raised; it should be addressed straightforwardly by the consultant. Questions by the consultant later in the meeting should concentrate on diagnosing the prospect's needs and objectives in seeking a consultation.

2. *The proposal.* If the initial interaction of prospective client and scientific consultant has been even marginally favorable, the sales discussion should lead to the suggestion that a written proposal be prepared (by the consultant, usually at no expense to the prospective client). Proposal writing is a learned skill, and can often be critical to the negotiations leading to the signed consulting contract. Proposals are sales devices—they suggest a plan of action to solve a specific problem, they identify the conceptual base of the proposed activities, they point out why the consultant at hand is the proper choice to carry out the study, and they inform without offering too much free advice. As such, they can constitute both an art form and an important part of the business procedures of scientific consultants.

   Proposals for consulting contracts are not too dissimilar from other types of scientific proposals, such as those for grants and for responses to government RFPs. They begin with an executive summary, then move on to an introductory section describing the goals and objectives of the study, the background of related information, the general approach to be followed, and the reasons why the present consultant is the only choice for the contract. The background information section is particularly important in proposals for scientific consultation—probably more so than for other kinds of consultant work—because scientific expertise and state of the art knowledge are the principal articles of trade, so the competency of the proposer must be demonstrated clearly.

3. *The contract.* Once the proposal has been accepted by the client, and negotiations about details or modifications have been completed to the satisfaction of both parties, a written contract or letter of agreement can be drawn up and signed. The document may be simple or elaborate, but it should contain enough information to prevent any future misunderstandings. It is an instrument designed to ensure that the specific responsibilities and expectations of client and consultant are clearly communicated. Specifications for the time of completion of the work and delivery of the final report in a mutually agreed on format are important elements, as are terms and conditions of payment. In general, it seems preferable to have too much detail in the contract rather than too little; this minimizes conflicts later on. Large contracts should specify periodic interim or status reports, describing what has been accomplished and what remains to be done to complete the project. Boilerplate forms for routine consulting contracts are available in some books,[5,11,18] but large contracts should probably be prepared with a lawyer's advice and assistance.

GOVERNMENT AS A CLIENT: MARKETING AND SELLING SCIENTIFIC CONSULTING SERVICES TO PUBLIC AGENCIES

One reality of technical consulting is that much marketing effort must be targeted, directly or indirectly, to a vast array of government bureaucrats. Other than the required minimal personal interactions with the Internal Revenue Service, consultants may find themselves in the presence of government representatives in three distinct situations (and variants thereof):

1. As advisors to *local* (city, county, or state) *politicians*, or their representatives or lawyers. These politicians come in all guises: as elected or appointed officials, or as members of innumerable commissions, authorities, councils, or committees. Some consultants may develop reputations as mediators, synthesizers, or conciliators in local disputes involving scientific as well as political components. Some consultants even enjoy this "grass roots" kind of interaction with the political system.

2. As suppliers of data and other information to *government administrators* at all levels, from a mid-level regional program leader of a regulatory agency to a special fact-finding committee appointed by a deputy assistant undersecretary of that agency. Drafting, enacting, and enforcing myriad rules and regulations concerned with the environment are particularly active bureaucratic areas at present, requiring expertise that is sometimes beyond in-house agency capabilities. This can provide a window of opportunity for the

savvy and informed consultant, if he studies Internet offerings and if he has some carefully nurtured agency contacts. Two major sources of frustration in interacting with federal agencies that have funds for contracts are: (a) the transiency of bureaucrats assigned to award and manage the funds, and their lack of familiarity with the science involved, and (b) the extreme fragility of any federal contract commitment, with possible impacts of budget cuts and program cancellations or redirections on funding that has already been approved.

3.   As *petitioners* for funding for contracts or for grant-supported studies in areas of interest to federal departments, agencies, and administrations (e.g. USDA, NOAA, EPA, USDI, COE). Paid functions include (in addition to data collection and analyses) service as an expert witness, membership on advisory boards or commissions, participation in grant evaluations, and many others.

Some points to remember about consultant–government interactions in the general area that could be described as "marketing" are:

- Bureaucrats come in all flavors, but can be immediately characterized as *politician-bureaucrats* (appointed at the request or insistence of an elected politician) or *career bureaucrats* (appointed on the basis of competitive examinations, professional qualifications, or longevity in temporary positions).
- Politician-bureaucrats have most of the power within an agency. Career bureaucrats at middle levels have little or no *directly assigned* authority, but they may have power, in their small area of responsibility, to affect, indirectly, decisions by

their politician-bureaucrat supervisors about contract awards or renewals.

- Career bureaucrats at middle levels are usually the agency interfaces with the outside world, as politician-bureaucrats abhor any public contact (except in carefully orchestrated situations,) and upper-level career bureaucrats are fully occupied in responding to administration and congressional demands for information and advice. Sensible consultants will recognize these realities and will cultivate working relationships with government where the actual work of the agency is done (the middle levels of any bureaucracy). Most professional networks will contain a sprinkling of bureaucrats with science backgrounds, and national meetings of scientific societies will always attract them in numbers, despite recent budget restrictions on professional travel.

- Information, verified or only rumored, is an important commodity within bureaucracies. Consultants attuned to the right levels can gain access to future plans and proposed actions of the agency well before they become available publicly.

- Most of the principal federal funding agencies, such as the Environmental Protection Agency (EPA) or the National Science Foundation (NSF), have developed lists of elements that they expect to find in any proposal submitted to them, and have published extensive guidelines to be followed carefully. A successful search for contracts or grants may hinge on adherence to agency wishes in this respect.

- Other factors that may influence success or failure in preparing proposals to acquire federal funding include: use of any available insider information on current emphasis of the agency, beyond that printed in the invitation for bids (IFB) or the RFP; willingness and ability to slant the proposal to best fit the perceived expectations of the agency; and use of advance information about the members of the review panel (so their papers can be cited and referred to in the text of the proposal). Acquisition of such insider information can be gained by intensive networking, or by deliberate cultivation of colleagues employed by government agencies.

- Government agencies that have funds for contracts do not like to deal with small sums or little companies. They prefer to contract with big organizations (megaconsultants) for large packages of project money, to be subdivided and managed by the large company as subcontracts. Small consultants should accept this reality, and address most of their interfacing and marketing efforts to the appropriate (middle) levels of the megaconsultant firm rather than the government funding agency. (Agency contacts should, however, never be abandoned or allowed to wither.) Aggressive networking with colleagues within the superconsultancy can again be a method of choice.

CONTRACTING PROCEDURES OF THE FEDERAL GOVERNMENT

Consultants who have not attempted to extract contract or grant funds from federal agencies can be confused, frustrated, repelled, or overwhelmed by the complexity of the process and the mountain of paperwork that is involved. The money is there, though, for those willing to tread the maze of procedures, jargon, and directives that can lead to its release. Three principal routes can lead scientific consultants to the source: (1) the IFB, (2) the

RFP, and (3) the grant proposal. A good discussion of procedures is available[19] and is summarized here:

1. The IFB specifies the work to be done, and the requirements that bidders must meet. Bidders complete a standard form, which includes their bid. Bids are opened at a specified time and the contract goes to the bid that is "most advantageous to the government."

2. The RFP differs from the IFB in that the agency knows what it wants, but invites proposals describing the best methodology to reach that endpoint. Factors other than a low bid are taken into consideration by the contracting officer or selection committee in awarding the contract.

3. A number of federal agencies disburse funds through a third channel—grants to individuals or institutions. Most of these are for research, and most are awarded to universities. Some, however, are available to consulting ventures (from the Small Business Administration, for example) or to research consortia that may have consulting firms as joint participants. Selection criteria are broad, and advice from evaluation committees is a normal part of the process.

Each government agency maintains a "Bidders Mailing List"; IFB or RFP invitations are sent automatically to those on it. Two federal agencies—the General Services Administration (GSA) and the Small Business Administration (SBA)—have field offices that can be especially helpful to consulting companies; SBA will even assist in obtaining subcontracts from larger consulting firms.

The enterprising and successful consultant should explore all avenues of potential funding—even those that only occasionally lead to unexpected income. One good example of this is work funded by the SBA. The "Small

Business Innovation Act of 1982" (SBIR Act 15 U.S.C. 638 PL 97-219) was enacted on July 22, 1987, and implemented by SBA Directive No. 65-0.1.1, dated August 1, 1993. The Act requires that certain federal agencies establish a Small Business Innovative Research (SBIR) program by reserving a portion of their extramural research and development budgets for awards to small businesses, including those operated by minority groups. One of the goals of this program is to fund small start-up businesses that will eventually operate without federal funds—other than those obtained through grants and contracts. The small business must be independently owned and operated, organized for profit, not a dominant performer in the area of specialization in which it is proposing to work, and with a principal place of business in the United States.

Each federal agency participating in the SBIR program has its own requirement for the type of business that it will support. Some may require the manufacture of a product useful to the agency or to industry. Because most consultancies do not market a wholesale or retail product, it does not appear on the surface that research proposals by a consultant would be suitable for SBIR funding. However, like many activities that do not appear appropriate for the consultant, there is a flip side to the coin. The Act does provide the prime contractor with authorization for arrangements between the company and universities, nonprofit organizations, and consultancies. *Here is a situation where the consultant may gain from advising and conferring with the owners or operators of small businesses (including those that are minority or woman owned).*

•   •   •

So here, in brief, are some of the marketing and sales activities that must be part of the working life of every successful scientific consultant. Academically oriented professionals, reading this chapter, might well be appalled by the pervasive tone of commercialism that emerges. They could well wonder where the familiar laboratories and seminars and intense technical discussions that characterize *their* professional existence have disappeared to. Then, maybe, after some reflection, the academicians might admit that this consultant cadre has an important role to play, carrying science to the level of practical application in real-world situations. To do this successfully, the scientific consultant must don some of the armament and play some of the difficult and sometimes hardball games of the marketplace, however far removed such practices may be from the hallowed halls of academic science. He pays a price in reduced technical creativity and productivity. Some scientists are ready and even eager to pay the price and enjoy the benefits—as long as they do not sacrifice ethics.

As a final homily, we offer this: success in scientific consulting can be achieved by a proper amalgamation of technical competence and marketing–sales skills. Neither can be substituted for the other, and neither can survive without the other.

NINE

Completing the Consulting Assignment

steps in fulfilling the consulting agreement:
information gathering, data analysis and
synthesis, drawing conclusions, preparing
recommendations, and submitting the final
report • the importance of adequate
communication • withdrawal activities
after the consultation ends

M ost of this book on scientific consulting is actually about *consulting*, and not about *science*. The
present chapter on performance of contract work
is as close to describing applications of technical expertise
as we will come in our examination of scientific consulting. The previous chapter brought us through the prelimi-
naries—the dances that, if well done, lead to contracts. It
is now time to look at how the consultant actually *does* the
work for which he is paid. As with other descriptions, this
one is best subdivided into phases, beginning with the
proposal—already considered in Chapter Eight—which

summarizes the approaches to be followed, and is essentially a work plan, to be augmented immediately after contract signing by an activities flow chart and a detailed time schedule.[10]

The earliest hands-on phase of contract performance is logically an *information gathering* one. For some projects, data collection and statistical or content analysis constitute the principal foci of the work; for other projects, data are important primarily in improving the quality of the consultant's conclusions and recommendations. As information gathering is an essential component of all consultations, some general guidelines seem sensible at this point:

- The *quantity* of data that needs to be collected should be assessed carefully. Too little will raise questions about validity of conclusions drawn from it; too much may place an unnecessary financial burden on the consultant.
- The *quality* of the data should never be in question. Quality control measures must have high priority in any project design.
- Any scientific studies conducted by the consultant must be tightly controlled, with impeccable experimental design and with procedures carried out by knowledgeable technicians.
- Information gathering can be slow, with few visible early products; periodic progress reports to the client can be important in quieting unease about apparent inactivity during this phase of contract performance.
- The manner in which data are gathered can provide clues about the professionalism of the consultant. Use of current testing and experimental technology and computerized analytic methodology should be expected.

- Some clear marks of a professional approach include a thorough literature search, utilizing electronic retrieval techniques; and a review of any unpublished data in the hands of the client or regulatory agencies that may have bearing on the project.

THE "SCIENCE" IN SCIENTIFIC CONSULTING

The subsequent phases of the consulting project, after adequate data and other information have been collected, include (1) data analysis and synthesis, (2) drawing conclusions, and (3) preparing recommendations. These steps are closely integrated and sequential, and to us are the most interesting and exciting aspects of contract performance. This is where scientific training and experience are particularly critical to the consulting process, and where intangibles such as professional credibility can count the most.

DATA ANALYSIS AND SYNTHESIS

Analytic methods used in science are, almost by definition, quantitative. Data of value to scientific consultants are always objective, whereas other kinds of consultants have more freedom to use anecdotal or other nonquantitative information in their analyses. Sampling design can be a critical element in analyzing data sets (consultants may otherwise be accused of slanting findings from surveys by subjective selection of sampling locations and times).

Synthesis follows analysis; it involves attempts to assemble often disparate results of investigations into a cohesive structure from which conclusions may be drawn. Synthesis also includes an examination of interrelationships and interdependence of data sets, to identify patterns, trends, and interconnections. Priority ranking is directly involved—making judgments about the relative importance of each data set, and the priority it might receive in problem resolution.

DRAWING CONCLUSIONS

Analyzing and synthesizing data will provide a vague outline of a whole landscape, which may be clarified and sharpened by preliminary attempts to draw conclusions. Draft conclusions should be tested repeatedly against the only realities—the data sets themselves—and only then should they be stated in definitive language that may be meaningful to the client. Several guidelines and admonitions are particularly relevant at this phase:

- Conclusions should be drafted that are based on objective analysis and synthesis of data, entirely uninfluenced by any preconceptions or expectations of the client.
- Conclusions should be based on all available data, but should not extend beyond the reasonable confines of those data.
- Conclusions from consultant's studies should be able to withstand the same critical review that is characteristically required for publication in refereed journals.
- Conclusions should not depend on selective choice of data sets to be analyzed.

PREPARING RECOMMENDATIONS

The sections of the final contract report labeled "Conclusions and Recommendations"—and maybe the "Executive Summary"—are probably the only parts of the report that will have the client's full attention as a consultancy draws to a close. Of those sections, the recommendations will be most meaningful, as they will indicate a course of action to resolve the problem that drove the client to employ a consultant in the first place. This implies that the recommendations should be carefully conceived, framed, and written; that they specify actions that are achievable by the client; and that they offer reasonable hope of problem resolution.

For projects involving complex variables, use of mathematical models to predict outcomes of selected actions can be a valuable tool in making recommendations. Such models can be especially useful in examining a broad array of technical problems in many disciplines.

The client should be involved wherever possible in formulating recommendations, since he will eventually act or fail to act on them—singly or in their entirety.

THE FINAL REPORT

Just as the outcome of the initial meeting of consultant and prospective client is critical to all that follows, the final contract report is crucial to all that precedes it. The report represents satisfactory (preferably more than satisfactory) consummation of the current relationship and a possible avenue to any future relationship. It is an indispensible part of any contract services supplied by the scientific consultant. Most of those services are *intangible*, dealing as they do with data analyses, conclusions based on available information, opinions, and advice tempered by the background and experience of the consultant—but the final report is *tangible*. It exists in a neatly packaged form, with the all-important findings of the consultancy presented crisply and understandably, and structured to demonstrate that the objectives described in the contract have been fully met.

The final report should provide *guidance*; this is what needs to be *communicated* to and *accepted* by the client. The acceptance phase stretches all the way back to the marketing component of the interaction—to the credibility of the consultant. The report must, therefore, be a gem, free from jargon, identifying the key findings of the project, and offering options and recommendations for actions by the client. On a practical level, timely production and delivery of the final report should be a specified part of contract performance, without exceptions.

Final reports can have several kinds of emphasis, depending on the nature of the primary readership. Although mixtures can and do occur, three principal types of final reports have been described.[1] They are (1) the report for executives, giving a broad overview of the consultation and its findings, with recommendations and options for action, (2) the technical report, containing detailed information on techniques, data sources, and operational plans of use to middle management, and (3) the report for publication, designed to be of use to the client organization, but with broader industry perspectives as well. Each type calls for a particular kind of writing, but all require clarity, precision, and brevity.

The final report should always be submitted to the client (and staff) at a formal presentation ceremony. The program for that meeting should include, but should not necessarily be limited to:

- An expression of appreciation to the key staff members who contributed to the success of the work—including client's staff as well as the consultant's staff
- A review of the highlights of the project, and a summary of important findings and recommendations

- An optional (at the discretion of the client) open discussion of the findings and recommendations in the report
- An optional proposed action plan from the consultant suggesting ways of implementing the recommendations[1] (inclusion of this agenda item should be *completely* at the discretion of the client)

A presentation of this kind provides a strong suggestion that the active contract period has ended, but that the consultant's interest in, and involvement in, the project will continue, although at a much diminished scale, as described next.

WITHDRAWAL ACTIVITIES AFTER THE CONTRACT ENDS

The end of a successful consultancy has been compared by some authors to a divorce, in which a relationship is terminated with mixed emotions (such as regret, abandonment, relief, hostility, anxiety, depression). But, as one expression has it: "It ain't over 'til it's over" (or words to that effect). Follow-on activities that can be significant after contract termination include:

- Postcontract meetings with the client to see if recommendations have been, are being, or will be implemented, and, if so, what the consequences to date have been.
- Self-evaluation of the contract performance by the consultant—as objectively as possible—especially from the viewpoint of "How could I have done a better job?" The evaluation should be in the form of a typed document for the record, presenting the entire history of the project, including positive and negative aspects.

- Postcontract discussions with the client that serve several purposes: They may disclose deficiencies in contract performance that can be corrected by the consultant, they provide reassurance to the client that he has not been abandoned, and they can permit the consultant to assess the value of the implementation measures that were recommended.
- Staying in touch with former clients to maintain visibility for repeat business and referrals. This might include such approaches as obtaining testimonials, or asking if the clients can be used as references in proposals prepared by the consultant.

At some time after the consultation is history, a final informal meeting should be held, to indicate that the project is ended, but not the relationship. At this time, any leftover business-related items can be cleared up (the bill, for example) and possible future projects broached—all (hopefully) in an atmosphere of mutual satisfaction.

THE OVERRIDING IMPORTANCE OF COMMUNICATION THROUGHOUT THE ENTIRE PERIOD OF THE CONSULTANCY

Most clients, once they have signed a contract with a consultant, expect the results to be available at least by the preceding week, if not sooner. They do not want to hear that scientific studies take time to complete, even if they sense that their demands are unrealistic.

One proven method of reducing those demands is to provide constant, at times overwhelming, doses of communication—by phone, fax, mail, or personal conferences—about the status, problems, and achievements of the consultancy. Clients should be approached as participants in a joint venture with the consultant (which they are), and should always be fully informed, *insofar as they wish to be*. The relationship must be frank, open, and mutually agreeable, if the contract work is to be successful. Failure to achieve an acceptable level of rapport is often identified as being near the top of the list of client complaints.[1]

Every book on business aspects of consulting will contain suggestions about improving communication links with customers. Some that seem especially relevant to scientific consulting are:

- *Avoid any hint of the kinds of superior attitudes* that characterize some scientists when they deal with intelligent but uninformed lay people. Impatience, condescension, annoyance, obfuscation—all will guarantee absence of repeat business.
- *Avoid the use of technical jargon* in any communication with a client. This is an extremely difficult habit for scientists to break, but it must be broken.
- *Treat every person involved in the consultancy with respect and appropriate deference*, keeping in mind that, to the client's staff, the consultant is often viewed negatively at first, as an intruder.
- *Inform the client of progress frequently*, especially when any phase of the contract study is completed.
- *If a problem develops, provide adequate warning to the client*, and try to work with him in effecting a resolution.
- *Be sure to distinguish between communication necessary to the consultation and that which violates the boundaries of proprietary information*. This is especially important in conversations with the client's staff or with competitors, as well as with colleagues. The person who signs the contract should

be the sole recipient of proprietary information, unless he designates others who can be included in that communication link.

- *Provide ample opportunity for open discussion of costs incurred by the consultancy*—and even initiate such discussions if any changes occur in projected expenses.
- Whenever appropriate and permissible, *encourage a broader dissemination of the results of a consultancy*, to the public, to other industry members, or to the scientific community—possibly by publication in technical magazines or journals. Scientific consultants appear to do too little with this method of communicating.
- Although just a tad beyond the perimeter of "communication" as it is normally interpreted, the consultant must be *available* to the client. This may include periodic visits to the client's facility, establishing a temporary field office at that facility, being willing to confer with clients at their request on short notice (within reason), and responding quickly to telephone messages.

The take-home lesson on communication is, from our perspective, that it is an essential element of every consultation, and of every phase of that consultation. Any errors should be on the side of "too much" rather than "too little," and full advantage should be taken of all forms— oral and written.

●   ●   ●

Scientific consultants spend so much time on nontechnical business-related activities—marketing and sales, managing staff, planning for expansion, analyzing costs and income—that it is almost a relief to find, as we have in this chapter, that shreds of science do survive and persist in such a commercial milieu. Steps in completing the consulting assignment include all of the functions that scientists are hired to perform (and are uniquely qualified to do so), such as valid approaches to data acquisition and statistical analysis, professional evaluation of relevant published literature, review of current status of thinking and concept development in the area of concern to the assignment, and preparation of conclusions and recommendations based on objective examination of all available information. For brief shining periods during the contract performance, the scientist emerges from the dense thicket of business practices to apply his technical skills to the problem at hand—to bring to bear all of the expertise that has been so slowly and painfully acquired throughout a professional career. The existence of these brief moments, we think, is the compelling reason for the willingness of technically trained people to be involved in consulting.

TEN

Maintaining
Professional Competence

a problem for all consultants: staying current
in a specialty • acceptance of the reality
that consulting requires a change in attitude
about maintaining competence • some
approaches to maintaining competence •
an alternative view—the generalist

The scientific consultant is unquestionably a businessperson whose company products and services are technical information and science-based advice. The reality of this statement has to be accepted by every practitioner. Once accepted, then the logical sequence that follows is (1) the science on which the business depends must be current and (2) to ensure that currency, the consultant must maintain his technical competence. These dicta are easy to state but extraordinarily difficult to achieve. Just reflect for a minute on the chapter about marketing and selling, or the one on managing.

How can any scientific consultant, whose workday must include attention to and sometimes hours devoted to such business-related responsibilities, be expected to maintain professional competence? Potential clients can and do expect it and it is one of the core requirements for long-term success in technical consulting. Regardless of how routine some procedures become in satisfying the "boiler-plate" specifications of a contract, there must always exist in the consulting organization a nucleus of cutting-edge expertise and familiarity with all aspects of the specialty area of consultation.

METHODS FOR
MAINTAINING COMPETENCE

A key point here is that professional competence can be maintained reasonably adequately without major participation in hands-on field or laboratory research. The substitutes—and they are not perfect—include: dedicated time for library research, especially with current journals; participation in seminar groups in the specialty areas at a nearby university; auditing relevant courses at that university; and periodic sabbaticals spent in government or academic laboratories or field stations involved in research on topics within the consultant's specialty areas. Additionally, some of the activities mentioned in Chapter Eight under *indirect marketing* can help in the struggle to maintain professional competence. They include participating in the meetings, committee activities, and governance of professional societies, presenting papers at those meetings, and writing and publishing articles in journals and science magazines on broad issues in selected discipline areas and in science generally.

The battle for continuing scientific competence within the strictures of a consulting company environment is rough and never-ending. The day-to-day demands of running a viable consulting venture can at times seem overwhelming, leaving little time for the science on which the organization is based. But then, similar time-devouring activities exist in other enclaves of science—government laboratories with their crushing load of bureaucratic paperwork, industrial laboratories with frequent changes in research direction and total product orientation, and universities with sometimes onerous faculty committee and teaching requirements. None of these activities, though, seems to have the same immediacy or the life-and-death quality of those consuming the time and energy of the consultant.

A significant subset of the problem of *maintaining* scientific competence is the problem of *acquiring* that competence within the infrastructure of consulting firms. This dilemma of course confronts all of the bright young bachelor's degree people who are recruited, before their time, to do the drudgery-level work on which many contract performances are founded. The problem is almost intractable; the best solution is to return to graduate school to build credentials and competencies that will permit truly professional participation in consulting as a career, if that choice is made. The time spent in early servitude is not entirely wasted, though, because it provides an insider's perspective on what consulting is like, and whether it is worth the apparent financial advantages to scientists. The early experience also provides an opportunity to evaluate the factors contributing to success or failure of other people's consulting ventures, and, most importantly, it offers a rare opportunity to scrutinize in some depth the way of life of a consultant.

One pronounced negative aspect of science as it is practiced by consultants is the proprietary nature of their findings from any original research they may do for a client. Often the contract specifies that all such information is the property of the client, and its release is subject to approval by the client (which is rarely given). This restricts or prohibits publication of scientific findings by the consultant, and may even result in assigning of patent rights to the client. The consequences of these contractual limitations are twofold: restrictions on publications result in a weak curriculum vitae if the scientist should leave consulting, and other scientists deeply resent the intrusion of the claim of "proprietary information" during discussions at scientific meetings, which are presumably devoted to open exchange. The consultant could be cast by some colleagues as a parasite, acquiring information but contributing nothing to the flow of knowledge at society meetings and conferences.

Our conclusion, from the information that we have been able to assemble, is that too many consulting scientists do *not* maintain an acceptable level of scientific competence. They may become expert in aspects of *consulting methodology*, but their knowledge of conceptual advances, new techniques, and current literature in their scientific specialty area, and in complementary technical areas, erodes quickly. We think that much of this erosion is a consequence of the unavailability of time to be involved in all of the activities normally required of a scientist— browsing through journals, carrying on active research, attending seminars, attending symposia, participating in activities of professional societies—so all are sacrificed in whole or in large part on the altar of business and profits. Despite firm resolutions and written daily or weekly schedules that set aside hours for professional enrichment, the reality is that most practitioners become totally engulfed by constant pressures from the business side of consulting—proposal preparation, marketing and selling, travel to confer with clients, report writing, employee relations, or resolution of financial crises. Science, as most of us understand it, cannot possibly prosper in such an environment.

ACCEPTANCE OF LOSS IN COMPETENCE

If this somewhat gloomy conclusion has any validity—and we think it does—then how is the scientific consultant to come to terms with the nearly inevitable erosive process? A balancing act, trying to succeed as a scientist and as a businessperson, could prove too stressful, so *acceptance of some loss in competency should be made by the consultant*, just as it is by the scientist who accepts a full-time role as laboratory director or program coordinator. Career objectives change for many reasons, so the eager but naive scientist in his early thirties may not be the same professional in his fifties. Attitudes and value systems metamorphose with the passage of time—as do levels of competence—this is the reality that we should face.

We think, though, that there are methods to be tested in the struggle to maintain scientific competency. These are expansions of or additions to those already mentioned. Some that offer the greatest promise are the following:

- Solo professionals, once their consultancies are solvent, should set aside one specific day of the week when the office is closed, when telephone messages are received only by the answering machine, and when the consultant is busy with the affairs of science—with journals, technical seminars, society affairs, library research, or college teaching. Any exceptions to this time reservation would have to be the consequences of genuine crises. (Of course this idealistic plan would have to be evaluated ever so carefully in advance, as we

are talking here about diverting one-fifth of a normal workweek away from billable pursuits.)

• Solo professionals, after achieving profitability
and diligently ascending the consultant's learning
curve for a few years, should consider and should
plan for a *sabbatical* of from three to six months.
This period should be spent in technical renewal—
auditing university courses, preparing scientific
papers for publication, attending an international
conference, writing a book, participating in a
short-term appointment or internship in a government laboratory—anything with a genuine flavor
of science and without the urgency of business.

• For those fortunate enough to require less than
eight hours' sleep and who are willing to forego
family obligations and all outside activities, a regi-
men of nightly journal reading and technical report preparation may be feasible.

*One approach to maintaining competency and contacts
with science was suggested by Dr. L. T. Whitman, a
successful long-term consultant who practices by choice
in a small seaside town. He was naturally concerned
about the isolation, the difficulty in maintaining contacts,
and the real problem of keeping up with developments in
his specialty. One of his responses to those concerns was
the formation and leadership of* monthly professional
consultants' forums *to which scientific consultants in
his region were invited. The participation was multidisciplinary, with announced topics or issues for discussion. The most popular agenda items were "brainstorm-
ing" sessions on real-life problems proposed by the
participants in the forum—with an attempt to reach some
consensus on a plan of action. As hoped, benefits of the
sessions included increased awareness of the existence of
counterpart consultancies in the region and their areas of
specialization, some general indication of the nature and
extent of other forms of consultant work in the region, and*

greatly increased communication relative to new clients and contract possibilities. One unexpected dividend was increased respect *for the various competencies that were represented by members of the group, and for unique technical problems faced by practitioners from other disciplines. Another unexpected consequence was a sharp increase in the number of joint multidisciplinary proposals, once the participants had a chance to evaluate the competence and professional attitudes of their colleagues from other specialties.*

Dr. Whitman was enthusiastic about the forum approach, and indicated future or alternate directions that his or other groups might take—such as panel discussions on environmental regulations that included invited lawyers, or panel discussions on suburban development that included invited politicians. Other suggested approaches included exploration of a "case history" series of presentations in which past consulting contracts carried out by individual participants could be reviewed (with full protection of proprietary information) and commented on by other members of the group.

- A very demanding approach to restoring technical competency is to teach a graduate course in a scientific specialty area. For an active consultant this should probably be tried first as a seminar course without a lab, and it might even be team-taught with other professionals (just to spread the responsibility). Encounters with bright young graduate students can be both stimulating and daunting, and can be an excellent basis for self-evaluation of personal competence in any specialty.
- One good use of the colleague network—especially that part of it that includes academic professionals—can be to seek entry to membership in project review panels, grant evaluation committees, or assessment groups of various kinds. These are often formed at the request of a federal agency, but

membership is usually based on expertise in the subject matter area and does not normally exclude consulting scientists. Participation provides two things: a felt need to be conversant with current knowledge and new developments in a specialty area, and access to peers who are involved in or who chair the many national (or even international) groups that provide scientific oversight services in every conceivable discipline.

Our general feeling, in this matter of maintaining scientific competency, is that scientific consultants must try harder to be *scientists* as well as businesspeople. After all, the career choice was theirs, and their clients expect a high degree of professionalism, which includes current technical knowledge in the discipline of their consultancy.

Before we leave this topic, though, we want to point out that there is a completely different perspective that can be taken on the entire matter of maintaining technical competence—one that has been accepted by many consultants. Its essential statement is that *a scientific consultant does not need to be and should not be expected to be in the vanguard of the research community*, but he should be aware of *current developments and the published literature* in the speciality area(s) of the consultancy. The consulting role is distinct from that characteristic of most scientists, as it emphasizes synthesis and interpretation of existing information, rather than creation of new knowledge. If this line of reasoning is acceptable, then the scientific consultant should not be judged by the same criteria that are applied to academic or government scientists, whose primary responsibilities are usually in research.

As technical information increases in volume and complexity, a division develops and widens naturally between the *specialists* producing new data and concepts in any discipline and the *generalists* (including the consultants) who package available information from many sources and apply it to practical problems and issues. This trend will undoubtedly accelerate in the future; we should encourage the full expression of those distinct roles for professionals, rather than trying to force them all into the same stereotype of "the scientist." We should probably also temper any judgment about the correctness of the choices of roles by scientists, as both sets of activities—research and application—serve useful societal goals.

•   •   •

Scientific consultants normally have much the same graduate training as research scientists, but have chosen to apply their technical knowledge to real-world problems. Consulting practice requires major commitment to business matters unrelated to science, and the consequence of that requirement must be drastic reduction in time devoted to activities typical of scientists in a generic sense. It follows that reduced competence, as judged by general criteria applied to all scientists, may well be the outcome. The insertion of other criteria, such as ability to synthesize and interpret large data sets, and the ability to make scientific information meaningful to the public and its agencies, can, however, provide a better balance in evaluating the contributions of scientific consultants to society.

Special Topics in Scientific Consulting

This, the third and final part of the book, contains nine diverse chapters:

Part Two provided a core of information about the *operational* aspects of consulting; Part Three explores subjects extending from legal matters to the future of consulting, with intermediate stops to discuss the dark side of consulting, international consulting, the kinds of scientists who become consultants, and other substantive matters that can help form the completed tapestry of consulting practice. It is our firm expectation that the "nuts and bolts" elements already considered in Part Two will integrate magically with the special topics to be discussed in Part Three, thereby forming a reasonably comprehensive examination of consulting as conducted by those professionals with scientific backgrounds.

ELEVEN

The Legal Side
of a Scientific
Consulting Practice

areas of consulting business activities that call
for legal assistance: document preparation
and litigation • scientific consultants
as expert witnesses: encounters in courtrooms
and hearing rooms

The professional existence of most academic scientists is remarkably free from any contact with the legal universe of lawyers, legal documents, courtrooms, or hearing rooms. Some brief interactions may be necessary for patent applications, for a rare appearance as an expert witness, or in equally rare disputes over perceived abuses of intellectual property (claims of copyright infringement, or plagiarism), but otherwise academic scientists are largely untroubled by legal matters in the pursuit of their career.

This blissful state of affairs is decidedly not available to those members of the scientific community who elect to be consultants. That decision changes the ground rules radically, and ensures that legal considerations will become part of the scientific consultant's professional life. Lawyers and the legal system will intrude, and become significant, in two principal areas: (1) business activities and (2) presentation of testimony as an expert witness.

A recommended course of action for a new consulting venture is to hire a young, aggressive, knowledgeable lawyer as a consultant and advisor (preferably on a limited retainer basis), and to do it early—right after a young, aggressive, knowledgeable CPA has been hired (also on a retainer basis). As the consultancy expands, these people (or their successors) can become integral elements of the management team, either as partners or as long-term consultants. A lawyer can do much to reduce conflicts and avoid litigation, and, in this way, protect the business from unwarranted damage. Advice from a good trial lawyer can be of great value in preparing scientists to be effective expert witnesses.

CONSULTING BUSINESS ACTIVITIES THAT REQUIRE LEGAL ASSISTANCE

We are all part of an increasingly litigious society, so scientific consultants, as businesspeople, must play by the same game rules as their cohorts in other kinds of businesses. These rules always involve legalistic caveats, restrictions, strictures, definitions, interpretations, limitations, exclusions, and inclusions, so a level playing field requires knowledge of (or availability of advice about) anything related to the business that has legal implications.

Legal assistance is necessary to every consultancy in two general areas: (1) oversight of documents and (2) litigation involving the company. Each of these functions requires some elaboration here.

DOCUMENT OVERSIGHT

Despite some natural reluctance to augment the financial advantage of members of the legal profession, we have to point out that there are certain business functions of a consultancy that require legal assistance. Most of the activities involve preparation or review of documents. For this, the occasional services of a competent attorney are necessary, mostly to provide scrutiny and advice about the following kinds of paperwork:

- Documents to establish a partnership or to incorporate the business
- All agreements and contracts with clients
- All nondisclosure agreements
- All contracts with subcontractors and agreements with other consultants for joint conduct of projects
- All reports containing recommendations or advice
- Copyright applications for certain documents developed and published by the consultant

Standard forms for many of these categories exist, or they can be prepared *de novo* by people without legal training, but a lawyer may be able to offer insights about deficiencies or omissions before misunderstandings occur. This can be especially true for consulting contracts and agreements with subcontractors, in which precise responsibilities of each party must be clearly defined. Surely, some arrangement can be made by every consultancy for at least minimal legal scanning of those documents that may influence the well-being of the organization.

LITIGATION

Beyond the routine but important legal review of all documents related to the consultancy, informed legal assistance becomes critical in two kinds of somewhat uncommon events:

- Civil lawsuits initiated by the consultancy
- Civil lawsuits brought against the consultancy

In both kinds of events, discussions, negotiations, and compromises are certainly preferable to formal court proceedings; in fact, most consultants will go to remarkable lengths to avoid court cases. Occasionally, though, the situation becomes confrontational and irreconcilable, and this is when the legal system becomes a participant.

Lawsuits initiated by the consultant often result from attempts to collect long-overdue major bills from former clients, or to recover advance payments made to a non-performing subcontractor. Legal actions against the consultant are principally initiated by dissatisfied or disgruntled clients, or clients who claim unsatisfactory contract performance to avoid paying the consultant's bill—or at least to reduce the size of it. Variations in the details of legal actions against the consultant are almost endless, but each one has a negative effect on the consultancy, regardless of motivation or outcome. Each one, fairly or unfairly, reduces the perceived credibility of the firm, whatever the reality may be or whatever the final decision may be.

One fairly recent development (during the past two decades) has been a substantial increase in malpractice suits against consultants.[19] Such litigation is usually brought by dissatisfied clients, or by third parties who claim damages as a consequence of faulty advice given by the consultant to the client. Any legal actions can have severe negative impacts on a consulting business that depends ultimately on its own credibility, but they may at times identify inadequate contract performances. Often such actions reflect an abysmal failure in communication on the part of the consultant during the project, and an unwillingness to correct deficiencies in contract performance after it is completed. Most reputable consultants try to protect themselves by providing consistently high-quality service and insisting on constant communication with clients, to reduce the likelihood of misunderstandings. Those same professionals will usually try to find some compromise, or will do any remedial work that seems reasonable (and even some that seems unreasonable) in an effort to avoid litigation. If, despite corrective steps, the malpractice action goes to court, it is always reassuring to have an informed attorney ready to plead the case, but with the recognition that a decision favoring the consultant is never a clear victory.

SCIENTIFIC CONSULTANTS AS EXPERT WITNESSES

One of the positive consequences of the environmental movement during the past two decades has been the emergence of experienced courtroom and hearing room-wise scientists from government, industry, and academia who have the background and the facts to hold their own in adversary proceedings or in regulatory hearings. Before entering the courtroom or hearing room, the scientific consultant, in any specialty area, needs several high-level qualifications:

- An established reputation as an expert, with a clear and current expertise in the specific area of legal controversy, and a complete familiarity with relevant published information
- More than passing acquaintance with legal concepts and courtroom procedures—particularly

with hearsay information, data and their abuses, and limits of expertise
- Painfully acquired *experience* in dealing with lawyers and with their legal universe and worldviews, which are totally foreign to those of most scientists

Some useful approaches for the scientific consultant include auditing selected courses in law schools, or attending relevant hearings and cases as an unidentified observer. A legal concept that is most difficult for scientists to comprehend and accept is that *lawyers want to win cases, and are not unduly concerned with a search for truth*, unless it is of advantage to their cases. It can be a great source of frustration to uninitiated scientists to learn that their valid and conclusive information may never be allowed to be presented, or that their testimony may be brought into question by seemingly extraneous considerations, or that they may be discredited as experts by technicalities. For the consultants who become involved in any legal or regulatory proceedings, the ultimate in skill will be required. Basic procedures include the following:

- Establish *competence* as indicated by training, degrees, experience, research, and publications.
- Establish *credibility* by demonstrating that data and conclusions are based on the use of standard methods, producing results within acceptable confidence limits.
- State facts and conclusions drawn therefrom clearly, distinctly, and succinctly.
- Offer clearly identified opinions and interpretations if requested, but *never* extend beyond the confines of the best available information, regardless of pressures.
- Where possible, in giving hearing testimony, insert a carefully prepared, scientifically sound,

signed document containing a summary of your remarks into the record.

The prudent scientific consultant is well advised to treat the courtroom or hearing room as a jungle, populated by such major predators as (1) lawyers who would impugn or destroy scientific reputations without a moment's hesitation, (2) hostile expert witnesses (possibly also consultants) who have the credentials and experience to cast doubt on the testimony of the uninitiated, and (3) hearing examiners who may have an agency position to defend, regardless of the evidence.

Encounters with legal minds range from informal hearings on patent applications through formal hearings conducted by agency examiners or fact-finding hearings conducted by district courts, to subpoenaed testimony in civil court cases involving claims for damages from such events as toxic chemical spills or vessel groundings. Some ground rules apply to all: enter the gates of any legal coliseum with great caution and always with professional counsel; never underestimate the intelligence of any person involved; never make comments for the record that cannot be supported by data, or that are beyond your area of expertise; don't give the court or hearing examiner a minilecture in your area of expertise, regardless of the temptation; where possible, come to the hearing with a prepared signed statement, to ensure that your complete testimony will become part of the record in the event that you are prevented from giving it orally; make certain that every word of the prepared statement is defensible and founded on fact; and, if possible, have the prepared statement examined by a lawyer before it is submitted.

For those scientific consultants with genuine expertise, with willingness to learn, with agile minds, and with a suitably thick and keratinized epidermis, here is a stimulating and demanding testing ground.

With the increasing involvement of scientists and

engineers in various kinds of legal proceedings and regulatory hearings, many professional societies and organizations have felt it necessary to develop codes of conduct and lists of instructions for their members who might become participants in these events.[20] Issues considered range from ethical concerns to very practical matters of comportment as an expert witness in a courtroom environment. Some of the available material is surprisingly detailed, especially that produced by groups such as the National Society of Professional Engineers, the American Institute of Professional Geologists, and the American Fisheries Society. Sifting through this good and voluminous information for gems, we have retrieved and assembled a short list of 20 admonitions, cautions, warnings, and suggestions, to help guide the scientific consultant along what may be at first unfamiliar pathways (but not unfamiliar for long). The list can be subdivided into three categories: (1) client relations, (2) investigations, and (3) courtroom behavior. Understand at the outset, though, that books have been written on these topics, so what we have retained here is but a tiny fragment of the total mass of information that is out there.

CLIENT RELATIONS

- Before agreeing to participate as an expert witness, make absolutely certain that you are competent to deal with the subject matter of the case.
- Give honest impartial information, always within a framework of ethical practice, which places truth above all other considerations.
- Advise your client, well in advance of any legal proceedings, of the nature of your findings and conclusions, and of their possible effects on the legal action at hand.

- Do not divulge information developed for a client to others, unless legally required to do so.
- Maintain data, analyses, syntheses, results, and conclusions in confidential files, to be used in preparing your testimony.
- Dissociate yourself from any procedure that is or appears to be fraudulent.
- The credibility of a professional can be weakened if he is constantly on one side in conflicts, be they those of industry, government, or environmentalists.

INVESTIGATIONS

- Express opinions only when they are based on adequate information—which usually means that a detailed study must be made.
- Make thorough investigations and assemble good documentation, but do not prepare or use misleading exhibits, graphs, or tables.
- Scientific consultants hired for a court case will be expected to have extensive interactions with the client's lawyers, and may be asked to prepare questions and answers (interrogatories).
- Expert witnesses are often subpoenaed to give depositions under oath that may be used later in a court case.

COURTROOM BEHAVIOR

- Find out as much as possible about the principal actors who will be performing in the courtroom or hearing room—the judge or hearing examiner, the lawyers for government agencies, industry groups, and public interest organizations, and especially the other expert witnesses (some of whom may be hostile).

- Insist on a conference with a friendly lawyer before giving testimony, to receive a preview of what is expected during the session.
- While in the courtroom answer questions briefly and deliberately; do not volunteer too much information; and use layman's language as far as possible.
- Remember that expert witnesses are permitted to use notes in giving their courtroom presentations.
- Take full advantage of the fact that expert witnesses are permitted to include explanations and qualifications in their responses to questions during cross-examinations.
- Always keep in mind that, as an expert witness, you are testifying as to facts and the conclusions that can be drawn from them. Your opinion is important, but speculations should be avoided.
- Be prepared for attempts by the opposition lawyers to discredit you or your testimony as an expert, by obtaining conflicting statements for the record.
- Beware of trick questions by opposition lawyers that require a "yes" or "no" answer; request the court to allow you to qualify or explain your answer.
- Do not necessarily agree with appeals to authority (other experts, books, journal articles) by opposition lawyers; instead cite the authorities on which you base your opinion.
- Use the courtroom episode as a learning experience, to ensure that you will be better prepared for future events of this kind. Try to get opinions from the client's lawyers about the effectiveness of your testimony (and any shortcomings).

- Finally, keep in mind that while you are addressing the court you are representing the scientific community in an obviously alien environment. Do it superbly.

We recommend strongly that if the role of expert witness is to be a common one, it should be played as a professional and not as an awkward ingenue. Read the specialized texts referred to earlier, observe the courtroom conduct of really good expert witnesses, prepare test performances of your own, and try to penetrate legal minds whenever possible.

•   •   •

Here, then, are three disparate compartments of a consultant's existence where legal assistance may be necessary: (1) when professional advice about legal documents is needed, (2) when business-related litigation may be imminent (malpractice suits in particular), and (3) when participation as an expert witness may be part of contract performance in civil cases or in regulatory hearings.

Scientists who would be successful consultants should (in addition to being technically competent and effective businesspeople) acquaint themselves with enough legal information in the areas mentioned to know when it is time to seek professional advice, and to recognize the vulnerability created by absence of legal support.

TWELVE

The Downside of
Scientific Consulting

---

downsizing and its consequences • reasons
for failures of consultancies • clients from
hell • dirty tricks by competitors • the evils of
remedial and second-opinion contracts • bill-
collecting problems • fragility of consultants'
products • perceptions of malfeasance

Judging from the reported high level of failures, full-
time scientific consulting is clearly a high-risk business. Based on long observation, we think that this
problem has its foundation in the genetic background, the
training, and especially the mind-set of scientists. Most of
them are not business-oriented, and many of them actively dislike anything related to business practices. They
are the ones who belong in universities, government research laboratories, or some types of industrial research
laboratories—leaving the rough and tumble of consulting
to the small fraction of their cohorts who, because of

family background, desire for a better living standard, or maybe some kind of inherited trait, are comfortable in the intensely practical world of the consultant. This minority, who might be called "atypical" scientists, comprise the group from which business successes are drawn—the scientists willing, able, and preconditioned to adapt to a sometimes harsh new environment, and to carry their technical expertise with them.

In the 1990s we have watched with some horror the increasing popularity and effects of a phenomenon euphemistically called "downsizing" (eliminating employees). Scientists have not been immune, as evidenced by the hordes of applicants for even mediocre scientific positions, or by the obscenity of highly trained professionals being forced to take low-paying jobs outside science. Consulting can be perceived by at least some of these displaced or frustrated scientists as an interim alternative to unemployment, even if they have little or no backgrounds in business methods. These are the ranks from which some of the consulting business failures are drawn—professionals ill-equipped by training or inclination, but driven by economic necessity, to enter a subdivision of scientific employment that is utterly foreign to them.

There is another group of scientifically trained people who have been affected negatively by current economic conditions. These are the bright energetic young men and women with bachelor's degrees who compete, without adequate credentials, for entry-level professional jobs. During the 1970s and even in the early 1980s the lower ranks of the larger scientific consulting companies were populated with people at this level of training. They were hired to do the field surveys or the routine data collections and chemical analyses needed for specific contracts, and were then terminated, sometimes to be rehired on another contract project and sometimes not. Some of them escaped into graduate schools; others survived marginally from year to year and contract to contract, without any real job security. The market even for this level of participation in science has contracted beginning in the mid-1980s, although it has not disappeared altogether. It is still a reasonable temporary expedient and training ground for upwardly mobile entry-level individuals on their way to graduate school and true professionalism.

REASONS FOR FAILURES
OF CONSULTANCIES

No meaningful chapter on the downside of scientific consulting would be complete without confronting the question "Why do consulting ventures fail?" We have already offered, early in this chapter, our opinion about the most important reason for failure of scientific consultancies—*the wrong kinds of scientists* (the non-business-oriented ones) *are often in charge,* and are not willing or able to adapt to a new environment in which skills in marketing, cost analysis, sales, and management are elements governing success or failure. Huddled beneath this umbrella statement are such specific perceptions as "Marketing and sales activities are repugnant to many technically trained professionals, and are often avoided or ignored" or "Business planning is useful, but to most professionals their reputations and contract performances are perceived as more important ingredients of success" or "Management activities, especially those related to financial and personnel matters, are important, but to many consultants they are subsidiary to the science involved in a project."

A more arguable reason for the failure of full-time scientific consulting ventures is *unfair competition from a superabundance of part-time consultants who have other sources of income*—either as university professors or as recently retired professionals. Competition from members of either of these groups is heavily weighted by several factors:

- Their additional sources of income—salaries or pensions—reduce the need to emphasize profitability and marketing.
- They are often parts of long-established networks that assist in steering contracts in their direction.
- Overhead expenses for them, as individual practitioners, are minimal.
- They often have exceptional reputations in their specialty areas.
- The university professors in the group have a superb source of cheap labor—graduate students.

Other reasons for the failure of consulting ventures have been proposed:[11]

- Some professionals need to be surrounded by organizations and support staff, and do not function well as individual practitioners.
- Some individual practitioners fail to maintain continuing marketing and sales momentum.
- Some individual practitioners commit to excessive overhead expenses, or withdraw too much from current income for personal expenses.
- Some scientists communicate poorly with clients or potential clients. They are great believers in the mistaken thesis that technical jargon will impress clients or prospective clients. Inadequate communication is a universal contributor to problems in any human endeavor, and one that stands out clearly in any discussions of managerial inadequacies—in consultancies or in other scientific organizations.

This depressing recital of the ingredients of failure for consultancies could go on and on, but it won't. We'd like to shut it off with one more reason of our own: Differences in *perceptions* of a consultant's expertise and competence can be overriding in decisions made by potential clients about hiring or not hiring a particular professional—whether those perceptions reflect reality or not. Additionally, choices made by potential clients among consultants may be affected by a number of considerations other than perceived or real competence. Friendships, aggressive marketing, and even the graduate school attended by the consultant may influence the selection process.

CLIENTS FROM HELL

Operating a service business, which is what consultants do, can expose the unwary, or naive, or financially stressed practitioner to an awesome array of cheats, liars, and thieves—in addition to all of the honest, sincere, and reliable people in this world. As part of our continuing emphasis on the downside of consulting in this chapter, we want to identify type specimens of the undesirables, and then discuss defenses against them that are available to ethical scientific consultants. Jostling for position in our rogues' gallery of clients or would-be clients to be avoided are these:

- The make-believe client who does not plan to hire any consultant, but invites preliminary discussions and/or proposals from a number of them, with the objective of obtaining free information, advice, or action plans that can be useful to his in-house staff.

- The would-be client who requests proposals from a number of consultants, even though he may have preselected one. The other consultants, unaware of this device, act in good faith by preparing proposals. This deliberate waste of professionals' time may be merely to satisfy company or agency policy that requires several bids.
- The would-be client who wants to award a contract to a personal friend or relative, but who invites other proposals that can be extracted or modified or copied and used by the favored candidate.
- The client who asks repeatedly that additional work be done by the consultant, without additional funding.
- The client who consistently nitpicks and tries to micromanage the day-to-day activities of the consultant.
- The client who is suspicious and hostile about every dollar claimed in the consultant's vouchers, and who insists on detailed explanations for every item.
- The client who does not pay on time, or who does not pay at all unless brought into court—and then claims that the consultant's work was unsatisfactory.
- The client who has an undisclosed hidden agenda for the information developed in good faith by a consultant.
- The client who tries to have the consultant modify conclusions or interpretations of data to better suit his (the client's) needs.

Fortunately, the perceptive consultant has defenses against falling into the clutches of undesirable customers—although there are always new tricks to cheat

ethical practitioners. Some workable protective measures
are to:

- Conduct a preliminary screening of prospective
  clients, before any meetings are held or proposals
  prepared. Networking among colleagues may disclose positive or negative information about previous consultant interactions—assuming that the
  colleague is willing to talk frankly.
- Include, as part of the early interactions with all
  prospective clients, the completion of a standard
  credit form, with provision of references that can
  be (and should be) checked.
- Look in local and state tax records for clues about
  the would-be client company's finances and length
  of existence.
- Look for information about the prospective client
  company from chambers of commerce, trade associations, or better business bureaus.

These and other strategies can reduce the number of
time-wasting interactions with deadbeat or pseudoclients,
but the barriers are never foolproof. Despite reasonable
caution about selecting clients, it is still possible for a
consultant to become involved with people who have a
varied menu of activities bordering on the unethical—
such as

- Contracting with a new consultant after a previous
  one has submitted a report unfavorable to the client's position—without informing the new consultant about the earlier work
- Expecting significant fee reductions from consultants in times of financial stress in the client's business, or expecting substantial additional work to
  be done after a contract is signed

- Recruiting members of the consultant's staff during or after the term of a contract

So, carefully selected clients are an essential base of the scientific consulting business, even though the selection process may be blurred or modified by financial considerations (especially during periods of contract scarcity).

"DIRTY TRICKS" BY COMPETITORS

Financial problems, business failures, and unsavory clients are only part of the downside of scientific consulting. We reviewed in Chapter Seven the ethical circles that surround the professional, but we did not explore the fascinating area of ethical misbehavior—so-called "dirty tricks"—inflicted on the ethical consultant by his *competitors*. Here are some (and remember that these competitors are presumably professionals too):

- Starting a rumor campaign suggesting that the consultant's data are unreliable, that the consulting practice is about to close for financial reasons, that the consultant's billing practices are suspect, or that the consultant's fees are excessive
- Deliberately hiring away key consultant staff members by promises of inflated salaries, unusual perks or bonuses, or provision of superior facilities and equipment
- Deliberately underbidding a choice contract, with every intention of submitting supplementary requests for funds later in the contract period
- Unfounded "nuisance" complaints to professional organizations and scientific societies that the business or professional practices of the consultant are unethical

Of course, this kind of behavior characterizes only the pathological fringes of consulting, but it occurs often enough to have been mentioned a number of times in our interviews.

THE UGLY TWINS OF CONSULTING: REMEDIAL AND SECOND-OPINION CONTRACTS

As we are wandering around in the pits of consulting's downside, it might be appropriate to describe what we call "remedial" and "second-opinion" consulting. The remedial component is understandable enough: A previous consultant has not completed the work required by the contract, because of illness, business failure, ineptitude, disagreements with the client, or the like. A replacement consultant is hired to complete the work and submit a final report. Clouds are already on the horizon, though. How good are the data already collected, and are they immediately available? Is the design of the study adequate or should the contract be amended or replaced? Is the price structure of the original contract in accord with the policies of the new consultant? Is there a deadline to be met, and is it feasible? Is the client apt to place unreasonable demands on the new consultant (as may have been the case with the previous consultant)? This kind of consulting should be reserved for those who are absolutely desperate for work.

The uglier twin of remedial consulting is second-opinion consulting—in which the original contract work was completed but the work or the conclusions drawn from it were not satisfactory to the client, who now wants the job repeated and another report submitted. The new contract work may well be done in a hostile atmosphere often characterized as adversarial/confrontational, with the possibility of unseemly squabbles. Pressure may be applied on the new consultant by the client to adopt an advocacy position, and the likelihood of legal action is high. Before such a second-opinion contract is signed, the second consultant should ask some key questions:

- What is the complete history of the proposed project?
- Have other consultants had contracts and then been dismissed?
- Have related studies been conducted by other consultants, by university scientists, or by government agencies, and if so, what were the findings?
- Is the client trying to employ the new consultant so as to reach a desired preconceived conclusion?

Unless the answers to these questions indicate strongly that this is a straightforward request for a second professional opinion, with no hidden agendas, the second consultant should reject it, or face the great likelihood of an unpleasant and potentially litigious contract effort, with results that may be unsatisfactory to all concerned.

Variations in the problems inherent in second-opinion consulting seem almost endless. Many of them involve attempts by unsavory or untrustworthy businesses, realtors, developers, private profit groups, or money laundering enterprises to enlist the assistance of naive or unsuspecting consultants in schemes that may be illicit or actually illegal. Because the authors of this book have backgrounds in environmental sciences, we are most comfortable with illustrations drawn from that area of practice.

- An investment group of shoreline developers in a southeastern state went ahead, unilaterally and without permits, to destroy substantial stands of mangroves—against the specific advice of an environmental consulting firm that had been hired, then fired. When the illegal activity was brought to the attention of the appropriate regulatory agency, the Department of Environmental Resources Management, the developers were profuse in their apologies but insisted that they were merely "trimming" the mangroves. They humbly offered to begin reparation and mitigation, and to hire another consultant to provide guidance for the project. We ask: "What sensible environmental consultant would want to be inserted in this no-win situation—*after* the damage has been done, the problem exposed, and a regulatory agency aroused?" The malefactors did find one, a retired government bureaucrat, but his contract was soon canceled after much acrimony, because his proposed remediation measures would be too expensive. Our last bit of information is that the developers are awaiting a legal decision and are still searching for a more gullible consultant to give them "better" advice. Meanwhile, the mangroves have been "trimmed" out of existence, the shoreline looks like a disaster zone, and the entire project is in abeyance.

- A competent but very young university assistant professor was given a contract by a chemical company to examine the biological effects of its factory effluent on shellfish stocks in the vicinity of the ocean outfall. Initial findings were that populations had been severely reduced in an extended area around the outfall, and that high levels of abnormalities were present in survivors. The news did not please the client company. The young consultant's contract was terminated abruptly and the company hired another more senior scientist with a reputation for charging large fees, conducting minimal studies, and reaching broad conclusions that usually fitted the customer's needs. He concluded that the population reduction was probably a consequence of several years of above-normal seawater temperatures, that the abnormalities seen were genetically determined characteristics of the subpopulation sampled, and were probably *not* induced by chemical contamination from the company's effluents. The second consultant had been in the business for three decades, so he had a form of longevity-created credibility in environmental matters, especially in hearings conducted by state natural resources agencies and the federal Environmental Protection Agency. The first consultant was bright but a relative novice; she was scheduled to learn a hard lesson in the hearing room: Clients pay for advice that they want to hear, even if the background studies are trash.

TRYING TO GET PAID

Too many respondents to our questionnaire indicated that one of the truly unpleasant aspects of being a small consultant was trying to collect overdue bills. Reluctance of clients to pay on time, or to pay at all except under extreme pressure, negates the satisfactions that would otherwise accrue to the consultant for completing a contract—and could put the consultancy in a serious financial bind if the overdue bill is a big one.

Fortunately, there are protective measures that the consultant can take against doing business with clients who can't or won't pay. They include:

- Having every contract or letter of agreement tightly written and scrutinized in advance by a lawyer to forestall attempts by the client to avoid payment because of some minor technicality
- Being certain that the total fee is stated, together with when it is due (for example, one-half on signing and one-half on delivery of the final report—or within thirty days from receipt of the final report)
- Including a statement in the contract that the full fee is due even if the client changes his mind and cancels (thus allowing for some consultant-controlled negotiation, if necessary)
- Being very selective in the choice of clients, with such approaches as checking with networking colleagues on the reputation of the would-be client, or requesting credit references, or determining the age of the would-be client's business, from state incorporation records
- Expecting all new clients to fill out a standard credit questionnaire before any commitments are made
- Delivering the final report in person, with a scheduled follow-up meeting with the client to get a reaction to the report—especially if there are complaints—and to remind the client about contract provisions for payment

Use of some or all of these measures should help to reduce the trauma of bill collecting from recalcitrant clients. Other, more extreme, steps have been described.[21] The core of the problem seems to be that frequently in lean times consultants may feel forced to overlook the risks, and thus become vulnerable to the kinds of nonpaying clients who would normally be rejected.

THE FRAGILITY OF CONSULTANTS' PRODUCTS

Consultancies differ from most businesses in that their products are intangibles—information, opinions, plans, conclusions, evaluations, recommendations, and interpretations. Because they lack physical substance, the products of a consulting contract are fragile and subject to many abuses. Results of investigations may be misunderstood, misconstrued, or ignored by clients. Furthermore, advice and opinions from consultants may be subverted to meet the needs of a client's hidden agenda.

Our questionnaire responses indicated that more than half of all respondents had faced a situation in which their findings had been ignored or deliberately misinterpreted, or modified to more closely support the preconceptions of the client. The consultant is, of course, prevented from publicizing the contents of the final report, so the frustration level is high, and mounts even higher if the client uses his version of the consultant's conclusions as a stamp of approval for actions contrary to the ones recommended in the report. This kind of frustration is especially hard to tolerate if the consultant's credibility is at stake—as it usually is, to some degree.

PERCEPTIONS OF MALFEASANCE

A less obvious component of the downside of scientific consulting is the active dislike for such practitioners that exists among many colleagues who are involved in research and teaching—the so-called "academics." These "purer" professionals have a list of grievances and complaints against scientific consultants that was discussed briefly in Chapter Seven on Ethics, but seems important enough to be reexamined here. The list is headed by the following perceptions:

1. Consultants develop data that will support or help to validate a client's position.
2. Consultants reach conclusions and interpret data in such a way that the client's position is always supported.
3. Data are gleaned from the published literature or from the "gray" literature at no cost to the consultant, then repackaged and sold to a client at a high price.
4. Data developed by consultants are almost always "proprietary," and are not available to the larger scientific community in any form, published or otherwise.
5. Consultants with a record of consistently producing data and conclusions favorable to clients tend to persist and prosper, while others disappear.

Perceptions of such ethical fringe practices have led to charges by colleagues of "scientific streetwalking," "selling your scientific soul to the devil," and "industry whore" leveled at some consultants who find too consistently in favor of their customers. Whether these charges are based on perceptions or realities, they lead to *lack of acceptance* of consultants by their peers, and they must diminish any satisfaction that an ethical consultant may find in his work.

The pervasiveness of antipathy toward scientific consultants that is felt by academic (and government) scientists should not be underestimated. The sources of dislike are doubts about the objectivity of investigations and concerns that interpretations of data support a predetermined position too consistently. The most positive perception of many scientists is that consultants tread a thin line between advocacy and objectivity in their practices, but to some observers consulting scientists are often *advocates* and not unbiased professionals (as, for example, in some performances as expert witnesses). In the eyes of some academic scientists, consultants do not *act* like scientists (with their insistence on the proprietary nature of their findings), they do not *talk* like scientists (with their preoccupation with subjects such as marketing techniques and profit and loss), and, some say, they do not *think* like scientists (as they always seem to be giving a sales pitch or a public relations spiel). Negative feelings may be expressed in print by academics who have encountered consultants whom they consider to be unduly influenced by economic considerations. We think that part of the poor image stems from confusion about the kinds of consulting firms that are out there—especially those that are most vocal in highly visible controversies such as land usage. These are often *public relations firms* that are not science-based, or that have a very tenuous association with science. Their strongest suit is *advocacy*, for or against specific issues—advocacy that is denied to ethical scientific consultants.

It has been our observation, supported by only limited examples, that cadres of scientists that have developed (and are being perpetuated) in a number of specialty areas make interpretations of data to fit the needs of those who pay their consulting fees. By the consistency of their findings in favor of their clients, it is reasonable to wonder if those scientists have not overstepped the boundaries of scientific objectivity. Such individuals are shrewd, though. They have learned how to speak in terms that do not render them susceptible to refutation in hearings or court cases, or that could be proven to be misrepresentations of data. Their standard (and almost unassailable) responses are "This is my opinion, based on the available data" or "This is my interpretation of the data available to me." Members of these suspect cliques of scientific consultants cause damage to and reduce the status of the rest of the community of scientists.

•   •   •

We will not go on about the unpleasant underbelly of scientific consulting, regardless of temptations for further elaboration. We have touched on some of the principal sources of unhappiness—business failures, unethical competitors, dishonest clients, and negative stereotypes of consultant ethics. The negative components are real, and very much with us, but it is time now to resurface and breathe some fresh air in brighter fields of consulting activities.

THIRTEEN

Possible Escape Routes, if Consulting Should Not Work Out

---

why do some scientific consultants cease being consultants, and where do they go?

The discussion about career changes, begun in Chapter One, focused exclusively on moves *into* consulting, but there is, of course, the expected countercurrent, moving scientists at all levels *from* consulting to other types of professional activities. Some favorite destinations for former consultants are:

- Graduate school in science or some other professional specialty (e.g., law, medicine, public administration)

- University or college teaching
- Federal or state government agencies, as career bureaucrats or political appointees
- State or local government offices, as planners or technical specialists
- High-technology research and development or production ventures (as founders, cofounders, or employees)
- Nonprofit public interest or activist organizations, as researchers, public interaction specialists, or fund-raisers

It might be instructive to follow the sample exit pathways from consulting that we have just listed, and to offer a few comments on each one.

GRADUATE SCHOOL

This departure route is common among the junior professionals hired under short-term agreements, usually with no fringe benefits. Often the move is accompanied by the realization that a bachelor's degree constitutes inadequate preparation for a truly professional career in science. Interestingly, though, the graduate training selected by young former apprentices may not be in science at all; law and public administration are alternate specialties of choice. Graduate school can be a career choice for older consultants as well. It is not unusual for mid-career professionals to take sabbaticals, or at least to audit a few graduate-level refresher courses in their field of specialization, or in complementary subject matter areas. For some professionals, this searching behavior may be interpreted as an indication of unease with the existing job situation and a prelude to a career change.

UNIVERSITY OR COLLEGE TEACHING

Consultants with full professional credentials (Ph.D.'s) sometimes make a gradual transition to teaching. The change may begin with a request to teach a specialty course in the evenings at a local community college, and may then escalate to a part-time or adjunct appointment there or at some not-too-distant four-year college or university. Consultants who find out that they have above-average teaching abilities may continue to do the part-time thing indefinitely, as a source of pleasure, stimulation, or additional income, or they may wind down (but not completely discontinue) their consulting work and accept a full-time academic appointment.

FEDERAL OR STATE GOVERNMENT AGENCIES

Scientific consultants in areas such as public health or environmental regulation often have continuing contacts with midlevel federal or state government bureaucrats—especially with those who have scientific backgrounds. Perceptive consultants are always very careful to include such acquaintances in their extended networking circles, primarily to keep current on the status of regulatory actions in the various agencies and to get early notice of the availability of agency funds for consulting contracts. The relationships with bureaucrats become mutual when consultants provide unbiased free information about the worth of competitors and about the technical merit of draft proposals. It is not unusual for news about position openings in the agencies to reach networking consultants early, especially if they have indicated interest in changing careers.

STATE OR LOCAL GOVERNMENT OFFICES

The professional activities of scientific consultants often result in close working relationships with the inhabitants of the myriad offices of state and local governments—city engineers, local environmental protection agencies, state natural resource departments, local and state planning offices, and so forth. Some consultants may participate, through contract work, in special projects of those public entities, and may find that they enjoy the usually low-key local atmosphere and the "down-home" flavor of interactions, peppered with "laissez-faire" attitudes toward business and decision making. If they can fit comfortably into that kind of system, and if their career aspirations permit it, some consultants may take full-time paid jobs with state natural resources or environmental protection offices or with city and county planning offices.

HIGH-TECHNOLOGY RESEARCH AND DEVELOPMENT

We have already characterized consultants repeatedly as "entrepreneurs," in the sense that they establish and manage their own companies. But, for some, the entrepreneurial spirit may carry them far beyond consulting, into research and development (and eventually commercialization) of new high-tech-based products. During the past several decades we have witnessed the emergence and expansion of R&D ventures formed by one or more scientists—to develop new products that satisfy society's needs. Lately, emphasis has focused on products resulting from genetic manipulation, and on disease control with new drugs and techniques. The evolution of such high-tech enterprises often includes an interim period when the scientist is employed as a consultant for a large corporation, before he elects to take the high-risk step of forming a new product-oriented company.

NONPROFIT PUBLIC INTEREST ORGANIZATIONS

Consultants often find that their principal income comes from contracts (or subcontracts) with federal regulatory agencies, with international agencies such as the United Nations, or with large industries. The nature of their contract work may be such that they have frequent interactions with representatives of public interest organizations—all of whom have a major cause or issue to which they are committed. All of the representatives of those organizations that we have met are very intelligent and very vocal—descriptors that also fit many scientific consultants. It would not be difficult at all for a consultant with those qualifications to make the transition from operating his own practice to an intermediate or even a senior position with one of the large number of nonprofit public interest groups that exist today.

•   •   •

These, then, are some of the preferred career destinations for scientific consultants who make up the flow of talent away from consulting. What we see at this point is a highly dynamic situation best described as "flux"—the movement of professionals at any age or career stage into or out of consulting. Entries seem to peak at three points: early career, midcareer, and postretirement; departures usually follow a similar pattern. But precise analysis can be confounded by those individuals who are, and who may remain, partly in and partly out of consulting, such as the university professor who consults intermittently, or the career consultant who teaches part time at a local college. What we have concluded so far is that the ultimate reasons for choosing or leaving consulting as a professional occupation are unique to each person, and consist of a mix of personally weighted factors such as a subjective as well as objective assessment of qualifications and interests, opportunities for entry or departure, evaluation of rewards (financial or otherwise), and spousal attitudes.

We want to make the special point here that part of the career flux just mentioned is that of moving from scientific consulting to nonscientific jobs that may require little or no technical background. This may happen when consultants have been deeply involved in contracts that emphasize management techniques, public relations, political interactions, employee training, or other nonscientific areas. If these peripheral specialties are pursued too long and too exclusively, consultants with scientific backgrounds may feel increasingly isolated from the technical mainstream, and may never return to it, except in dreams or fantasies. Those who do try to return face a daunting struggle to regain lost competence.

There is still another kind of career flux that can involve consultants. This is what we call the "revolving door syndrome." It afflicts a certain subspecies of consulting scientists who, every few years, move from college teaching to consulting and then back again. The reason given is that this is the way to maintain technical competence, as it is not feasible to do so as a consultant. The better-paying consulting years also help to balance the poorly paid teaching years to provide a higher-than-average long-term income.

To us, the most positive aspect of career moves, at any stage of development, is that *alternatives are readily available*, if some advance planning and preparation precede the decisions.

FOURTEEN

Megaconsulting Organizations

the magnificent world of the superconsultant
corporation • universities as
megaconsultants • pros and cons of
employment with a megaconsultant firm

M uch of this book focuses on the individual practitioner and on small scientific consultancies that remain under the control of a single entrepreneur. This seems logical, as most scientific consulting entities are in these categories. But this is only part of the universe of consulting, for out beyond these small businesses are much bigger ones, variously labeled "megaconsultants," "superconsultants," or "umbrella" consultants. These are large profit-making organizations (usually corporations) often with complex internal management structures, with in-house technical capabilities, and with skills in technical management of a shifting cadre of subcontractors (other consultants) who supply much of the scientific expertise and capability.

Megaconsultants of this nature and size—firms such as Battelle, Dynamac, Versar, Dames and Moore, and Taxon—submit proposals for large consulting contracts, usually to large industries or to national or international agencies, or they have long-term continuing relationships (through contract renewals or extensions) with agencies like the U.S. Environmental Protection Agency (EPA), the U.S. Army Corps of Engineers (COE), the U.S. Agency for International Development (USAID), or the National Oceanic and Atmospheric Administration (NOAA). The relationships with these funding sources are stable enough to support a sizable in-house technical staff, and to maintain a list of specialty subcontractors to whom part of the money can be assigned. Monitoring subcontractor performance and preparation of integrated reports become major responsibilities of the in-house staff members, usually exceeding any involvement by them in direct field or laboratory data acquisition. The superconsultant corporation thus acts a *manager* of a significant chunk of agency or industry funds, thereby assuming responsibility for effective completion of contract requirements (and removing many of the nuisances of direct contract and subcontract management from the funding agency).

FUNCTIONS OF MEGACONSULTANTS

The megaconsultants fill many roles, most of them well beyond those expected of smaller groups:

- They prepare broad proposals covering large contract packages.
- They subdivide a large funded project into chew-

able segments—with a predetermined balance of in-house and out-of-house subprojects.

- They find and hire qualified and effective sub-contractors, drawn from a fluid but often extensive list of smaller consulting firms.
- They form and maintain advisory committees (usually in cooperation with the funding agency or industry).
- They maintain quality control for all aspects of the project.
- They maintain a timetable for completion of phases of subcontractor work and report preparation.
- They conduct periodic reviews of subcontractor work performance.
- They control public relations activities connected with the contract.
- They package the findings of a number of sub-contractors in an integrated final report.
- They are available for interactions and command performances with politicians at the request of the funding agency.

During the course of the megacontract, the agency or industry (the funding source) will have only carefully structured interactions with the megaconsultant, and virtually none with the subsidiary smaller consultants. The executives of the megaconsulting corporation sign contracts ritually with agency executives; the megaconsulting firm designates a project manager; the agency assigns a liaison person; formal conferences of representatives of all concerned parties (sometimes even including the sub-contractors) are scheduled periodically, to review findings and to offer advice useful in planning later phases of the project; and a glossy, often voluminous, final report is submitted on the data specified in the contract.

It would not seem too unkind, at this point in the description of the megaconsultant activities, to ask "Where is the *science* in these large organizations?" It does exist. Some of it is in the in-house staff, whose attention is, unfortunately, diverted almost totally to subcontract management duties; but most of the scientific expertise resides within the small consultant groups or individual consultants who have prepared proposals and have been awarded subcontracts by the megaconsultant for specific pieces of the project. The large consulting firm supplies the *managerial* expertise, especially the project managers with scientific backgrounds, but the *technical quality* of contract performance still depends on the best choice of subcontractors.

Another question that would not seem unreasonable at this point in the discussion would be "Are megaconsultants really consultants, or are they merely profit-making business entities that hire scientists and scientific consultants as *laborers*, and then lay claim to their findings in a final contract report?" We tend to favor the latter interpretation.

A recent development in megaconsulting is one in which university faculty or administrators may become enmeshed in umbrella-consultant activities, in a search for bigger and bigger pieces of a diminishing research grant pie and greater control over their own destinies. Some universities have sought and have received contracts from federal agencies such as the EPA and NOAA that they then manage by overseeing subcontracts or grants* awarded by them to faculty members at their own or other academic institutions.

---

*Grants differ from contracts or subcontracts only in minor and poorly defined ways. Contracts tend to be more formal and more specific in designating the work to be completed and the products expected, whereas grants permit a somewhat greater degree of flexibility and a reduced degree of accountability. Grants are awarded by a funding entity on approval of a proposal; contracts also require a proposal, but are usually followed, if the proposal is accepted, by a document stating precisely what is to be accomplished, and when.

Examples of this, in the northeastern United States, would be management of undersea research contracts from NOAA by the University of Connecticut, or management of aquaculture research funds from the U.S. Department of Agriculture by a unit of the University of Massachusetts at Dartmouth. Private nonacademic consultants may or may not be afforded access to these funds (usually not), but the quasiacademic organizations created to manage these agency contracts do resemble megaconsulting firms very closely.

ADVANTAGES AND DISADVANTAGES OF EMPLOYMENT WITH SUPERCONSULTANT CORPORATIONS

When scrutinized from a more personal perspective, employment with a megaconsulting company can be seen to have advantages and disadvantages. Some advantages are:

- Salaries can be better than in most other areas of scientific employment.
- Large agency contracts may have long-term projections, even though federal budgets must be approved annually; this supplies a modicum of stability and job security.
- Individuals with exceptional abilities in computer analyses and project management can expect excellent wages and relative immunity from sudden dismissal.
- The management hierarchy of megaconsulting organizations is often broad enough and transient enough to permit upward mobility for outstanding performers. Occupants of key operational slots in the corporation depart suddenly for various

reasons, creating vacancies that must be filled quickly—often from within the organization—to ensure timely contract completion.

There are of course disadvantages to employment with a large consulting corporation:

- Opportunities for research are minimal or non-existent.
- Geographic locations of major projects may require project management staff to move from place to place at central office insistence.
- Time demands on technical management staff may be sudden and excessive, if subcontractor performance is inadequate or reports are delayed.
- Project managers are well paid, but they are subjected to interminable hours in meetings and conferences, to days on end in travel status, to unreasonable deadlines for evaluations and report preparation, and to repeated geographic dislocations.
- Competition for the better positions in the corporate hierarchy—as in any corporate hierarchy—can be severe and nasty, and totally dependent on continued peak performances.

•   •   •

The authors of this book have had, during the past three decades, extensive contacts with employees of mega-consulting firms—usually with scientifically trained people at the project management level, or with the thinly spread senior research scientists who help maintain technical credibility. Characteristically, the managerial people are bright, aggressive, vocal, and young. Their academic training is frequently limited to the master's degree level, but most of them see broader career horizons in non-research but science-related jobs (in administration, public relations, politics, or public service). Their tenure with a megaconsulting corporation provides them with an intense and valuable learning experience in one commercial phase of scientific applications. A few prosper; many are repelled by overwhelming management- and deadline-dominated aspects of the work. The consultancy goes on, though, filling an expanding need for technical organizations capable of bidding on large contracts and delivering acceptable products.

FIFTEEN

International Consulting

---

consulting for international agencies •
consulting for foreign governments •
consulting for foreign or multinational
industries • gaining access to the fast track
of international consulting • attitudes and
sensitivities of foreign nationals

M ost of the discussion thus far in this book has
focused on scientific consulting as it is currently
practiced in the United States. There is, of course,
a wider faster track, with different rules and other perspectives. This we can call "international consulting" or
even "global consulting." It is characterized by the application of specialized knowledge to problems and needs
outside the borders of this country. Consulting in foreign
nations is a diverse and too little publicized export product of U.S. technology, and is a logical activity in an era

223

when economic advancement is a key political objective worldwide.

Scientific consulting beyond our national borders can be subdivided for discussion purposes into (1) consulting for international agencies, (2) consulting for foreign governments or their agencies, and (3) consulting for foreign or multinational industries. In some countries, the relationships of government and industry are so close that any such artificial pigeonholing is not realistic (as, for example, the effective intertwining of government and industry in Japanese fishing and aquaculture operations). For now, though, the three major categories can be useful for descriptive purposes.

CONSULTING FOR INTERNATIONAL AGENCIES

The larger international agencies and programs, such as the Food and Agriculture Organization of the United Nations (FAO), the World Health Organization (WHO), and the United Nations Environmental Program (UNEP) have in-house staffs of experts and program managers, but they also depend on short- and long-term research and development contracts with national authorities in specialized fields of science. These imported experts have been and are especially important to international programs based in developing countries, providing infusions of technical skills and knowledge where such commodities may be in short supply.

CONSULTING FOR FOREIGN GOVERNMENTS OR THEIR AGENCIES

This form of consulting is in some instances a subset of the previous category, in that the offices and laboratories of regional programs (in specialty areas such as agriculture, aquaculture, hydraulic engineering, or disease control) or international agencies may be within the affected countries, even though funding is international. In other instances, however, scientists may contract with and be paid directly by a foreign government, to augment the expertise needed to solve (or at least to address) a particularly pressing national problem of the moment (such as water quality, hydroelectric power, deforestation, aerospace development, irrigation, insect control, or airborne pollutants). This can be an extremely sensitive kind of professional interaction with local counterparts and with local politicians, so the consultation may have sociopolitical ramifications far beyond the wording of the contract.

CONSULTING FOR FOREIGN OR MULTINATIONAL INDUSTRIES

Technology-based industrial development now characterizes most countries of the world, but the technical competence to support this vast expansion can at times be spread very thinly. This is particularly true in Third World countries lacking the cadres of competent specialists needed to plan and construct an industrial infrastructure. It is at precisely this point that scientific consultants can enter the scene, bringing with them knowledge and experience, acquired in industrialized countries, that can move new ventures in emerging economies ahead rapidly.

There are, of course, other alternatives. Multinational companies need only to reassign in-house technical staff members to new subsidiaries in foreign countries, or U.S. companies may form joint ventures with existing foreign firms, with an initial major contribution of technical knowledge from this country. Often, though, the services of consultants are called on—as, for example, when in-house specialists refuse to move, or when they are fully committed to product development programs here in the United States. Then too, some consultants can provide unique skills in evaluating and assessing risks—skills that may not exist in the parent company.

So, to some scientific consultants with broad career objectives, the prospect of joining the fast track of international consulting can be intriguing—all that foreign travel, contacts with foreign scientists, opportunities to make impacts on developing industries, generous consulting fees, and the good feeling of being accepted as an expert and an authority (even if only in a country that no one has heard of). The international circuit also has its downside, which we will explore fully later in this chapter. For the moment we can point out only a few very real problems: (1) deterioration of professional competence in an environment that can be devoid of frequent contacts with close colleagues, in a geographic location characterized by absence of libraries and other forms of intellectual stimulation; (2) the many personal problems that can be created by extended or frequent commitments in foreign countries (e.g., high and persistent stress, family disarray caused by prolonged absences, and psychological effects of isolation), and (3) the high prevalence of unstable governments around the world, with increasing danger of terrorism and other forms of violence. But these are defects to be considered further downstream.

Probably the first question to be answered by a prospective international consultant is "Why? Why do I want to get involved in that kind of consulting?" We have listed a few incentives in the preceding paragraph, but there are others:

- *Expansion of a regional or national practice.* Some scientific consultants see international activities as a logical extension of an existing more localized effort confined to the United States. Furthermore, they use their existing practice as a financial and professional base for initial probes and then larger projects in foreign countries of their choice. The combination of national and international projects provides an opportunity to select the proportion of each that they feel most comfortable with.

- *Adequate funding sources.* The market for specific kinds of technical expertise is great in the developing countries of the world, and broad programs have been developed by major international agencies and foundations to apply that expertise, often with the assistance of scientific consultants from the industrialized nations. Here, then, is an opportunity to participate in what can be described as a "growth industry" with substantial long-term funding.

- *Application of scientific expertise.* Many scientific disciplines and specialities (such as epidemiology of infectious diseases, insect control, or fish population dynamics) encompass a body of concepts and information that can have universal application, with some modifications. There are still regions of the planet where that technology has not yet been applied—but should be.

- *Humanitarian incentives.* Some established scientists like to see, occasionally, how their knowledge can be used to address basic world problems, and can lead to improvement in conditions of existence for some human populations. They feel that results can be more clearly discerned in human environments that are less complex than those in the United States.

Other rationales exist for involvement in international consulting—including an overwhelming interest in a particular scientific specialty as developed in a foreign country, the relative sophistication of a science-based industry in a foreign country, the availability of clients in a foreign country, the opportunity for joint consulting ventures with foreign colleagues who are also consultants, and the emergence and development of a new science-based industry in a foreign country with an inadequate technological infrastructure.

After the "why" question has been resolved, a sensible sequence of chapter development should spur us to ask "how"—"How do I get on this international fast track anyway?"

Participation in international scientific consulting can be, as we have indicated, a logical extension of a successful local practice, or it can be a consequence of the intervention of pure blind chance—or any combination of the two. This is obviously not a very enlightening answer to the question, and we can do much better:

- Exceptional competence and peer recognition at home can contribute significantly to decisions by others that favor selection for international consulting plums—but for this recognition to be meaningful abroad, foreign colleagues must be made aware of any status achieved at home.
- Participation in international societies, meetings, symposia, conferences, or workshops can provide visibility and contacts that may lead to contracts.
- Communications with, close professional relationships with, and even joint research projects with foreign colleagues can be valuable when and if your credentials are examined by potential international clients, whether governmental or private. The foreign colleague may be able to provide assistance through his contacts in whatever administrative hierarchy makes the decisions at the moment.

- Some industrialized nations (such as Japan) have established sites for business, cultural, educational, and other information on the World Wide Web. Information appearing on such sites may be of relevance to consulting possibilities in those countries.

- Some colleagues in the United States may already be on the international circuit—especially through being part of the scientific advisory structure of regional or global technical councils, commissions, or other quasigovernmental and/or quasiregulatory organizations. Those colleagues, if favorably disposed, can be of great help. They can recommend that you be added to the roster of advisors-participants, and you will then perform superbly.

- Other colleagues in the United States may be on advisory or review boards of the larger international funding agencies, public or private (e.g., FAO, WHO, UNEP, World Bank, Ford Foundation, Rockefeller Foundation). They may, if approached properly, be willing to propose your name to the appropriate administrative officers or panel chairpersons of those entities. The United Nations, with its numerous scientific bodies and with projects all over the world, is an excellent organization for the development of international contacts, but it is often difficult to know what is going on, except by chance or by overhearing a corridor conversation among those actively involved and already "inside."

- So much of participation in international consulting depends on a continuing working relationship with either a State Department-funded agency (e.g., U.S. Agency for International Development) or a U.N.-sponsored agency (e.g., UNEP Regional Programs). Entry is best gained by being seconded by a colleague who has already performed well as a consultant for one of the funding offices. Participation in the activities of these groups can also be possible through such routes as submission of research proposals with international cooperative activity at their cores, or being invited to give a specialized paper in one's area of competence. Often an initial involvement, if carried out with exceptional skill, can lead to continued association with the organization.

- The United States, like other industrialized nations, is party to a great number of international agreements and compacts that have strong scientific components—such as the International Whaling Commission. Delegates to the regular meetings associated with such agreements (who are often politicians and not scientists) like to have a cluster of national experts behind them in the session chamber as "scientific advisors." Scientific advisors usually function as paid consultants during the meetings, although the financial terms of employment are variable—from zero in the case of federal government scientists to standard billing plus expenses in the case of full-time consultants. This is a distinct and demanding kind of international science that deserves brief mention. Scientific advisors are in attendance to provide authoritative detailed information to the delegates on extremely short notice. Often there is only one expert present to represent each discipline of science involved in the discussions; that expert will be expected to be available at all times during the sessions and to have answers *then*, not later. It is an all-or-nothing arena, suited only to those with a high level of expertise, instant and total recall, and a keen analytical mind—but it can be an extremely exhilarating environment for the qualified. Some important ground rules for scientific advisors include the following:

✓ Remember that the meeting is *political* and not scientific; decisions will consequently be based principally on political considerations and not necessarily on scientific rationality.

✓ Bring key reference material with you, but don't count on it to help you provide the kind of instantaneous response that will be expected of you.

✓ Keep the official delegate informed—insofar as information is wanted. This responsibility includes gleanings from corridor conversations, if relevant.

There is an added advantage to this kind of meeting, in that delegates from other participating countries also bring their scientific advisors, and outside the formal sessions there is ample opportunity to mingle and to discuss scientific matters (assuming language compatibility, which to an American usually means "Can he speak English?"). Some of these scientific counterparts can make good dining and drinking companions. Often such contacts lead to future international scientific conferences, workshop plans and proposals, or consulting contracts.

• One additional potential access route to international consulting, which we have heard about but have not tried personally, is to enlist the aid of key staff members of national legislators or their oversight committees and subcommittees. These people can make appropriate representations to the numerous international agencies of which the United States is a member or an observer. The relevant staff members must be presented with a

well-developed package of qualifications and any
supporting documentation of expertise. (We have
to point out, though, that these are not auspicious
times to talk science to the Congress, which in
October 1995 *abolished its own major link with
science—its Office of Technology Assessment.*)

There are, of course, many other routes to participation in international science; some of them can be
planned, but most are entirely fortuitous. There are, for
example, countless bilateral and multilateral panels, joint
committees, and commissions that consider a broad spectrum of international issues with scientific content. They
usually hold regular or special meetings or conferences to
which they invite national experts. The various government agencies participate continuously in such international discussions of mutual problems, and again they
frequently invite national experts—some of whom are
there as consultants.

Sensitivities abound during any participation in
science-associated foreign meetings of intergovernmental
commissions or councils with or without regulatory responsibility. Participating scientists, whether academic,
governmental, or consultant, are present in an *advisory*
and not a *decision making* capacity; they must obtain national approval to be present, as well as approval of the
sponsoring organization; and they are expected to remain
inconspicuous in the general (political) sessions.

> *The rigidity of guidelines that can govern participation in
> international science-related council meetings was per-
> manently impressed on the senior author of this book in
> the early 1980s during an annual meeting of the Interna-
> tional Council for the Exploration of the Sea (ICES). This
> organization, based in Copenhagen, is the oldest and most
> prestigious intergovernmental scientific advisory group*

on ocean affairs that exists. Its principal purpose is to offer scientific advice on fisheries and environmental matters to member countries that border the North Atlantic.

I was there principally to present to the Council a report of one of its many technical working groups, which I had chaired for almost a decade. Unfortunately, my name had been omitted inadvertently from the delegation list for the United States. I sensed that I was in big trouble when I presented myself at the registration desk. My name could not be found; no admission badge or meeting documents had been prepared for me; no mail slot had my name attached—I became an instant nonperson, almost like a U.S. tourist who had wandered in off the streets of Copenhagen.

Things went downhill from that early confrontation at the registration desk. A crude temporary visitor pass was prepared for me grudgingly by a staff member after our head of delegation had been summoned and had guaranteed that I was real, but I received no meeting agenda, and, worse still, no invitations to the various embassy and Council receptions (which pained me severely because these were very elaborate affairs and the social highlights of the meeting). As might be expected, after the bureaucratic posturing was over, I was allowed to present the working group report, but I felt like an intruder during that entire period, and I resolved to never appear again at an international meeting of that genre without full credentials and a State Department identification badge.

Deeply held sensitivities also exist on a national level in many parts of the world. If ignored, they may affect the award of a consulting contract or the success of contract performance. Foreign scientists and foreign governments are acutely aware of the status and stature of science in their respective countries. They are also aware that functionaries from the United States, whether scientists or not, have a great propensity for assuming control and domi-

nating any activity, despite sometimes elaborate camou-
flage arranged by the State Department, and despite
requests from that timid agency that U.S. nationals maintain low profiles in most negotiations.

Conferences and negotiations in foreign countries
must be conducted in the presence of an almost worldwide inferiority complex engendered in foreign nationals
by the participation of U.S. counterparts. Those feelings
of inferiority can foster anger in foreign participants
when U.S. members fit an unfortunate but commonly
held stereotype (aggressive, sometimes rude, domineer-
ing, unwilling to compromise, smug, superior). The harm
that that anger can do to productive interactions is significant, and must be recognized and guarded against by any
consultant who ventures into other countries.

The act of importing a consultant from far away can
be construed by the indigenous population as lack of faith
in the competence of national scientists (which may be
true). A more realistic and less self-defeating view is that
the imported consultants bring with them the accumulated technical knowledge of the industrialized nations.
It's all there, for a price, as a tremendous potential boost
to an emerging economy. Technical skills and the equipment to support them are readily transferable from one
country to another; scientific consultants provide one vehicle for such transfers.

After the "why" and the "how" of international consulting have been considered—however briefly—we can
next examine a few aspects of actually conducting a consulting practice with a foreign component. Doing business abroad requires the application of a number of
commonsense social rules—not unique to technical consulting, but still relevant to the proper interactions of
professional and client.[18] Some (of many) points of concern are these:

- Negotiations with foreign nationals require skill and experience. Tiny behavioral nuances—such as the nature of a handshake or the kind of eye contact—can effect success or failure of the meeting. Most industrialized societies have learned to accept (but not necessarily to enjoy) some of the foibles of Americans, but Third World representatives may be less tolerant about ignorance of their customs.
- Rigid rules of civil intercourse must prevail in all negotiations and at all times, as consultancies may take place in countries that are willing to accept aid but are hostile toward the United States. Any breach of the rules may result in termination of the project and/or dismissal of the consultant.
- Differences in languages can easily result in misinterpretations and misunderstandings that unless corrected immediately, can result in termination of the project.
- U.S. scientists, because of lack of indoctrination, are prone to follow customs that are intrusive and repellent to many foreigners. We speak too loudly, we rarely listen to reasonable arguments, and we are apt to take hard positions for or against a specific action.
- Female scientists from the United States may be assigned (or elect to work in) countries where females are held in low esteem, and are treated with little respect, regardless of their capabilities. This can be a challenging kind of assignment, and is one that more and more women are opting to accept.
- What we in the United States usually consider to be "bribes" are an accepted way of doing business in most countries of the world. One of the most

common forms is payment to a third party for an introduction to someone who is a business prospect. Every international consultant will encounter this custom sooner or later.

- Most educated foreigners can speak and understand English to a greater or lesser extent, but are not comfortable with prolonged technical discussions in that difficult language. Consultants without fluency in a prospective client's native language should bring an interpreter, preferably one with a scientific background.

- Consulting activities in foreign countries usually involve staff people in addition to the client. The consultant should try to determine as early as possible the roles of each participant, and to accord proper deference.

- One of the greatest aids to successful entry into foreign consulting can be a fellow scientist who is also a friend, and who lives and works in the target country, where he has developed a network of other professionals. Care must be taken, however, not to push the relationship too hard.

- U.S. citizens who do business in foreign countries can have the support of a vast panoply of government and private agencies and institutions—such as the Small Business Administration, the World Bank, the United Nations, the Chamber of Commerce, International Professional Associations, and many others. Routes to their services may be convoluted and bureaucratic, but they exist; those organizations are on the ground there, and they should be asked for assistance.

National attitudes toward consultant services vary from country to country. Most of the developing countries have become familiar with the United Nations practice of supplying experts as consultants in fields such as agriculture, and can see benefits from so-called "counterpart programs" in which a national scientist works closely with a visiting expert. Politicians and administrators in those countries can make some impact on the selection process for consultants, especially if they or their technical advisors have prior knowledge of the capabilities of the candidates.

There is, as was intimated early in the chapter, a prominent downside to international consulting. Some negative features include the following:

- U.S. companies and agencies have found that Americans in general to not adapt well to foreign assignments. They are too used to elaborate amenities (such as running water) and are persistently deficient in foreign language aptitudes.
- Many of the international funding sources are being reduced or eliminated, so consultants are finding fewer prospective clients in today's world.
- Consultants from other industrialized countries can be fierce competitors for some international funds (those controlled by the United Nations, for example), and such competitors can be favored in the many bilateral development programs in developing countries.
- Competition for foreign contracts can also be severe among consultants who are U.S. nationals, as the numbers of qualified and interested people increase annually, and as international assignments have prestige value in most careers.
- There is a continuing effort by global companies and some international agencies to compensate consultants (and other expatriate employees) in

the local currency, which may fluctuate in value enormously, or may not reflect the cost of living abroad, or the additional taxes that must be paid.
- Sequential foreign consulting assignments may increase visibility in the countries where the work is done, but may reduce contacts with U.S. colleagues and networks—which could create problems when new contracts are needed.

Despite these and other negative aspects of international consulting, it can be a career objective for the uniquely qualified scientist. Recognition and acceptance of cultural, language, and social barriers that need to be overcome can be important to the success of consultancies in foreign countries, especially if accompanied by confidence in personal technical expertise and a sense of adventure. The risks of encountering intractable problems or financial disasters are significant, but the rewards to the qualified and prepared can be great.

•   •   •

This chapter on international consulting would not be complete without some brief description of a category that we label "world-class professionals"—even though "world-class" has become a somewhat hackneyed buzzword for anything that is exceptional. These people exemplify the best that a country has to offer. They are astute, urbane, perceptive, interesting professionals who have survived a severe selective process within their own countries. Most of these world-class professionals are politically aware, diplomatic by instinct and training, sensitive to the nuances of interpersonal relationships, and usually excellent scientists. Furthermore, they are frequently found in leadership roles where science interfaces with political processes in various international panels, councils, commissions, and advisory boards. Careful study of these world-class scientific consultants should be made whenever the opportunity exists to observe them in action; this can be an unparalleled learning experience for the developing international consultant.

SIXTEEN

Junior Professional Members of Scientific Consulting Organizations

---

reasons for an early career decision to become a consultant • moving up in the system • encountering the "glass ceiling" • exercising options—returning to graduate school

---

The professional staffs of all but the smallest scientific consulting organizations usually consist of technically trained people in two broad categories: the senior members, with experience, credibility, and advanced degrees in their areas of specialization, and the junior members, with less experience and with little if any graduate training. The senior staff does the client contact work, the proposal drafting, the technical planning, the data analyses, the project supervision, and the report writing; the junior staff does the data collection and collation, the literature reviews, the field surveys, and the lab analyses.

This chapter focuses on the junior professional staff members—those eager, usually young, and relatively inexperienced individuals, male or female, who do the many routine but essential chores that contribute to outstanding contract performances.

A personal question that obviously requires some exploration early in this chapter on junior professionals is "Why did you make a decision to join a consulting company so early in your scientific career?" We asked that question in some of our interviews with younger staff people, who gave us a variety of reasons:

- The most common response was that the job was strictly temporary—a breather before graduate school.
- Another common response was money—lack of enough of it to begin or to continue graduate work, with all of the attendant poverty and starvation.
- Still another reason could be translated as the "effects of imprinting," usually as a consequence of working as a student assistant (graduate or undergraduate) for a professor or mentor with a consulting contract.

Some other responses that appeared less frequently were:

- Dissatisfaction with perceived financial horizons of academic or government employment without a Ph.D. (or even with it), as compared with the apparent open-endedness and possibilities for rapid advancement in a consulting firm.
- Desire for firsthand involvement in practical science-related issues of today (e.g., environment, health, urban development, food production)

rather than in the more theoretical and basic aspects that are more characteristic of academic science.

We suspect, though, that in a significant proportion of cases, jobs were available in consulting organizations to people at bachelor's or master's degree levels, but were less available to them in other areas of scientific employment.

OPTIONS AVAILABLE TO JUNIOR PROFESSIONAL STAFF MEMBERS

Junior professionals do, of course, have options that depend on a mixture of academic experience, personal career goals, performance on the job, and the availability of niches in the hierarchy of the consulting organization. Effectiveness and enthusiasm in completing assigned routine tasks and occasional contributions of good ideas for improvements can facilitate some degree of upward mobility, if the company structure is such that it can accommodate promotions from within. Acquired skills in subcontract monitoring and specialized technical courses are also helpful, and increasing proficiency in computer applications is a present-day necessity. At the entry level, work assignments may be in areas other than those covered in undergraduate training, so while a broad range of science and math courses may be desirable, the ability to get up to speed quickly in other related disciplines can be important too.

We offer a few specific suggestions for moving beyond entry levels in larger consulting firms:

- Find a mentor among the more senior members of the organization. This may happen spontaneously as a result of assignment to a subunit of the company; if it doesn't, take some diplomatic steps to encourage it.

- Indicate your interest in being upwardly mobile, unobtrusively, by such methods as regular perusal (during lunch breaks) of the technical journals to which the company subscribes, always being a little early rather than a little late, or always completing work assignments, even if it becomes necessary to stay a little late in the evening.
- Do assigned jobs superbly, then quietly look for additional tasks.
- Don't participate in prolonged corridor discussions of topics irrelevant to the job.
- Always have something appropriate, meaningful, and positive to say at staff meetings—but don't get long-winded.
- Follow company policies in all aspects of job performance; if that becomes impossible because of personal standards or unreasonable requirements, leave.
- Accept better and more complex work assignments readily, but expect added compensation after a break-in period.

It is almost a truism, though, that for most of the choicer positions in science, a Ph.D. or D.Sc. degree is the metaphorical union card. This is an absolute in academic science; it is somewhat less critical in government research, and even less so in industrial research. The credibility gained by possession of an earned doctoral degree can enhance admission to the upper levels of consulting organizations as well, even though other factors, such as job performance or managerial competence, may be overriding. Without the degree, the likelihood is high that a non-Ph.D. will eventually bump into a counterpart of the "glass ceiling" that midlevel professional women have often encountered and rightly complained about. Clients of consultants need assurance that they are dealing with skilled professionals, and degrees possessed by key consulting staff members are among the criteria that will be used in making choices among competitive bidders—however fair or unfair this practice may seem.

So the bright upwardly mobile young professionals in consulting firms need to be cognizant of the limitations to advancement imposed by the lack of that final degree. Its absence may not constitute an *absolute* barrier to the upper tiers of the company's professional ranks, but it is a very real impediment. Its significance may not be obvious at the middle levels of the hierarchy, where technical and management skills are being developed and where much jostling for space in the institutional pecking order is taking place, but eventually someone in a power position will scrutinize the earned degree credentials of the staff before reaching a decision about promotions to a senior-level job. We think that decision will usually favor a person with the most complete academic background.

All of which, somewhat circuitously, brings us to another critical decision point—when the junior professional in a consulting organization exercises (or fails to exercise) his option to go to (or to return to) graduate school. On the positive side, the decision to stay with the company will be tempered by a host of modifying considerations such as the attractiveness of a steady paycheck, the promise of a promotion, a good work environment, increasing family responsibilities, opportunity for professional growth through on-the-job training, or a compatible supervisor. The negative side also surfaces, especially during the long dark hours of sleepless nights, in the form of questions such as "What is the long-term viability of the company?" or "Will I still be doing routine data collections and related scut work a decade from now?" or "Do I really want to be a research scientist (or teacher), or would I be happier as a manager?"[11]

We, as authors of this book, probably should not try

to force the decision of any newcomer, as the variability in circumstances is so great. We can, however, examine and try to interpret the findings from our questionnaires and limited interviews with junior professionals in consulting companies.

Admitting to occasional preconceptions on our part, but trying desperately to suppress them, we think we see some trends in the data. Probably most important is that *a majority of the younger professionals queried do not see a career in consulting as a lifetime goal.* Consulting is more often viewed as a stopgap, a job, a temporary vantage point from which to scrutinize options for a future in science. Many of our younger respondents list only bachelor's or master's degrees in their curricula, and these were in areas sometimes only marginally related to the principal specialties of the employing firm.

Another trend that we see is *the frequency with which computer literacy and broad undergraduate training in science are emphasized* as being among basic qualifications, even for entry-level jobs. Consulting companies seem to expect applicants to be familiar with statistical treatment of data, with use of sophisticated analytical equipment, and with field sampling methodology. Employers will often favor applicants who are or have been students of well-known academic specialists in specific research areas, or who have served internships in industrial laboratories or in nonprofit environmental organizations.

INCENTIVES FOR ADVANCED PROFESSIONAL TRAINING

Still another trend in the interview data was the frequently expressed *need for further training—at least at a basic level—in disciplines that impinge on scientific consulting practice, especially engineering, law, and economics.* Undergraduate science, as taught in the United States, does not equip graduates to interact adequately with graduate engineers—who are often in charge of consulting organizations. Even though science and engineering are frequently thought of as closely connected parts of a whole, the disciplines have too many different conceptual bases to permit easy integration. Science is concerned with *understanding* the physical universe, whereas engineering deals with *applications* of tested principles. Often the entire hierarchy of environmental consulting firms will consist of engineers, and the contracts they accept will have a strong engineering emphasis.[22]

Similarly, an undergraduate degree in chemistry, physics, geology, or biology will not equip a junior-level professional to appreciate or to participate in the legal and economic considerations that are part of many contract specifications. A background in environmental regulations, state and federal; a knowledge of land use practices; some rudiments of economic theory and jargon—all are customarily beyond the training of the new science graduate. Fortunately, some proficiency in these subsidiary areas can be acquired by the aggressive newcomer through part-time studies and technical literature, but never enough to feel really comfortable with.

•   •   •

Our final advice to young partially trained professionals employed by consulting companies or other industrial organizations, or government agencies, in subprofessional roles is *to move on when it is time to do so.* Don't become trapped in what is and may always be a semiprofessional job, regardless of its title and its apparent short-term benefits. *Escape into graduate school* before the passage of time reduces opportunities to do so and narrows the horizons for alternative kinds of participation in a scientific or other kind of occupation. Graduate studies can be in one of the fields of science, or in business administration, or in law, or in economics—any discipline that equips people with energy and intelligence to participate *as a professional*, and that can build on a basic science background.

SEVENTEEN

University Faculty Members as Scientific Consultants

---

full-time faculty members and part-time
consultants • research grants versus research
contracts versus consulting contracts • the
consultant as a mentor to graduate students

A special breed of university scientists is active in industrial and government consulting. This group consists of faculty members with credibility in their fields of specialization, and acquired ability to design a project, collect data, then assemble, analyze, and synthesize the data relevant to a client's needs. Many faculty members (and their assistants) with technical skills act as part-time consultants for industrial or governmental organizations. Today's demands for expertise are in expanding "high-tech" specialties such as immuno-chemistry, molecular biology, and genetic engineering,

249

and it is rare to talk to academic specialists in these emerging areas who are not consulting or have not been approached for paid advice. Environmental consulting has also been popular during the past two decades, coincident with increased public concerns about actions of industries that pollute or otherwise modify ecologically sensitive natural areas, and with the passage and enforcement of more and more laws and regulations protecting our water, air, and land from degrading practices. It seems generally true that as the regulatory agencies become more powerful, the demand for consultant services increases.

Biomedical consulting is also a "hot" area for scientific consulting, but only for those with exceptional qualifications—academic training in narrow specialties, and servitude as apprentices in the laboratories of research leaders in such specialties. Consulting in biomedical areas requires a unique combination of recognized expertise and good business sensitivities, and even these stringent qualifications need to be augmented by an acquired background in the employ of major pharmaceutical companies.

There are strong incentives for academic scientists and scientific consultants to join other specialists in forming high-tech ventures that are research-based but oriented toward product development and sales. Drug companies that sell highly specialized (and prohibitively expensive) new drugs have long been favorites for investors. Many of the smaller research-based entrepreneurial firms with an effective drug have formed partnerships with larger companies to develop other promising drug candidates more rapidly.[22] All of this provides strong pressures for university faculty to become involved in such high-risk high-profit ventures. Some faculty members consult with drug companies on a retainer basis, some may be given stock options, and some may even become involved in company management.

THE NEAR-UNIVERSALITY
OF PART-TIME CONSULTING
BY SCIENCE FACULTY MEMBERS

Universities vary greatly in their attitudes toward extramural involvements of their faculty in part-time consulting; some permit substantial amounts, and others none, but most research institutions now have guidelines of some kind. Many universities, such as Harvard, Yale, and Stanford, allow one day a week for industrial consulting. Some require disclosure of consulting arrangements and financial interests, and some even suggest minimum consulting fees for their faculty members. Problems of primary loyalties and commitments arise when faculty members are paid with stocks or stock options in the company; when they become officers in industrial concerns for which they have been consulting; or when they become the principal executive officers of private consulting ventures. Universities are often slow to react to excesses, but eventually they do. A good example of one possible sequence of events is in the consulting career of Dr. E. A. Randall.

Dr. Randall is an excellent scientist-cum-consultant/ entrepreneur. After a decade of effective research and teaching at a major university in the 1970s, and after successful management of several large federally funded multidisciplinary projects late in that decade, he founded (and incorporated in another state) a private consulting venture to take advantage of the then-increasing environmental concerns, and their impacts on the operation of chemical and electric power companies. This was a time of regulatory actions requiring environmental impact studies before project approval. His company was available, it hired credible professionals, and it prospered. With a small permanent staff and with several field offices, its operations spread over much of the East Coast. A key to its success seemed to be a pool of part-time university faculty members and a much larger pool of postdoctoral assistants, graduate students, and undergraduates hired for short-term work. Professor Randall is an energetic, highly organized, gregarious man, recognized for his earlier research, and for his commitment to the university as well as to his company. The university was tolerant (some members of the faculty would say too tolerant) but eventually he was asked to give up either his tenured position or the management of his private business interests. He elected to sever his academic connections, and claims to this day that the decision was the correct one.

Professor Randall is a scientist-businessman—exemplary of a group of excellent professionals who have an added dimension that involves them in high-risk ventures, for power or profit or both. Their backgrounds may be in research, but their principal commitments quickly become managerial and administrative.

Members of this group of scientist-businesspeople are somewhat atypical, though, when compared with the much larger category of *part-time scientific consultants* who are, and who remain, full-time university professors. Members of this group of part-time practitioners consider their academic commitments to research and teaching to be primary, with any consulting activities limited to a time available status. Consulting contracts that they may seek are normally related closely to their ongoing research projects, and structured so they do not interfere with responsibilities to the university. Dr. E. S. Allison is one of our best examples of faculty members in this category of full-time professor-part-time consultant.

Professor Allison is a conscientious effective teacher and an excellent mentor for graduate students. He is a senior member of the faculty at a major private university, but he still carries a full teaching load of graduate and undergraduate courses. His field of specialization—aquaculture—has recently undergone remarkable worldwide ex-

pansion, as limits to continuing seafood production from wild stocks are being recognized and often exceeded. He does intermittent contract studies, mostly for groups interested in investing in production facilities in this country or in industrial development in other countries. His consulting activities include field surveys and feasibility studies, and his advice to clients can be a major consideration in their go or no-go investment decisions.

Professor Allison is able to weave his consulting assignments and experiences into his graduate courses, making extensive use of a case history approach. He is also able to hire (with the department chairman's permission) some of his students as temporary assistants, to do some of the fieldwork and laboratory analyses that are relevant to his contract studies but that do not interfere with the students' academic program. Some of his more perceptive students have even been able to find thesis topics in the research required by the consulting contract, and have in some instances found other sources of funding to expand the scope of their part of the project.

Dr. Allison seems to have achieved a balance of academic involvement and occasional paid consulting that suits his long-term career objectives. Critical to this balance is successful integration of consulting activities with his graduate teaching program.

RESPONSES OF
UNIVERSITY ADMINISTRATORS

Universities (and even some four-year colleges) have made efforts to accommodate the wishes of their faculty members who want to consult. This flexibility is understood by academic administrators to be a method of retaining good professionals, who might otherwise move to institutions with more liberal consulting policies. Some actions, in addition to providing "released time" for consulting, that university administrative officers have taken include the following:

- They have approved, on a case-by-case basis, reduced or no overhead charges for some exploratory consulting contracts that may lead to large full-overhead joint projects later on. Off-campus consulting by faculty members appeals to some industries because the cost of the project does not include overhead, but the university affiliation can be used. The clients almost always want the university affiliation of the consultant to appear on the report, to give more credence to the results. Furthermore, they may feel that if the consultant does not produce on time, or does an inadequate job, or (heaven forbid) even comes up with a finding that the client does not like, they can obtain satisfaction from the consultant's department head, dean, a member of the board of trustees, or even from the university president.
- They have recommended that funding for some consulting projects be made as a grant to the university rather than as a consulting contract to a professor, if institutional laboratory equipment or secretarial services are to be used. This device can work in favor of the faculty member-consultant for some projects with possible risk of injury—for example, those involving commercial fishing shipboard time—in which university insurance might not cover cost of injuries to a consultant working on his own, but would cover grant-supported research.
- They have been unusually tolerant of changes in proclaimed scientific research interests of their faculty members, in response to changing popularity of certain "scientific fads" (and availability of

funds for studies in those trendy areas). In our specialty area—environmental studies—for example, we were amazed a few decades ago, when aquaculture was in its ascendancy, to observe the numbers of biology faculty members with diverse research interests, who were preparing grant proposals and seeking consulting contracts in aquaculture—clearly an area peripheral to their former professional activities.

- They have concluded that competent short-term studies (such as those conducted by faculty member-consultants) should be a definite part of the community-oriented activities of the university— provided that such studies are "good science," even if temporally and spatially limited.

- In the area of environmental issues, some university administrations have concluded that it is a reasonable function of their faculties in the relevant sciences to suggest ways to reduce environmental damage, and to participate in fair public discussion of environmental problems and proposals. The administration's concern is that in the absence of advice based on scientific expertise, developers and polluters will turn directly to political means to achieve objectives that will result in environmental degradation.

- They have noted that financial support for faculty, staff, and students has been generated by consulting contracts, and that such funding has helped some faculty members to survive between larger grants—which are becoming increasingly difficult to find.

- They have been, understandably, concerned about the contents of agreements made by faculty member-consultants—especially about the time involved in carrying out the contracted work. One university stated the matter clearly as follows: "[E]very attempt should be made to estimate accurately an investigator's time to be spent on the task. Failing this, some clause should be added to the agreement, which permits an increase in costs if the project takes more time than originally envisioned. This is particularly important when the additional time is a consequence of continually expanding terms of reference dictated by the private company involved."

It is important in this chapter on university faculty members as consultants to examine, in a little more detail than we did in Chapter Fourteen, the distinctions between research grants and consulting contracts. *Research grants* are very familiar to academic scientists. In its usual form, the grant process begins with a proposal submitted to a funding source (usually a part of the federal government or one of its quasigovernmental commissions) where it is approved or rejected. If approved, the proposal serves as a vague sort of contract, vulnerable to modification as the work progresses. A *consulting contract* is initiated in the same way—with submission of a proposal, and with its acceptance or rejection. Unlike a research grant, however, a much more formal document— the consulting contract itself—is inserted into the sequence of events preceding the appearance of money. The existence of the contract with its many specifications for work performance, imposes a degree of rigidity on the relationship of donor and recipient that is absent from the research grant.

We are making an issue of this because many academic scientists do not seem to comprehend (or they choose to ignore) the distinction between a grant and a contract, even though their research may be supported by a mix of both. Furthermore, their *self-perceptions* may be that even though some of their research may be funded by contracts, they are *not* consultants. Often it is not until they seek to modify the terms of a contract (or, worse still, they fail to follow contract specifications) that the true nature of their role and responsibilities is impressed on them by the client.

It is not surprising, though, that distinctions between grants and contracts can become blurred. *Flexibility and rigidity are characteristics imposed by the managers of the funding source, regardless of what the paper trail specifies.* Thus, research grant awards may require detailed interim reporting and periodic evaluations, whereas, conversely, consulting contracts may consist of no more than a brief paragraph, lacking any specific language and not even requiring a final report. With such ambiguity, academic scientists have reason to be confused, and to make their own interpretations of what is really required. They understand clearly that, after all, documents are not meant to be impediments to science, and that they, the scientists, supply the critical ingredient—professional expertise.

> *Professor H. H. Harlow is an archetypal representative of the academic scientist who becomes enmeshed in the various procedures and documents required to extract funds from granting/contracting sources. A senior faculty member at a major Midwestern university, he has had a long history of excellent biological research. Much of his research support has come from state or federal natural resource agencies, and for most of his distinguished career he has been feuding with the temporary heads of those agencies (and with countless midlevel agency bureaucrats) over the nature of his relationship to them. The offices from which Dr. Harlow has received his funding are operational units of line agencies, which deal with contracts and not with grants. Contracts are of course much neater from the perspective of a bureaucrat: The contractor promises a given body of work and delivers it on a specified date, summarized in the form of a final report. Dr. Harlow was never able to get through to people with that mind-set that research is just not amenable to*

*those strictures—but he continued to take their money.
He also continued to ignore deadlines for interim and
finals reports, but his findings were so valuable that the
agencies eventually began accepting any handwritten
note or letter as a contract report. Finally, almost as if it
was responding to his pleas for rationality in how research should be funded, the principal federal agency with
which he was involved set up a remarkably well-financed
office that dealt only with research grants. The old contracting requirements were reduced (but not eliminated),
and a new and gentler environment was created—one
more compatible with Dr. Harlow's concept of how research support should be managed.*

The more astute and experienced university professors who moonlight as scientific consultants are occasionally or frequently called on as expert witnesses in
hearings conducted by agencies such as the U.S. Army
Corps of Engineers, the U.S. Environmental Protection
Agency, and the Food and Drug Administration. Others
appear regularly as expert witnesses for utility companies, petroleum companies, or forest products companies. Sometimes, unfortunately, the thrusts of their testimony and conclusions are predictable, based on past
performances and the best interests of their current clients. Fortunately, though, most scientific consultants will
present unbiased conclusions based on the best available
data.

THE STUDENT–MENTOR RELATIONSHIP
WHEN THE MENTOR IS A CONSULTANT

An associated phenomenon that we have seen reen-
acted often is *the propagation by the consultant/professor of
graduate students who, after suitable apprenticeships, perform
the same kinds of predictable industry or agency support func-*

tions as their major professor. This is an entirely logical evolution, and the financial returns are attractive. These activities usually don't interfere with Ph.D. programs—in fact, some thesis topics may be outgrowths of consulting projects. Contract payments support graduate fellow-ships and research assistantships, and—poof—a whole new generation of scientific consultants emerges. But a small worrisome element here has to be the totally prag-matic approach to research and to science that is instilled in these naive eager newcomers during this kind of matu-ration process.

We should not dismiss too lightly the role of funds from consulting contracts in the shaping of future genera-tions of scientists. Attitudes about interpretations of re-search data, about statistical methodology, about scien-tific ethics, and about the sociology of science are being imparted to these newcomers by their major professors—their mentors—along with funds for tuition and living expenses.

We can see positive and negative facets of the use of consulting contract funds to pay graduate and under-graduate students. On the positive side, such funding does provide support for tuition and living expenses, and exposure to applied science. On the negative side, partici-pating as a student in that kind of science, rather than in basic studies supported by grants from major funding institutions and agencies, seems to reduce or eliminate contact with and training in more fundamental and ideal-istic aspects of science. Graduate school experiences can be influential—even critical—in setting a future course in the practice of science.

Maybe, though, we underestimate the perceptive ca-pabilities of graduate students. They have one important objective—to acquire the advanced degree that is crucial to entry into the professional universe. A significant sub-set of that objective would be to acquire the knowledge and background to enable pursuit of the kind of science that is most personally rewarding. Graduate students have one first hand and continuing example: their mentor's approach to the practice of applied science, as supported by consulting contract funds. They may have *other* examples in the observed professional activities of members of the department who also have consulting projects. They undoubtedly have *still other* examples in professors who depend exclusively on research funding from governmental granting entities such as the National Science Foundation, the National Institutes of Health, the National Sea Grant Office, the National Aeronautics and Space Administration, and other agencies that tend to support research of a more fundamental nature. These observations will be incorporated into the complex mix of factors to be evaluated by the student in answering the difficult question "How do I want to practice science, once this purgatory of graduate school is ended?" That answer will help define any future professional career, so it can't be reached without careful introspection and as much background information as can be assembled.

•   •   •

It seems perfectly permissible to end this discussion of the slightly ambiguous role of the academic scientist in consulting activities with a question: "What is the proper role of the university professor?" He is grossly underpaid, he knows that some private consultants are billing for more than $1000 a day, and he wants to be part of this bonanza. The solution seems simple—participate! Charge those exorbitant fees, stretch those ethical boundaries, find in favor of your client every time, get new contracts, and live! Don't retreat to your 8 × 12-foot university office and pontificate about the purity of science. We don't really believe that most academically based consulting scientists would subscribe to such a totally pragmatic and unethical code of practice. The alternatives should be clear, especially to academic scientists. Participate, yes, but never to the extent of compromising the value systems on which science is based, regardless of temptations. And make certain that your graduate students understand fully that consulting is only a narrow and somewhat mercenary *application* of scientific expertise, and not at all representative of the true horizons of science as a wonderful and satisfying human endeavor.

EIGHTEEN

Retirees as
Scientific Consultants

_____

the growing pool of recent retirees as a logical
source of consultants • advantages and
disadvantages of postretirement
consulting • major problems facing
postretirement consultants

_____

The immediate preretirement period is for many scientists a time of introspection, occasional melancholy, and planning for a postretirement career—preferably in some science-related activity, and preferably with pay. The authors of this book have both been down that path, so we can write about it as certified experts—or at least as professionals who have considered the available options and who have made choices about how to invest our time for the foreseeable future. We have both elected involvement in consulting activities, either intermittently (C.S.) or full-time (T.S.). We both have other science-related projects (such as writing this book on scientific consulting), and we both encounter scientists, active or retired, every day. In addition to focused and structured interviews with consultants for the purposes of the book, we have talked with professionals of all ages about attitudes and options related to retirement. Once we got beyond the stock responses of "I'm never going to retire" or "I'm getting out just as soon as I'm eligible," we began to appreciate the true range of options available to the retiring scientist. We felt that a reasonable way to begin a chapter on retirees as consultants would be to position the consulting options within the larger spectrum of postretirement occupations.

POSTRETIREMENT OPTIONS

The possible postretirement routes to be taken, and the many secondary branches of them, kept multiplying even as the list of options was being prepared. We cut it off after a while, and these are the survivors:

- The "out really means out" segment of the retiree population, who clear their desks, sell or donate their journal collections, give any usable equipment to a junior colleague, and disappear from the halls of science with scant traces and no regrets.
- Those who prefer to stay close to their specialty and their colleagues, who refuse to abandon a way of life completely, who have no hobbies outside science, and who retain emeritus, senior scientist, or volunteer status. They may act as co-principal investigators on a younger investigator's grant, or they may write books, but they remain part of the organization.

- Those who retain emeritus or senior scientist status, but, with the help of institutional affiliation and their own earned credibility, act intermittently and informally as consultants—in the sense that they may accept pay for advisory functions, or for participating in review or evaluation committee activities.
- Those who retain or do not retain institutional affiliation, but who consult on a formal basis, forming their own companies, maybe hiring staff, maintaining financial records, and working part or full time, at their own discretion.
- Those with a technical specialty that is in current demand, and who, even after retirement, receive annual retainer fees from relevant industries for advisory activities on an intermittent basis.
- Those who establish their own foundation or institute—nonprofit and tax exempt—contributing their own funds or soliciting grant support, carrying out specialized personal research or funding other scientists to do so, and in some instances paying themselves or family members and colleagues who are on the staff.
- Those who become affiliated with foundations (church related or private) that operate nationally or internationally to support specific causes or humanitarian activities (e.g., Volunteers for America)
- Those who serve as paid members of the board of directors of one or more foundations or institutes—positions that provide annual stipends as well as travel expenses.
- Those who become affiliated with (and may even take paying jobs with) international agencies, institutes, or commissions, such as agencies of the United Nations or its many subsidiary bodies. Functions may be advisory, or the scientists may

act as national representatives at periodic meetings. Retirees with special skills may, on occasion, be appointed to augment official governmental representation on international bodies, to help ensure unprejudiced nonpolitical deliberations.

- Those who continue to perform, under government or industry contract, science-related functions such as editing journals or preparing operations manuals, which were being done by them before retirement.

- Those federal scientific bureaucrats at an executive level who, after retirement, are awarded consulting contracts by their former agencies to locate and deliver scarce expertise needed for agency projects, or to organize specialized workshops or conferences on topics relevant to agency missions.

- Those recent retirees who have spent the last decade or two in executive levels of government agencies, and are particularly well placed to move to the executive levels of a large consultancy— transporting all of the acquired expertise in negotiations, all of the contacts at upper governmental and industrial levels, and all of the intertwined networks of peers, to the new position. Consulting at this level is almost exclusively advisory, based on an entire career devoted to synthesizing information and making administrative decisions.

- And finally (in organizations without a mandatory retirement age) we have those who refuse to retire, who continue to perform effectively, and who cling to their desks to the last day, until they are removed from the premises by physical force or who expire in the middle of a scientific experiment (we have heard of such individuals, but have never witnessed a departure of that nature).

ADVANTAGES AND DISADVANTAGES
OF POSTRETIREMENT CONSULTING

Where along this spectrum of postretirement options the fickle finger will point for any scientist of a certain age depends on about half a dozen factors: the degree to which continuing involvement in science is seen as desirable, the nature of the immediate preretirement job situation (favorable or unfavorable), a personal assessment of the energy investment required for the option selected, the extent to which the career successes in science have been internalized, and the policies and attitudes of the employing institution toward retention of older employees. We will assume for the purposes of this discussion that the option for consulting on a formal full-time basis has been selected by the retiree.

Most of the sole proprietor scientific consulting organizations that exist in the United States today are headed by a scientist who has retired from another kind of professional activity—industrial research and development, government research, or academic research and teaching. This is an entirely logical progression, as much of the success in consulting can depend on expertise and credibility acquired earlier on those other playing fields of science. Retirees, either voluntary or involuntary, are usually equipped with some form of annuity, pension, termination settlement, investments, or savings that provide the initial funding for a sole proprietor business venture. Consulting start-up costs can be nominal, but a regular retirement income or savings may be critical during the interval preceding achievement of profitability of the enterprise, and may be important later, during periods of contract scarcity.

To many scientists on the edge of retirement, then, consulting seems to offer an irresistible option. This ap-

pears to be an opportunity for a continuing career in a
scientific specialty in which a high level of competence
has already been established, in which professional networks have been developed, and in which some demand
for services is apparent. What could be a sweeter choice
for the later years of a scientific career?

> *Dr. Salinger was a well-known environmental biologist
> who planned to do consulting work shortly after retiring.
> Friends advised him to develop a business plan at least six
> months before his retirement date because life as a consul-
> tant would be a new experience. The first thing he did was
> to begin watching the newspapers for advertisements on
> consulting seminars. He attended several seminars, read
> over the handouts carefully, and signed up for a business
> accounting course offered in the evenings at a local com-
> munity college. He then contacted several personal
> friends, an accountant, and a lawyer, only to learn that it
> would be to his advantage to start a small corporation
> rather than to consider himself self-employed; as a corpo-
> ration, he and his wife could then use some of their
> savings to purchase stock to provide some of the start-up
> funds needed for supplies and equipment. When retire-
> ment became a reality, Dr. Salinger was able to imme-
> diately enter a consulting career because he had estab-
> lished his business well before retiring. On the basis of his
> success as a productive scientist, his first tasks were to
> submit research proposals to several large federal and
> state agencies. The proposals requested modest amounts
> of financial support with little overhead or direct and
> indirect costs as he thought that the smaller the costs the
> more likely it would be that he would be funded. After
> four or five proposals were rejected, in spite of the rela-
> tively small amounts of money requested, he sought the
> advice of several of his former colleagues, only to learn
> that most large agencies were less concerned with costs
> than with the reputation and stature of the applicant and
> his institution. Rather than becoming discouraged by a
> growing number of rejections, he decided that the one*

element missing from his business plan was a section on different ways of obtaining funding, and an analysis of the kinds of clients served by successful consultants. He soon learned that one worthwhile approach was to offer his services as a subcontractor to large corporations and to successful university researchers. Success in this direction led to spread of information about his expertise by word of mouth from many of his clients. One important observation that he made was that presentations at scientific meetings rarely led to additional work as a consultant. The trade-off here, however, enabled him to keep in contact with fellow scientists and to keep abreast of new developments in his specialty.

Clouds appear on the horizon almost immediately, though. The existence of alternative income from annuities or other retirement plans can act to decrease the economic urgency that might otherwise provide an incentive for achieving profitability sooner rather than later. Absence of severe financial pressure can encourage a more casual approach to marketing, sales, and other business activities that are critical to the long-term success of the venture and so easy to neglect. Of course, the daunting stress levels associated with starting a business will be lower. That should be true at least until the rapid disappearance of initial funding forces greater attention to commercial activities, even at the expense of some of the more enjoyable scientific pursuits.

The full realization that the scientific consultant must be a businessperson, and must invest serious time in the business aspects of a professional practice, can come as a shock and disappointment. It is at this point that many scientists become disenchanted with the prospect of that kind of future, and retreat to some alternative science-related position. Either that or they hang in there and get training in business management at a local college or in specialized seminars, and actually *become* businesspeople.

These are the survivors, and from their diminished ranks emerge those who go on to become professional consultants.

> *One of our consultants planned her work as a consultant several months before she retired. Prior to retirement, she attended several seminars on consulting, completed a basic accounting course at a local college, and discussed her plans with a well-known consultant in her specialty. She then wrote a business plan reviewed by both an accountant and a lawyer (both personal friends), and applied for corporate status at both the state and federal level, including her EINs (Employer Identification Numbers). On retirement she was ready to enter the world of consulting with little or no lag time. This individual considered renting or leasing office space, and the cost of other overhead or operating expenses, and decided that it might be wiser to operate out of her home until she began to show a profit. First-year operating expenses (e.g., computer, printer, telephone, fax) used up most of her personal start-up funds, and at tax time she had to file forms showing a modest business loss. Furthermore, there were spaces on the forms to show 179 depreciation items, retained earnings, adjustments, and K-1 shareholders pass-through dividends. On learning of these unknown areas of expertise required by the novice consultant, she immediately made the decision to pay for the services of a certified public accountant—on the premise that nothing could be more stressful than trying to handle paperwork as an amateur, and risk penalties for inaccurate tax reporting.*

Retirees have so much going for them as scientific consultants:

- They have acquired expertise, competence, and credibility—all of the ingredients of choice that are important to prospective clients.
- They are usually parts of intermeshing networks

of other scientists in their area of specialization and often outside it.

- They may have long-term friendships with other scientists, senior administrators, government bureaucrats, politicians, business managers, and other categories of professionals.
- They may, if they come from industrial research and development, have intimate, detailed, and current knowledge of industrial design and operations.
- They may, if they come from government research and regulatory agencies, have experience with the needs and procedures of those agencies—especially those that use consultant services.
- They may, if they come from academia, have excellent close relationships with members of the key "in-groups" that exist in every scientific specialty, and with officers and board members of scientific societies.
- They are, as scientists, intimately familiar with problem solving, and with visualizing approaches to solutions of problems.
- They may have enough visibility in science to have instant name recognition, at least among colleagues in the same specialty; this translates into credibility in any consulting activity in which they are involved.
- They may have good contacts with highly respected research scientists or research institutes in their specialty area.

Retirees also have identifiable deficiencies as scientific consultants:

- Their current expertise may quickly become dated during the present period of explosive growth in technology, unless they wage a serious and continuing battle against obsolescence by maintaining and upgrading technical skills.

- They may have little or no familiarity with business practices and methodology, and they may not be inclined to invest too heavily in acquiring those new skills.
- They may, if they come from an industrial organization, have occupied various management or executive positions with their previous employer(s), so their technical expertise may be already obsolescent or obsolete.
- They may, if they come from a government agency, have spent most or all of their careers in stultifying bureaucratic jobs, with little or no direct contact with science.
- They may, if they come from academia, be authorities in extremely narrow subdisciplines of science that have little or no relevance to the real-world scientific problems faced by consultants.
- They will, as they age, have less energy to expend on plunging into new projects, less wonder about the universe to foster creativity, and less enthusiasm for the new and untested.

With all of these considerations, positive and negative, the retiree still plays with a strong hand. He has credibility, contacts, and expertise—all attributes that are not acquired easily and that are essential in the scientific consulting business. He may be deficient in understanding business techniques, but these are readily learned, to ensure success in the retiree's new career.

The retiree who has occasional need for laboratory facilities must often rely on contacts with other consultants or former associates. One of our respondents obtained a position as a visiting scientist at a laboratory where he could make use of equipment such as centrifuges, auto-

claves, and photomicroscopes, thus expanding the types of services that he could provide clients. In another situation the consultant learned of a nonprofit privately owned foundation that provided laboratory space and equipment for professionals in need of facility support. Rather interestingly, the founder of the organization was a retired physician who wanted to keep active and up-to-date in the medical and environmental sciences. This individual and his wife purchased a waterfront property with outbuildings that could be converted into laboratories, and enough space to set up a computer center. In addition to participating in some of the research carried out by his guest workers, the retiree organized an extensive computerized data base to use in on-line scientific abstracting services with participating libraries. In this way he maintained his own interest in research and continued to work as a consultant in medical and environmental topics.

Retirees who would be or are scientific consultants have many of the same needs as all other kinds of consultants:

- A need for an appropriate mix of short- and long-term projects (some long-term projects are essential)
- A need for positive cash flow, even when consulting is not the principal source of income
- A need to be selective about contracts that can be accepted—Are they within the consultant's area of expertise, or will others be required to augment capabilities?

Retired professionals who become consultants contribute significantly to an extremely interesting statistic, namely, that older Americans make up a larger and larger percentage of entrepreneurs among the 15 million self-employed people in the United States (13% of the total work force), according to economist Diane Herz with the U.S. Bureau of Labor Statistics.[23] Her analysis found that "the proportion of the nation's self-employed age 45 years or older has increased to 46%, or about seven million persons (1994 figures), up from 42% ten years earlier." There is a downside to these statistics, though. In another analysis,[24] Dr. Paul Reynolds of Babson College, a university professor of entrepreneurial studies, has estimated that half of all people 50 or older who start a business shut down or sell out within five years—the result of a variety of factors, including poor planning, unexpected competition, inexperience, insufficient capitalization, and the state of the national economy.

Our examination has indicated three principal problem areas for postretirement scientific consultants:

1. *Complacency* can be an easy consequence of the knowledge that a fixed monthly annuity or pension will arrive on schedule ad infinitum, to cover basic living expenses. That knowledge reduces the urgency of acquiring new contracts or of completing existing ones, and in the extreme can degrade a serious consulting venture to the level of an interesting hobby.

2. *Declining energy levels* are common characteristics of advancing age, regardless of heroic efforts by some to delay their onset or deny their existence. Some common symptoms are shortened workdays, frequent vacations, reduced marketing efforts, deferred project start-ups, or lengthened completion schedules.

3. *Technical obsolescence* is a danger that all scientists, regardless of their age, must guard against, but it can become a very real menace to consultants working alone. Lack of stimulation from frequent interactions with colleagues or the unavailability of local science libraries can contribute to a rapidly decreasing familiarity with current science,

except possibly in the narrow specialty area that is the focus of the consulting practice.

It does little good to warn about this triumvirate of dangers facing the postretirement scientific consultant without proposing some remedial actions, and we have some:

- To avoid the sin of complacency, an early decision must be made about the true nature of the consulting practice. Is it to be a *business* in every practical sense of the term, or is it to be merely a cover for an enjoyable postretirement *hobby*? The decision will be influenced, of course, by the actual need for income beyond that available from pensions or investments. It may also be influenced by a strong desire for continued active involvement in the practice of science. The decision does not need to be immutable, either, as the consulting practice can evolve in many directions depending on the interests of the practitioner.
- Responses to declining energy levels are more difficult to propose—beyond recognizing and accepting the reality that such declines are part of the human condition. Logical consequences of that recognition might be a scaling back of the yearly schedule of projects, or a gradual shift in project emphasis from hands-on data acquisition to more evaluative and interpretive products, or recruiting one or more partners to assume some of the responsibilities of the practice.
- Responses to dangers of technical obsolescence should center on motivation to prevent this unhappy development. All scientists face the problem, whether they are in universities, government, or industry. Solutions lie in acts of will—reading journals, participating actively in professional

The Scientist as Consultant

meetings, writing good scientific papers, participating vigorously in networks—all of the functions that are part of being a scientist, and that
need not disappear as a consequence of voluntary
or forced retirement, or remote work environments, or a need to augment income by consulting.

So here then are three evils that postretirement scientific consultants must guard against—complacency, declining energy, and technical obsolescence. There are, of
course, other problems to be aware of, but these are of
relatively minor impact relative to the big three. They
include, but are not limited to, pomposity, verbosity, exclusivity (limiting professional contacts to a closed circle
of colleagues of comparable age and achievement), and
false superiority (especially in interactions with junior
colleagues).

SPREADING THE RESPONSIBILITIES

Beginning a solo scientific consulting career after retirement can be a difficult and often exhausting process, if
the venture is to be successful. One device that reduces
personal energy expenditure and increases breadth of
available expertise is to invite one or more colleagues to
form a *partnership*, in which individual resources and
competencies contribute to a common pool and form the
basis for soliciting contracts. We outlined in Chapter
Eleven some of the legal steps that should be taken in
forming such a joint consultancy at any career stage; we
want to focus here on partnerships formed after retirement.

At first glance, a partnership of compatible peers,
each with expertise and credibility in a specialty, would

seem to approach an ideal for a professional organization. It does, for some, but for others it proves unworkable. Most of the problems result from inadequate communication and planning before the venture begins. Some measures that have been suggested to ensure at least a level playing field include the following:

- Well before any definitive steps are taken, assemble the proposed partners for a three-day retreat in a mountain cabin, to explore in great detail every conceivable aspect of the proposed venture.
- Appoint the most detail-conscious member of the proposed partnership to draft a written agreement (minimum 20 pages) that, after revisions by the other partner(s) and scrutiny by a lawyer, would be signed by each partner.
- One of the provisions of the agreement should be that it (and the partnership) will self-destruct after a stated period (possibly two years) unless deliberately renewed with written approval of all partners.
- Another provision could be for an annually rotating presidency, so that each partner would get to be boss at some point, but that power would be temporary.
- Still another provision could be an obligatory annual review of the agreement, with opportunity to change it if the decision is unanimous.

With enough forethought, and with the right mix of personalities, partnerships—especially those of mature professionals—should succeed. They have several advantages: combined credibility of all partners, capability to take on relatively large projects, shared financial responsibility, and creation of a tiny mutually supportive scientific enclave in a too-impersonal world.

Another slightly different approach to sharing responsibilities would be for the senior consultant to accept a younger professional as a junior partner. The association would be (at least at first) more in the nature of a mentor–apprentice relationship, so interpersonal rapport would be critical. If formalized as a partnership, with adequate stipulations about division of profits, responsibilities of each partner, and life span of the arrangement, such a partnership should succeed—at least for a limited period.

Still another approach to spreading the responsibilities of a consultancy is to form alliances with other solo practitioners in related specialty areas.[6] The concept includes a number of joint activities, such as proposal preparation and marketing, but permits each professional to retain autonomy in specified areas. Flexibility is provided by the wording of a joint agreement detailing the mutual activities to be conducted.

•　　•　　•

Retirement—voluntary or forced—from a position that involves active participation in a scientific specialty is an excellent time for a career change to consulting. It is distressing to us, as observers, to see people with decades of experience and often unique technical backgrounds suddenly disappear into the gray ranks of yardmen, gardeners, handymen, or hobbyists (unless, of course, this is what they really want to do with the rest of their lives). Retirees at any age have so many advantages as beginning consultants—credibility, contacts, current expertise—that a prompt transition to the new career is entirely logical. The extent of commitment, part or full time, is of course optional, as is the attractive aspect of partnership with one or more compatible colleagues.

NINETEEN

The Future of Scientific Consulting

THE NEXT DECADE

---

economic and technological changes that
indicate larger markets for scientific
expertise • recent trends in the roles and
methods of scientific consulting

The study of economics has long been referred to as "the dismal science," and that designation certainly applies to some assessments of today's business climate. A recent and somewhat gloomy economic forecast for the United States[25] included statements that have great relevance to the future of consulting:

- "[M]any leading companies are shedding [highly skilled workers] in a downsizing frenzy."
- "There is a malaise affecting professionals. Middle managers are hurting."

- "Manufacturing jobs [value added jobs] are losing ground throughout America."
- "A concern is that the future economic foundation [laid by federal spending programs] will be cut in the name of deficit reduction. This will include areas of crucial importance such as environmental protection."

These are some informed perceptions of the climate in which small businesses (such as individual consultants and small consulting ventures) will have to function in the immediate future.

TRENDS IN THE DEMAND FOR SCIENTIFIC CONSULTANTS

Despite these negative indicators, we think the short-term outlook for employment of scientific consultants, and for consultants in general, is clearly positive. Consulting is a growth industry, enhanced by rapid advances in technology and a continuing shortage of skills required to support industrial development. There persists, of course, a continuing dependence on business conditions in the United States and elsewhere, as downturns and recessions result in postponement or cancellation of some projects involving consulting services. In general, though, we are now in an economy that maximizes the role of the consultant—one that is characterized by dependence on temporary employees (one-quarter of the work force is now estimated to be temporary), by concomitant absence of long-term overhead investment in employee benefits, and by demand for instantly available expertise in rapidly developing new high-technology disciplines, as well as in related communications and management specialties.

In some scientific consulting areas (e.g., environment) the intensity of government regulatory activity determines the health of related consulting businesses. We have seen repeated examples of the reality of this dictum in following the politically induced fluctuations in promulgation and enforcement of environmental regulations by the EPA. When existing regulations are enforced and new ones imposed, scientific consultants are kept busy with data collection and interpretation; when budgets are cut and enforcement of antipollution measures is reduced (as at present), there is less demand for the services of environmental consultants, the entire regulatory process retreating to minimal levels.

Medical consulting is also affected by comparable trends. The tremendous expansion of health management plans, systems, and organizations (HMOs) has increased the demand for consultant services, as has the threatened and inevitable revamping of the entire government health care structure in this country (especially Medicare and Medicaid). Consultants provide advice, predictions, and options to hospitals, hospital groups, health insurance firms, physicians, HMOs, and even patients.

A significant aspect of the extensive reductions in permanent industrial jobs in the United States since the early 1980s has been the great increase in *temporary positions*, as we have already noted. Placement agencies to fill short-term clerical and data entry jobs have been a part of the employment scene for decades, but a more recent phenomenon has been expansion in recruitment of *professionals* for temporary jobs (usually for assignments of a few weeks to a year). This is a logical concomitant of the currently popular "downsizing" in that (1) the temporary position self-destructs at the end of a stated period, unless extended by management, (2) the temporary position does not usually carry with it any overhead expenses, such as health plans or unemployment benefits, and

(3) the temporary position can be used to buy expertise that does not exist in the newly leaner staff—expertise that is not required or cannot be afforded any longer on a permanent basis.

This recent trend, resulting in the appearance of a substantial cadre of "temps in gray flannel suits,"[26] may prove to be a long-term reality in the workplace of the future. Professionals in many categories (lawyers, physicians, even scientists) may find themselves moving, by choice or necessity, from one temporary position to another. Some may even begin to enjoy the flexibility, the opportunities for acquisition of additional skills, and opportunities for new challenges that short-term employment can provide. Others—undoubtedly a majority—look on temporary jobs as merely stepping stones to something more permanent.

Here, we think, is the important attitude that separates the professional in a temporary position from the consultant. The temp focuses on a future permanent position with some larger industrial organization; the consultant envisions a continuing series of short-term assignments (contracts) as a chosen way of life.

As consultants begin to form a larger and larger segment of the professional population—either by choice or as a consequence of industrial downsizing—a more aggressive and more structured kind of networking is appearing. This new phenomenon was described recently.[27] Its core is the *replacement of some of the support functions formerly provided by corporations with counterpart functions offered by informal professional associations of consultants in similar specialties.* Such organizations could be sources of career counseling and development, personal crisis support, apprenticeships, referrals, and even group purchasing and insurance. We can see other advantages to these advanced networking associations for consultants:

- They help to supply the kind of personal linkages that seem important to many professionals, and that may be absent from the daily lives of individual consultants.
- They can supply a supportive and generally sympathetic environment in which to explore privately with other individual consultants, problems related to ethics or business practices.
- They can create a continuing forum for detailed group discussions of problems common to all consulting ventures (such as maintaining cash flow, recruiting, client relationships, and staff training programs).

The concept of networking associations of consultants clearly fills a need created by the decline and disappearance of the support functions formerly supplied by corporations—career counseling, training, and (most importantly) bonding with professional colleagues. Consultants with a common specialty have much to gain by forming or participating in this kind of networking. The learning experiences, the contacts, and the personal relationships are all available, and are free.

Another aspect of the future of consulting concerns interactions with the legal system. The ever-increasing abundance, diversity, and complexity of litigation in this country (and in other parts of the world) require that scientific consultants either have additional training in law or have legal assistance readily available. Few consulting projects are free of legal implications; many are funded specifically to enhance a position in a regulatory hearing, or to establish a position in a civil court case. Other than by seeking additional training, scientific specialists must resort to often-painful experience as a participant in adversarial venues (hearing rooms, courtrooms, and liability cases against the consultancy)—experience that is often rich in stress and failure. The pace and variability of tomorrow's consulting practice may not permit the luxury of such an apprenticeship. Specific training in legal aspects of the consultants' role may become almost as important as technical knowledge.

EXPANDING ROLES FOR SCIENTIFIC CONSULTANTS

Leaving these generalizations about the future behind us—however reluctantly—we can now consider briefly a few specific components of scientific consulting that can be important in the next decade.

THE IMPORTANCE OF ACQUIRING NEW TECHNICAL SKILLS

Maintaining technical competence has been stressed repeatedly throughout this book as a continuing responsibility of every scientific consultant. But just *maintaining* competence is not enough; *acquiring new technical skills* is also almost obligatory in a world characterized by explosive growth in many scientific disciplines. The science learned in graduate school or in on-the-job projects is just not enough, and will not be enough in any future consulting practice. New techniques and equipment become available seemingly overnight, and concepts evolve as data bases expand. Consultants, as businesspeople, have difficulty in just keeping up with current technology, let alone exploring new developments—yet they must if they expect to survive and prosper. This is especially true with respect to the latest computer software innovations.

THE IMPORTANCE OF KEEPING UP-TO-DATE ON ENVIRONMENTAL ISSUES, AND ON NEW APPROACHES TO ENVIRONMENTAL MANAGEMENT

Environmental consultants comprise the largest group of scientific consultants in the United States—undoubtedly because of continuing public sensitivities about environmental degradation, and attempts by government agencies to regulate polluting industries and municipalities. For more than three decades consultants have been busy developing data bases to be used in preparing environmental impact statements, to support regulatory hearing arguments, to provide information relevant to environmental damage cases in courts, or to perform myriad other advisory functions related to environmental management. The work continues, the data bases improve, and the sophistication of the interpretations, the analyses, and the environmental modeling efforts improve.[5] The next decade should see further refinement of predictive models, especially for the nation's heavily impacted coastal zones, and the more widespread application of a relatively new concept—that of "environmentally sustainable development"—which will bulk large in any future environmental discussions.

A brief note seems in order at this point about the continuing role of the scientific consultant as an industry spokesperson. A venue for science–industry–government interaction that can only expand in the future is the courtroom or hearing room, as discussed in Chapter Eleven. Here the most qualified from the industrial research laboratories and the industrial consulting groups confront the best scientific spokespersons from the federal agencies, various citizen action groups, and private foundations. Industry representatives usually take a low-

key approach in issues relating to environmental degradation, trying to minimize the problems. The environmental action groups and the regulatory agencies, on the
other hand, want to get as much factual information into
the record and before the public as possible.

Polluting industries in particular are willing to spend
major sums to delay, impede, or prevent actions that will
force them to change processes or carry out cleanup measures. Part of the expenditure of funds is to buy scientific
expertise that can be counted on to support the industry
position, which is normally to minimize the extent of
demonstrable damage. The degree to which some industries will invest in "safe" scientific advice often comes as a
distinct shock to scientists unfamiliar with this aspect of
the behavior of some of their colleagues.

EMERGING ROLES FOR WOMEN AS CONSULTANTS, PROGRAM MANAGERS, AND PROGRAM DIRECTORS

The Woman Scientist, an earlier book in a long-running
series of publications about scientists as people,[14] reached
a number of upbeat conclusions about the improving
position of women in science—noting reductions in overt
discrimination, progress in achieving salary parity, and
improvement in publication comparability. It is interesting in retrospect that the book was silent about the role of
female scientists as consultants. That defect may reflect in
large measure the fact that most of the research—questionnaires and interviews—on which the book was based
targeted female scientists in academic and government
positions. But that isn't a good explanation. The truth is
that female scientists, even today, are not often found in
the ranks of consultants, even though their relative abun-

dance in academic and government jobs has increased substantially in the past two decades.

We did not address the gender imbalance during the research for the present book, but the disparity became apparent during the preparation of questionnaires for mailing. Available lists of consultants rarely included evidence of women in leadership positions, and lists of individual consultants were heavily male dominated. This early observation of unequal presence, even if it is in part a sampling artifact, will be modified, we are convinced, to become part of the general trend toward parity in numbers between male and female scientists that was apparent in the earlier study.[14] Beyond mere numerical equivalency, we also expect to see more women in key roles in consulting ventures—whether as individual entrepreneurs or as chief operating officers of larger organizations. The much discussed "glass ceiling" that has kept many women from upper management and executive positions in industry seems to have been operative in consulting companies, but should show more obvious signs of fracture during the decade ahead, as more and more women move into leadership positions in consulting organizations.

INCREASING DEMANDS FOR QUALITY ASSURANCE SCRUTINY OF METHODS, DATA, AND CONCLUSIONS OF CONSULTANTS

Concomitant with the expansion of adversarial roles as key elements of a scientific consultant's daily responsibilities has come an emerging emphasis on quality assurance. Some consulting firms now limit their practices exclusively to this kind of work—scrutinizing proposals and reports prepared by other consultants, to determine whether the methodology and the quality control are adequate, to evaluate plans and protocols for data collection and analysis, to suggest most effective data log forms and chain of custody procedures for field samples, and to prepare recommendations, options, and courses of action for clients.

The need for this quality assurance activity has developed because of real or perceived deficiencies in preexisting systems of control, in the form of:

- Wide variability in the competence of consulting firms
- Absence of government certification, licensing, or other regulations that pertain to consultants
- Difficulties that clients have had in evaluating the scientific merits of information presented to them by consultants
- Increasing disenchantment of judges and hearing examiners with incomplete or inconclusive data, controversial or conflicting findings of scientists (consultants or otherwise), and public quarrels among scientists about interpretations of data and conclusions to be drawn therefrom
- Unwillingness of lawyers to accept almost any pronouncement by a scientist, unless that scientist is part of the "home team" in a legal case
- Embarrassment of expert witnesses, which may be the consequence of increasing levels of scientific awareness, and even technical expertise, demonstrated by some lawyers

Emphasis on quality assurance yields more contracts for scientific consultants with recognized credibility and demonstrated skills in program evaluation in specific discipline areas. It also increases paperwork and reduces profits for the individual practitioner, because of the time required for the preparation of quality control forms. We have referred several times in this book to the increasing degrees of competitiveness in consulting as well as in other businesses. Quality assurance, properly conducted, should be a positive factor, favoring the competent and suppressing the less competent—helping to define that fine line between success and failure.

USE OF ELECTRONIC METHODS OF COMMUNICATION

Seen in retrospect, the science that was conducted even a few decades ago seems so leisurely and gentle, and somehow abstract. It really wasn't, of course, except by comparison with today's practices—typified by goal orientation, short-term projects, the mad scramble for research funds, media releases and overnight publication, computerized digestion, assimilation, and interpretation of data, and the almost instantaneous dissemination of information. This rapid dissemination of information is of great relevance to the activities of scientific consultants, and is one that will influence consulting practice significantly and progressively during the next decade.

Scientific departmental or project offices in the dark ages (before 1980) were equipped with electric typewriters, inefficient copying machines, assorted personal use recording devices, and possibly limited access to someone else's computer. Today all that has changed. Every desk has a personal computer; messages are faxed or e-mailed; and almost overwhelming amounts of information can be found on the Internet. These developments in communication and information availability can be and should be—and in fact are already being—incorporated into the consultant's business practices. Equipment and system use costs are of course substantial, but they are tax deductible as business expenses, so should not be major deterrents. A major investment of time—always in short supply for the professional—has to be made in learning how to take full advantage of the available information sources, without wasting hours in interesting but irrelevant (to business) items on the menu.

On the practical level, the increasing use of electronic communication is changing the nature of contract work in consulting. Use of the World Wide Web/Internet has become a source of contracts (some respondents to our questionnaires have identified such use as *very* important). Additionally, federal agencies are now putting RFPs on the Internet.

Questions about these new information sources that must be resolved in the short term concern the kinds of information that will be available on the Internet, how the information can be used legitimately, and how credit for it can be assigned. These questions are particularly critical to scientific consultants, who live in a commercial world where nothing is free and everything has a price—especially data. Scientists in general are rightfully very sensitive about priority of ideas, use of data that they have acquired, release of their findings, and a host of other items related to the almost universally held concept of "intellectual property." Scientific consultants, as businesspeople, will, if they are wise, tread very gently in this thicket, which has suddenly grown much denser because of new kinds of information transfer.

AN EXPANDING ROLE FOR CONSULTANTS AS INFORMATION SYNTHESIZERS AND ADVISORS

Some authors see in the immediate future a continuing trend in this country away from an industry-based to an information-based society. As the mass and complexity of information increase, the demand for professionals who can ingest, assimilate, and synthesize it, and then offer informed opinions and advice based on it, will increase. The consultants are perfectly positioned to exploit these trends in the decade ahead—to continue and to expand their critical service link between the information producers (research scientists) and the consumers (decision makers at all levels).

•   •   •

So, in summary, the next decade should be a good one for the best scientific consultancies. Competition will be increased, though, by an influx of new practitioners, and sources of government funding will be harder to find, but competent credible professionals will never be in oversupply. Consultants are already well positioned to participate in the national trend toward proportional increases in temporary employment for professionals as well as nonprofessionals. Additionally, the widening gap between complex new technology and the average level of public comprehension indicates an expanding role for scientific consultants in numerous specialties.

Conclusion

THE QUINTESSENCE OF
SCIENTIFIC CONSULTING

Scientific consulting, especially in the currently dominant area of environmental affairs, can be a volatile enterprise, with drastic fluctuations in demand for services. This selective force has led to the evolution of a cadre of professionals with high survival capabilities in times of economic stress in the consulting industry. The survivors have been aptly characterized as "being able to perform a variety of functions. They write lucid reports, supervise personnel, manage complex multidisciplinary projects, and wrestle with budgets. These employed scientists also communicate well, and they have demonstrated an ability to acquire new work for their company. Most importantly, they have shown an ability to apply their basic training to scientific inquiries in new issue areas."[28]

Environmental consultants, for example, must be familiar with the working language of a number of specialists—hydrologists, geologists, engineers, economists, and sociologists—and should also be able to communicate effectively with chemists (about pollution levels), biologists (about algal blooms and other phenomena), and public health officials (about potential health risks from contaminated waters). Furthermore, scientific consultants must understand and participate in business

293

affairs—finances, marketing, selling, profits, cost estimates, fee setting, human resources management, proposal preparation, and a host of other factors. Success
emerges from demonstrated competence in all technical
and business aspects of the industry and the ability to
meld the often disparate demands of consulting.

Many of these skills have received attention earlier in
the book, but it would seem sensible, in this final chapter,
to extract and restate a series of generalizations that seem
to embody our concepts and conclusions about scientific
consulting:

- Consulting is a *business* and must be conducted as
  such. *Scientific* consulting is still a business, but
  one bound by the rules and ethics of science—
  objective evaluations, weight of evidence, validity
  of conclusions, adequacy of data, currency of
  information—and the scientific consultant is an
  entrepreneur, selling his expertise, experience, judgment, and reputation for a price.
- Scientific consulting is a *service* business, supplying technical information and advice to clients for
  a fee. However, unlike many other businesses, scientific consulting is *not* based on the notion that
  the customer is always right, or that the customer's wishes have primacy. The guiding principle in providing scientific consulting services is
  more properly that advice and recommendations
  will be based on the information available, and
  will not be skewed to satisfy the preconceptions or
  needs of the client, regardless of the consequences.
- Successful scientific consultants are those who
  have achieved a viable mix of *technical proficiency*
  and *business skills*. Technical proficiency is a com-
  posite of competence, credibility, effective networking with colleagues, and ability to negotiate.

Successful business practices include careful attention to marketing and sales aspects of the enterprise, maintenance of correct business procedures and attitudes, managerial skills, and effective personal presentation.

- *Effective management* of a consulting organization is a *critical learned skill*, especially for scientifically trained entrepreneurs, who are not always noted for excellence in interpersonal relationships. As the consultancy grows in size, more and more of its success will come to depend on the work of technically trained employees, who tend to be highly individualistic and demanding in their expectations about the workplace, their salaries, and the company management. The best consulting firms are those that are managed to provide a productive and pleasant work environment in which a spirit of challenge and growth is fostered, and reasonable job security is assured.

- Scientific consultants, in the course of their practices, sometimes face difficult *ethical choices*, some of which push against the borders of acceptable professional behavior. Problems are frequently generated by a desire to satisfy a client's needs whenever possible. This client-oriented perspective may conflict with findings of the consultant's investigations, or with conclusions that may be drawn from the available data. The real problems, though, result from how scientific information is *interpreted* by the consultant, and the degree of flexibility that he exercises in that interpretation. Temptations exist to favor the client, although consultants almost always deny any unethical acts on their part.

- *Maintaining professional competence* is a particularly vexing problem for scientific consultants. The rapidity with which new information is developing today is daunting even for the academic scientist, and can be overwhelming for the consulting scientist who is trying to manage a business, maintain positive cash flow, market aggressively, and win new contracts. One sanity-preserving approach is to be very *selective* about efforts to maintain competency—about the journals to be read, the professional meetings to be attended, and even the colleagues to be included in networking. A necessary corollary to selectivity, though, is persistence. Once choices about continuing involvement in the affairs of science have been made, they should be followed, and not be allowed to disappear into the maelstrom of more mundane responsibilities (with some reasonable flexibility, of course).

- Most scientists spend entire careers without ever encountering the rough legal fringes of their profession—even in areas such as copyright infringement, fraud, theft of ideas, or plagiarism. This blissful freedom from the legal system is denied to scientific consultants, who must appear as expert witnesses in all forms of court cases and regulatory hearings. To do this effectively, an absolute requirement is training and/or experience in basic legal procedures, to avoid being eaten alive by the principal predators (lawyers) that prowl the courtrooms and hearing rooms. Some consultants acquire the skills to survive and even to prosper in this foreign milieu, but most consider it a negative and even dangerous aspect of their work. For those who perform well, the satisfaction of competing successfully with lawyers on their own turf must be great indeed, as must be the pleasure of injecting a little science into their alien universe.

- Most scientific consulting is done by individual professionals or by small entrepreneurial companies. This is where much of the expertise-for-hire resides as well. But hovering over these small operations are much larger management-oriented *megaconsulting corporations* that bid on large government, international, or industrial contracts. Those umbrella organizations then manage the larger projects or programs—usually by parceling out subcontracts to smaller consultancies, and then guiding the course of all subsequent activities—disbursing funds, reviewing progress, examining reports, conducting evaluations—assuming responsibility for effective use of funds from the donor entity. The internal structure of such megaconsulting firms can be elaborate; some scientific staff exists, but its activities are principally in project planning, data management, evaluation of subcontractor performance, and report preparation. Among the largest of such firms, some science is actually done by the in-house staff, mostly to demonstrate competence in selected technical specialty areas.

One of our overriding observations is that consulting does form a distinct career alternative for those technically trained professionals who find at some point that research and/or teaching do not provide all of the anticipated satisfactions. Consulting is not, however, a panacea for all professionals who become disenchanted with standard forms of employment, but it can definitely open new perspectives and possibilities for a number of them. We have tried in this book to describe the special kind of scientist who will survive and prosper in a stressful, demanding, and frequently rewarding occupation. That person will be energetic, intelligent, and well attuned to the realities of existence in a highly competitive world; that person will be a risktaker, but one well prepared to welcome new challenges; that person will be well versed in the fundamental principles and content of his chosen specialty, but will be eager to use that technical expertise in practical applications; and that person will respect the values of science but will also appreciate the norms of the business community that he has chosen to join.

Epilogue

We have just completed 19 chapters that describe consulting as part of the commercial side of science. Scientists as business people? Not likely! Yet many highly trained and competent professionals have decided that this is where their interests and futures reside. A persistent but rarely expressed question has to be "Why?" Why, with the array of scientific problems yet unsolved, and with only rudimentary solutions to many others, should men and women with ability and training turn away from research and teaching to the pursuit of dollars? We had hoped that producing this book would give us some measure of enlightenment, but there is no single easy answer. We have gained some insights from the interviews and the responses to our questionnaires, but the truth is elusive. Motivation for any specific behavior—especially by scientists—can be complex and easily disguised by facile explanations.

We have to conclude that money is at the base of some decisions by scientists to enter and to remain in the business of consulting. Scientific training plus entrepreneurial skills *can* lead to a financially rewarding career— often far beyond potential dollar rewards to be found in academic or government research. Also, there is the mildly disturbing reality that *some scientifically trained pro-*

fessionals do not want to teach or do research; they want the group interaction, the public involvement, and the power that are parts of the wider universe of business. Scientific training, for that kind of person, is merely a springboard to something more challenging and remunerative (but, unfortunately, somewhat peripheral to science as it is usually defined). Consulting does provide, though, the satisfactions of seeing science applied to significant current issues and problems—and the deeply personal rewards of *making a difference,* as a professional, in how society functions.

Our explorations have revealed many lesser truths about scientists as consultants—how they struggle against a loss of competence; how they work toward maintaining their roles in the professional community; and how they must always strive for ethical practices in their work and that of those who work for them. Inevitably, though, lurking in the background, is another poorly resolved key question: "How do you as a consultant reconcile scientific objectivity with the need to satisfy a client's expectations?" A standard, and we think too glib, response is that the data and the conclusions drawn therefrom cannot and will not be manipulated or slanted, but the reality is that interpretations of the data are often flexible and can be supportive of the client's position. Probes by us into this ethical twilight zone have not been satisfactory, but our suspicions of occasional marginal practices persist. Consultants should, in their reports, always strive for the utmost clarity and precision in their analyses and recommendations.

We leave the scientific consultants as we found them—scrambling to make a living in a highly competitive and stressful business-oriented occupation, with inadequate time to maintain a full range of professional pursuits, but convinced that this is the kind of career that best suits them. They consider themselves to be practicing scientists, even though much of their work week is pre-empted by marketing and managing activities. And they do provide, for a price, technical contributions to issues of importance to the society in which we live. The role of consultants in applying scientific expertise to problems of the moment should not be undervalued. Technical information expands daily, and there must be a corps of professionals who—for a fee—are able and willing to interpret that accumulated data for people without the background and experience to do so. From this perspective, it is easy to be optimistic about the future potential for science consulting. Technical information increases in quantity and complexity, and access to it is not simple, so the technology gap that the potential consumer perceives gets wider and becomes more formidable. This perception makes the services of a scientific consultant attractive and essential in a future world deluged with an uninter-rupted flow of information and technological advances.

Endnotes

1. H. L. Shenson, *How to Build and Maintain Your Own Part-Time/Full-Time Consulting Practice* (Manchester, NY: American Association of Professional Consultants, 1985).
2. B. Berelson and G. A. Steiner, *Human Behavior* (New York: Harcourt, Brace & World, 1964).
3. R. Teitelman, *Profits of Science: The American Marriage of Business and Technology* (New York: Basic Books, 1994).
4. D. O'Brian (D. Ousterhout), *30 Reasons Not to Buy or Start a Business* (Houston, TX: New Century Publications, 1994).
5. T. L. Greenbaum, *The Consultant's Manual: A Complete Guide to Building a Successful Consulting Practice* (New York: John Wiley and Sons, 1990); and M. McKeever, *How to Write a Business Plan*, 4th ed. (Berkeley, CA: Nolo Press, 1995).
6. M. D. Lewin, *The Overnight Consultant* (New York: John Wiley and Sons, 1995).
7. M. P. Follett, "How must business management develop in order to possess the essentials of a profession," in H. C. Metcalf and L. Vwik, Eds., *Dynamics of Administration, The Collected Papers of Mary Parker Follett* (London: Sir Isaac Pitman & Sons, London, 1941), pp. 117–145.
8. J. Naisbitt, *Megatrends* (New York: Warner Books, 1982).
9. D. D. Martin and R. L. Shell, *Management of Professionals: Insights for Maximizing Cooperation* (New York: Marcel Dekker, 1988); T. Peters and R. Waterman, *In Search of Excellence* (New York: Harper and Row, 1982); and E. Williams, *Partici-*

304 The Scientist as Consultant

pative Management Concepts, Theory and Implementation (Atlanta: Georgia State University Press, 1976).

10. R. E. Kelley, *Consulting: The Complete Guide to a Profitable Career* (New York: Charles Scribner's Sons, 1981); and B. R. Smith, *The Country Consultant: How to Make a Better Living and Live a Better Life as a Rural Business Consultant* (New York: New American Library, 1982).

11. H. L. Shenson, *Shenson on Consulting: Success Strategies from the "Consultant's Consultant"* (New York: John Wiley and Sons, 1990).

12. J. A. Raelin, "Examination of deviant adaptive behaviors in the organizational careers of professionals," *Academy of Management Review* 9 (1964), pp. 413–427; and A. Shapero, *Managing Professional People: Understanding Creative Performance* (New York: The Free Press, 1985).

13. D. C. Pelz and F. M. Andrews, *Scientists in Organizations: Productive Climates for Research and Development* (New York: John Wiley and Sons, 1976); D. C. Pelz and F. M. Andrews, "Autonomy coordination and stimulation in relation to scientific achievement," *Behavioral Science* 9 (1966), pp. 89–97; and M. B. McLeod, "The communication problems of scientists in business and industry," *Journal of Business Communications* 15 (1979), pp. 27–35.

14. C. M. Yentsch and C. J. Sindermann, *The Woman Scientist* (New York: Plenum Press, 1992).

15. S. Prasso, "Glass ceiling pierced when men are comfortable" (*Miami Herald*, 10 March, 1996), p. G-1.

16. W. Hendricks, *Coaching, Mentoring and Managing* (New York: Career Press, 1995); and T. Gabriel, "Personal trainers to buff the boss's people skills" (*New York Times*, 28 April, 1996), pp. F-1, F-6.

17. C. J. Sindermann, *Winning the Games Scientists Play* (New York: Plenum Press, 1982).

18. G. Kishel and P. Kishel, *How to Start and Run a Successful Consulting Business* (New York: John Wiley and Sons, 1996).

19. W. Brockhaus, "Prospects for malpractice suits in the business consulting profession," *Journal of Business* 21 (January 1977), pp. 34–40.

20. J. R. Dunn and G. A. Kiersch, "The professional fisheries scientist as an expert witness," *Fisheries* 1 (1976), pp. 2–4,

44–46; P. W. Huber, *Galileo's Revenge: Junk Science in the Courtroom* (New York: Basic Books, 1991); and W. A. Thomas, Ed., *Scientists in the Legal System* (Ann Arbor, MI: Ann Arbor Science Publishers, 1974).

21. G. G. Scott and J. J. Harrison, *Collection Techniques for a Small Business* (New York: Oasis Press, 1995).
22. R. Teitelman, *Profits of Science: The American Marriage of Business and Technology* (New York: Basic Books, 1994).
23. D. Herz (cited in Lewis, R., 1995), "Tough road for entrepreneurs," *AARP Bulletin* 36 (October 1995), pp. 8–9.
24. R. Lewis, "Tough road for entrepreneurs," *AARP Bulletin* 36 (October 1995), pp. 7–8.
25. G. Fields, "Outlook '96," (*Miami Herald*, 22 January, 1996), pp. 18–19.
26. M. O. Kirk, "Temps in gray flannel suits" (*New York Times*, 17 December, 1995), p. F-1.
27. H. Lancaster, "As company programs fade, workers turn to support groups" (*Miami Herald*, 28 January 1996), p. G-1.
28. R. B. Bogardus, "The consulting environmental biologist," *Fisheries* 8 (1983), pp. 16–18.

Questionnaire

(This questionnaire was mailed to names selected at random from lists of consultants and from scientific society membership lists.)

1. In what area do you work as a consultant? (Check one or more)
   ____ biomedical
   ____ environmental
   ____ educational (scientific)
   ____ advisory
   ____ research
   ____ marketing
   ____ advertising
   ____ Other

2. What type of consulting do you do? (Check one or more)
   ____ lab testing
   ____ product design
   ____ education
   ____ environmental sampling
   ____ Other

3. Who are your principal clients?
   ____ government

307

_____ state
_____ industry
_____ foreign
_____ academic institutions
_____ other consultants

4. What is your background?
_____ academic
_____ government
_____ state
_____ industry

5. How do you obtain clients?
_____ personal contacts
_____ published requests for proposals
_____ advertising
_____ brochure
_____ letters of inquiry
_____ word of mouth

6. How many years have you been a consultant? _____

7. Did you begin your career as a consultant?
Yes _____ No_____

8. Why did you become a consultant?
_____ financial
_____ freedom and independence
_____ maximizing qualifications and experience
_____ active career goals

9. How is your time in consulting activities spent (in percentage)?
_____ at office (or lab)
_____ outside travel
_____ conferences and meetings
_____ writing reports and proposals
_____ technical work
_____ promoting yourself

10. If you were beginning a scientific career, would you prefer:
    _____ academic
    _____ federal
    _____ state
    _____ private sector
    _____ self-employment

11. Why is your scientific consulting profession rewarding? (Check one or more)
    _____ financial
    _____ personal interest
    _____ utilization of talents
    _____ recognition
    _____ impact on client's decisions
    _____ other _____

12. How do you determine your charges?
    _____ hourly rate
    _____ fixed cost agreements
    _____ cost plus contract
    _____ competitive bidding
    _____ other _____

13. If you were just beginning a career, would you choose the consulting professions?
    _____ as a starting profession
    _____ as a later-in-career profession

14. Would you recommend a career as a consultant to persons entering the workforce? Yes _____ No _____

15. Are you ever required to sign confidentiality statements? Yes _____ No _____
    Do you object to your results being kept confidential? Yes _____ No _____

16. Are you allowed to have proprietary interests in proposed projects? Yes _____ No _____

17. Do you have royalty and profit agreements?
    Yes ____ No ____

18. Do you have primary responsibility for consulting
    activities? Yes ____ No ____

19. Do you participate in a broad range of consulting
    activities? Yes ____ No ____

20. Do you accept work on a problem when the result
    may conflict with your own interests?
    Yes ____ No ____

21. Are your findings ever misrepresented when pre-
    sented to others? Yes ____ No ____

22. Have you ever experienced difficulties in carrying
    out your work because of difficulties in dealing with
    foreign countries? Yes ____ No ____

23. Have you ever been cited as an authority when your
    findings are not presented accurately?
    Yes ____ No ____

24. Have you ever experienced other people claiming to
    have expertise based on information or materials that
    you have provided? Yes ____ No ____

25. Have you ever felt that your findings have been ig-
    nored because of political, economic, or social rea-
    sons? Yes ____ No ____

26. Have you ever agreed to work on a problem only
    to realize later that methodology was not effective?
    Yes ____ No ____

27. Is keeping current with new instrumentation or scien-
    tific developments ever a problem to you?
    Yes ____ No ____

28. Is most of your work carried out "in house" rather
    than by subcontracts or collaboration with others?
    Yes ____ No ____ Both ____

29. Do your results ever conflict with results expected by clients? Yes _____ No _____

30. What do you think are major problems for consultants? (Check all applicable)
   _____ getting paid on timely basis
   _____ reviews of reports by outsiders
   _____ time lags
   _____ criticisms and revisions
   _____ results not in agreement with those expected or desired by client
   _____ excessive overhead
   _____ maintaining continuity of contracts
   _____ subcontractors who misrepresent their capabilities
   _____ keeping up with current thinking on specific topics
   _____ maintaining skills with new technical developments
   _____ compliance with standards established for methods

31. Number of consultants within your organization: Full time _____, Part time _____, On call _____.

32. Do you have primary responsibility for consulting activities? Yes _____ No _____

33. Do you participate in a broad range of consulting activities? Yes _____ No _____

34. What type of consultant are you?
   _____ self-employed
   _____ sub S
   _____ C corporation
   _____ nonprofit
   _____ partnership
   _____ employee

35. Do you have a board of directors? Yes _____ No _____

36. Have you ever experienced difficulties brought about by bureaucrats or foreign governments?
Yes _____ No _____

37. Have you ever experienced other people claiming expertise based on information or materials you have provided? Yes _____ No _____

38. Do you think that consulting is more stressful than other kinds of careers? Yes _____ No _____

39. If you founded your own firm:
    a. How did you obtain your start-up funds?
    b. Who did you consult with for writing your charter?
    c. How did you get your first contracts?
    d. How did you determine your fees?
    e. How long did it take to return a reasonable profit?
    f. How do you solicit new business?
    g. How did you determine your accounting procedures?
       _____ cash
       _____ accrual
    h. Does bookkeeping and accounting take more time than anticipated? Yes _____ No _____
    i. Who does it?
       _____ self
       _____ paid accountant
       _____ family members

40. Do your consulting activities interfere with your home and family life? How?

41. Has consulting changed your earlier work habits? How?

Key Interview Questions

(These questions helped form the framework of interviews with consultants, although digressions were frequent and informative.)

1. How would you describe the consulting that you do?
2. How many years have you been consulting?
3. Did you begin your career as a consultant? (If not, what was the nature of your earlier experience in science that led you to consulting?)
4. Why did you become a consultant (financial, independence, maximizing qualifications and experience, active career goals)?
5. If you were beginning a scientific career now, would you prefer academic, government, industrial research, or self-employment (consulting or entrepreneur in high-tech venture)?
6. Is your scientific consulting rewarding in areas other than financial? (If so, how?)
7. Is keeping current with new developments or new instrumentation ever a problem for you? How do you maintain scientific expertise?
8. Do your results ever conflict with results expected by clients? (If so, how do you resolve such a problem?)

9. What, in your opinion, are some key factors in successful consulting?
10. Could you describe for us any unethical actions of consultants who are your competitors?
11. Are there other aspects of scientific consulting that should be discussed here—as being useful to future consultants?
12. Could you describe for us some of your most memorable experiences in consulting—either good or bad, positive or negative, successes or failures?

Consulting from the Perspective of Practitioners

A SUMMARY OF QUESTIONNAIRE RESPONSES

Early in the planning phases of this book, we realized that a standardized list of questions would be a good source of information, particularly if respondents could remain anonymous. The list turned out to be quite long (see Appendix 1) but we used it anyway—with very satisfying results.

Much of the material from the individual responses has been digested and then assimilated into the various chapters of the book, but we thought that, for added emphasis, it might also be summarized separately. This has been done in Appendix 3, clustering the summaries into major subject matter areas—as a kind of book within a book. Some early reviewers of the manuscript wanted greater visibility for the information, beyond a restricted place in an appendix, but we did it our way.

THE NEW CONSULTING VENTURE

THE NEW CONSULTANT

The aspiring consultant must sometimes make an early decision as to whether to start a career as a consultant, or instead to gain some practical working experience first. Most of the consultants who responded to our questionnaire suggested that consulting should be considered as a career *after* the individual has earned a reputation and has become established in his chosen professional discipline. The exception might be an individual whose *first* experience was as an *employee* of a large and well-known consulting firm and who then moved up the management or corporate ladder. The choice as to whether one should enter consulting as a profession often depends largely on individual circumstances. Caution is particularly important for those who plan to invest their savings as start-up funds for a new consultancy. Most successful consultants are those who have already achieved stature in their profession and have adequate personal contacts with potential clients. As pointed out by one of our respondents: "The successful consultant must have multiple capabilities, including good communication skills and experience in problem solving." The individual who begins a career in consulting must have solid technical credentials, self-confidence, communication skills, and effective person-to-person relationships. An equally important consideration is timing—how much demand is there currently for the specialty of the individual? Our respondents were in general agreement that consulting is a highly specialized profession in which successful individuals most often have proven track records in their areas of expertise and have both marketing skills and good business sense.

STRUCTURE AND FINANCES OF CONSULTING

The new consulting organization may be chartered as a C corporation, sub S corporation, partnership, limited partnership, nonprofit organization, or the individual practitioner may want to be considered self-employed. Each type of organization has its own advantages and disadvantages, making it essential that the individual seek professional advice from the outset. The charter is the first requirement for establishing a new business. It is a legal document that spells out the articles of incorporation and bylaws and must be approved by both state and federal agencies. We cannot emphasize the importance of this document too strongly; it contains rules and procedures that govern the operation of the new venture. Changes in government regulations, accounting procedures, hiring practices, and so forth are all highly regulated by state and federal agencies and often require interpretation by accountants and lawyers. The choice of an organizational structure depends largely on the number of officers or partners, the present and projected size of the organization, the number of full- or part-time employees, whether there will be a stock issue, and whether there will be a board of directors.

Once the organizational structure has been determined, some allowance must be made for growth. It is not unusual for a small family-owned business to have a humble beginning and eventually grow into a large organization. Initially, the small business may begin with a core of family members, add a few part-time workers, and then develop into a full-scale operation. Early on, it may be desirable to employ on an "on call" basis individuals such as retired persons, college students, or subcontractors. The advantage of having a list of "on call" specialists is that they are not employees—so they do not increase overhead costs or space requirements. Respondents in our study ranged from individuals with no employees to large companies with staffs of 100 to 400 people. The largest companies or corporations had offices throughout the United States as well as in foreign countries. The important point here is not to underestimate the potential for growth, and to change the company structure as necessary.

When the firm has been established and is ready to

open its doors for business, a system of billing clients must be determined. Charges may be based on an hourly rate, a cost-plus profit margin, or a fixed cost basis. The system must also be flexible enough to encourage an award when proposals are submitted on the basis of competitive bidding. When the company is just getting started it may be necessary to forego some profit so as to be a successful bidder and to obtain contracts that are needed to demonstrate the capabilities of the firm. It is not unusual for a small business to be turned down for a contract in excess of $100,000, but this can be offset by seeking work on a smaller scale. The small consulting venture business might, for example, succeed at getting ten contracts for $10,000 each, with profits based on $100,000 worth of business. The well-established consulting firm may have an advantage over the new individual entrepreneur, but this can be overcome over the long term by producing a superior product at a reasonable cost. The extreme example is the consultant who works in a highly specialized area with few competitors. That person fits the story about the consultant who was asked about her hourly fees. Her response was "ten dollars an hour more than anyone else; some clients think I'm better than anyone else in my field." Such a reputation is a luxury enjoyed by very few consultants!

CLIENT SOURCES

Most of the consultants whom we have contacted began their careers in either academic institutions or private industry. Almost without exception, they have recommended consulting as a career *after* having gained experience in a professional discipline. The consultant *must* have a skill, or have earned a reputation, in an area for which there is a continuing demand. The enterprising new consultant should have already established a list of potential clients, preferably through personal contacts and acquaintances, and know how to market his expertise. Consultants may respond to public announcements, requests for bids, and the like, but one of the surest ways to succeed is to develop a reputation for having produced high-quality results, and for submitting reports and analyses on a timely basis—and at reasonable cost. Business opportunities can also result from circulating an attractive brochure or newsletter that provides information on the organization, its staff, and its areas of expertise.

ORIGINS AND MOTIVATIONS OF CONSULTANTS

Most of the consultants we contacted did not begin their careers as consultants, and were instead equally divided between academia and the private sector. They generally agreed that skills should be developed and a reputation earned before attempting to market one's capabilities. More than half of our respondents had been in the consulting business for ten years or more and had specific goals in mind before becoming consultants. The most common reasons for becoming consultants were:

- Freedom to work as an individual
- Opportunities to maximize qualifications and expertise
- Professional growth
- Achieve career goals
- Financial well-being

One career objective of most consultants was to obtain job freedom and to utilize creative skills—all adding up to job satisfaction!

JOYS AND SORROWS

Entering a new business venture risks disappointment and frustration. Perhaps one of the biggest changes in lifestyle is the lack of a fixed hourly workweek. Unexpected delays in getting paid, unexpected deadlines, travel—all enter into the daily life of the consultant. Demands by clients, some unreasonable though paying well, may interfere with home life and family activities. However, job satisfaction and financial rewards may offset some of the negative aspects of a career as a consultant. Work habits as an "independent" income earner, rather than as an employee, are certain to lead to substantial changes in lifestyle, family responsibilities, and free time. Consultants enjoy having control over their activities, the freedom to make decisions, meet challenges, and produce meaningful work. However, success is determined largely by earning a reputation for reliability and integrity—characteristics that often come at a high price but lead to personal satisfaction.

REALITIES OF A CONSULTING PRACTICE

SPECIALTY AREAS

Success as a solo consultant is largely dependent on the skills and resources of the individual to respond to new demands for services. Science, in particular, has experienced logarithmic growth in almost every facet of human activity—ranging from land use to occupational safety to biomedical research. Almost every aspect of human life is subject to regulation, and compliance with rules and regulations. Today's world offers an opportunity for individuals with creative talents to enter into some form of consulting activity. One area of rather spectacular growth has been the protection of our natural resources—a topic that has extended into the classroom at all levels of education. Opportunities now exist for consultants to develop educational materials ranging from coloring books to college-level texts, to help land developers comply with extensive regulations concerning residential and industrial development to fulfill the requirements of environmental impact statements, and to participate in courtroom hearings. Global concern for the environment has provided opportunities for the established consultant to work with both foreign and local governments as well as special interest groups.

FINANCIAL MANAGEMENT

One of the biggest problems that many consultants must face from time to time is failure of clients to pay promptly. Financial problems often arise when the consultant fails to keep an adequate cash reserve to cover expenses when business is slow or when payments for contract work are late. At other times the consultant may not have money in reserve to work on a project when payment is to be made on completion of the work. One common practice, especially in long-term projects, is to receive payment on a "percentage completion" basis. The consultant may require a portion of the funding on acceptance of the proposal with invoices to be submitted at predetermined intervals. This kind of practice is employed by home builders or home improvement contractors and should be considered by consultants—especially by individual consultants or small firms. Money management is a skill and represents one area where the consultant must have good communication skills and a good head for business. Just as the home builder must be able to pay for construction materials and employees wages before the completion of the work, so the consultant must prepare for similar contingencies to avoid problems with cash flow. Overhead expenses must be met on a timely basis. Care must also be taken when a project depends on work performed by subcontractors or input from other consultants. The successful consultant chooses such firms or individuals on the basis of their past performance. Poor performance or delays in completing terms of an agreement can be embarrassing and jeopardize the reputation of an otherwise successful individual or firm. The success or failure of consultant "business" is equally dependent on the ability of the individual to provide a service for which there is a need and at the same time to possess the financial and management skills that ensure a successful venture.

SUBCONTRACTS

The senior consultant in a sole proprietorship organization has primary responsibility for managing and directing a project. Successful consulting, however, often depends on the ability to work on a wide range of activities—even those beyond the training and skills of that key individual. Success then depends almost exclusively on the wise choice of individuals or firms as subcontractors. Most of our respondents stated they have a complement of highly skilled individuals or organizations that may be contacted for cost estimates to be included in their proposals. Large firms with a staff of trained professionals often maintain up-to-date lists of individuals and organizations with expertise that is not available within their own organizations. Depending on the nature of a proposal, work carried out by outside firms may be subject to management fees. This type of activity allows the prime contractor to charge a percentage of the costs for managing and overseeing the work performed by subcontractors.

UNUSUAL FINANCIAL AGREEMENTS

Consulting activities do not ordinarily require the consultant to have proprietary interests or sign royalty and profit agreements with clients. When such a situation does occur, a lawyer should be retained to examine the documents and discuss their terms with all interested parties.

CONFIDENTIALITY

The successful consultant must have a reputation for maintaining the privacy requirements of a client. This may involve signing confidentiality statements and ensuring that other members of the firm understand and comply with the stated requirements. There may be occasions when a conflict exists for the consulting firm providing services to individuals or organizations. For example, environmental consultants might be involved with clients seeking to develop residential or commercial property but who are opposed by conservation or land preservation groups. Financial need may put the consultant into the position of representing the developers although he or she may have personal ties with the conservationists. When such a conflict arises the consultant must respect confidentiality agreements and not discuss the matter with *anyone*—especially not with friends, relatives, or others in the community. In general, it is wise to consider all aspects of a project before signing such agreements.

CONFLICTS OF INTEREST

Financial and ethical concerns may influence whether a consultant is willing to work on projects where the findings may conflict with his or her personal interests. About half of our respondents stated they would provide services regardless of such a conflict. The determining element here is whether or not the consultant is "business oriented" to the point that personal feelings do not enter into the decision-making process. Conflicts today are fairly common when issues concern protecting the environment, conserving natural resources, and managing environmental pollution. In a hypothetical situation a consultant who is an avid hunter or fisherman might hear that plans are in progress to clear a prime sporting area for development. The environmentalists will want to preserve the area, and be opposed by those who insist that development is needed to create jobs and to increase local government revenues. In such a situation the consultant may be approached for services by those supporting development. What if there is an attractive financial package for his services? A consultant who is financially secure may decline the offer and may even put forth some effort to stop the project. On the other hand, if financial need exists, the consultant may have to do some soul-searching before declining the opportunity. The question as to whether or not to accept projects that conflict with the personal interests of the consultant cannot be answered empirically; it depends on the situation or circumstances existing at the time that a decision must be made.

USE AND ABUSE OF DATA

There are times when the consultant cannot afford to be thin-skinned or overly sensitive about controversial issues—especially in courtrooms or at public hearings. Situations do occur in which reports prepared by consulting firms may be misquoted or misinterpreted by others. About half of our respondents stated there had been occasions when individuals presented themselves as authorities by using reports and information prepared by others. Perhaps even more significant were our findings that information provided by consultants may be totally ignored for political, social, or economic reasons. Instances where the consultant may feel ignored, insulted, or otherwise offended are most apt to occur when issues are of a confrontational nature involving lawyers and expert witnesses. [One of the best examples we know of concerned a long-running battle over the pros and cons of the disposal of wastes in the ocean. When a government agency (EPA) refused to issue ocean dumping permits because of potential harm to fish and shellfish, public hearings were held to discuss problems that would be faced by several large East Coast cities with no other means of waste disposal. Testimony that was presented failed to offer a solution and the final decision to continue ocean waste disposal on an interim basis had to be made in a courtroom. The hearing provided an unusual opportunity to listen to consultants, researchers, bureaucrats, and lawyers on both sides of the issue attempt to discredit one another. The amazing feature of the unfolding drama, to those of us in the courtroom, was that *both sides were using the same data sets, but were reaching very different conclusions.*]

WHEN THE CONSULTANT DISAGREES

Consultants are usually hired by clients who expect positive results! How does the consultant handle a situation where results are contrary to those expected by the client? Most of our respondents stated they had experienced this type of situation, but, unfortunately, did not elaborate on their handling of the problem. Conflicts of interest are not uncommon in today's world, especially in matters involving land use and urban sprawl, health care, education, or financial matters. Findings or recommendations of the consultant that are contrary to the expectations of the client must be supported by strong documentation and defensible arguments—not speculation or the personal opinions of the consultant. Whether or not the client will accept such findings probably depends largely on the reputation and credibility of the consultant or the consulting firm.

DEPLOYMENT OF PROFESSIONAL TIME

Depending on the amount of business being done by consultants, most of the workday is often spent writing proposals for new projects, or preparing final reports for clients. Time distribution, however, varies with the size of the organization, the number of employees, and the extent to which other individuals are capable of assuming responsibility. Meeting with clients, attending conferences or workshops, and time spent in the field are important elements in establishing a reputation and are essential aspects of the life of the consultant, but just how much time is spent in these pursuits also varies with the size of the organization. A small business may require the consultant to spend most of his time collecting field samples, conducting laboratory analyses, responding to telephone inquiries, and so forth—often leading to a considerable investment of time. However, despite this requirement, most consultants find their work financially rewarding; they enjoy utilizing their professional skills, and sometimes having important input to decisions made by clients. If the choice could be made to start a career over again, we were surprised to learn from the questionnaire responses that most consultants would *not* choose a career working for state or federal agencies. This unifying characteristic suggests to us that most successful consultants place a high value on freedom to work independently and utilize their skills, talents, and professional time to the maximum.

QUALITY ASSURANCE

One has only to look at catalogs, trade journals, and scientific publications to be overwhelmed by the "explosion" of new products available today. The scientific consultant must keep up-to-date on new developments in technology and instrumentation so as to maintain a "state of the art" reputation in his or her area of specialization. Almost half of our respondents reported having the need to modify or change their approach to a problem when a project advanced from the concept stage to actual operation. Just how difficult and time-consuming it may be to stay on top of new developments depends largely on the type of services provided by the consultant. One pitfall that may face the new consultant is accepting work from a client who routinely uses a quality assurance program to critique his or her final reports from consultants. The experienced consultant will ask the client whether or not a quality assurance review is required, and, if so, a copy of the review plan should be studied thoroughly prior to starting work on the project. Quality assurance requirements must be thoroughly understood, especially in projects where fieldwork or sample collection is required. For example, one of our projects had quality assurance specifications for keeping a daily log of when and where samples were collected, following an established procedure for labeling or coding individual samples, and signing appropriate change of custody forms when samples changed hands. There were also requirements for employing approved or standardized methods for processing samples. Some consulting contracts specify whether data or information on a particular topic require interpretation by the consultant. When interpretations or conclusions are required they must be valid and not include statements based on speculation or personal opinion.

One example of the training and communication skills required by a consultant before entering into complex projects is that of studies on air quality For projects involving indoor air quality, there exist extensive guidelines concerning use of standardized methods. By contrast, there are acceptable methods but not standardized ones for outdoor air sampling. In the latter case, temperature, solar radiation, changes in wind speed and direction, and air pollution must be considered—just to mention a few of the variables not encountered when sampling indoor air. In projects of this type, it is imperative that discussions be held with the client to decide on an approach that is acceptable to all parties. Large consulting firms often have a highly trained staff to participate in complex projects, whereas the individual or small firm may have limitations in the expertise available. In this case, the consultant should not rush to sign an agreement without doing his homework. Problems can be avoided, but not necessarily eliminated, by effective communication with the client and perhaps other consultants involved in the project.

Highlights of
Survey Findings

Examination of responses to our questionnaires, and the percentages of similar replies to individual items, enabled us to reach a number of conclusions about scientific consulting—recognizing some of the limitations of the data (one being a sampling emphasis on environmental consulting, which we feel is warranted as it is probably the most heavily populated consulting specialty area at present). Additionally, we have taken very seriously the comments made in the margins of the questionnaires by many of the respondents. These comments greatly augmented information that could be gained by simply following the format as designed.

We have assembled the following list of commonalities and general conclusions from our examination of the questionnaire responses:

- Use of personal funds and/or bank loans is the most common way of starting a consulting business.
- Consulting firms may or may not have a charter, but if they do, it is usually prepared with legal assistance.
- Initial contracts most often come from direct solicitation or word-of-mouth advertising.

- Most clients of scientific consultants are federal or state governments, private industry, or other consultants (as sources of subcontracts).
- Most consultants come from an earlier academic background, followed by those who worked previously in industrial research. Smaller percentages had worked previously for federal or state government agencies.
- Most contracts result from personal contacts and from referrals—so the consultant's reputation is vital.
- A well-planned and informative company brochure is considered essential.
- Most consultants (60%) did not begin their careers in consulting; experience and reputations were acquired in other kinds of science.
- Scientists usually become consultants for financial reasons; most also want freedom and independence, maximum utilization of skills, and opportunities to meet career goals.
- A majority of consultants spend most of their time on technical work and writing proposals and reports; very little time is spent at professional meetings, and the amount of travel fluctuates widely with the nature of the project, but is frequently very high.
- Most consultants recommend that new professionals start in academia or private industry. Many entry-level professionals prefer self-employment, but they recognize that they must first get established professionally and must build scientific reputations.
- Consultants find their work rewarding financially; they also find satisfaction in being able to utilize their talents and training. They take a personal

interest in their work, and usually feel that they make an impact on clients' decisions.

- Many consultants work on an hourly rate basis, whereas others use a fixed cost basis, or enter into competitive bidding. Still others use a cost plus basis. Competitive bidding requires the most skill, and a prior knowledge of cost determination methods used by the competition.
- Confidentiality agreements are required by most employers, and the work that consultants do should be and usually is kept confidential.
- Employees of consulting firms usually do not have a proprietary interest in company projects.
- Most employers do not provide royalties for employees, or profit sharing (unless a profit-sharing retirement plan exists).
- Most consultants, as well as many employees, of consulting companies assume primary responsibility for their professional activities.
- Almost all employees of consulting firms participate in a broad range of activities; those with a narrow range are usually those who provide a highly specialized service (e.g., chemical analyses, pathology).
- Consultants are sometimes required to make statements or offer opinions that are contrary to their personal feelings. Their employees must sometimes accept decisions with which they do not agree.
- Findings reported to clients may be misrepresented by the clients when used in making decisions. Half of our respondents identify this as a problem.
- Consultants' findings are often ignored for political or other reasons; about 65% of our respondents

have had this experience, so consultants can't be too sensitive about rejection.

- Consultants sometimes agree to work on a problem only to find that the methods to be employed do not work. This is a common problem today because of rapidly changing technology.
- Keeping up with advances in instrumentation and technology can present a challenge—depending on the nature of the specialties of the consultancy.
- Consulting operations may vary as to whether work is carried out by the company or by subcontractors. Successful operations often do both.
- Work performed for clients does not always satisfy their needs. This is a major problem in consulting today, especially when it comes to controversial issues such as land use (e.g., shopping malls, marinas, housing developments, industries).
- Getting paid on time is a major problem, especially when overhead expenses are high and cash reserves are low. Also, maintaining a continuous flow of work—smoothing the peaks and valleys—is of continuing managerial concern.
- Small consulting firms may or may not have a board of directors, but a board made up of people with credentials always looks good to prospective clients.
- Consulting for foreign governments or corporations may be difficult at times because of inadequate communications, or philosophical or ethnic differences.
- Consultants frequently encounter clients who claim personal expertise because of services they have purchased; some clients use findings of consultants to overstate their own knowledge of a subject.

- Stress varies depending on demands placed on consultants. The job situation, as reported by our respondents, ranges from "highly stressful" to "not much of a problem." Stress often comes from meeting short deadlines, too much travel, or complexity and difficulties of problems.

Undoubtedly there are other useful conclusions and observations lurking in the questionnaire responses, but we'll settle for these. Standard forms have value in supplying limited quantitative information, but we have found that structured interviews and conversations with consultants have contributed more to an understanding of their universe. The book, then, is an amalgam of data and interpretations from these varied sources. We are reasonably confident that it approximates reality.

Service Corps of Retired Executives (SCORE)

SCORE is an association made up of over 13,000 retired business owners or managers (some still work) who volunteer their services and expertise to assist individuals interested in going into business for themselves. It is an organization sponsored by the Small Business Administration. Volunteers serve as counselors who meet with individuals to identify business problems, and offer solutions. Workshops, offered for a small fee, are held periodically to take the prospective businessperson through all of the steps involved in setting up a business—including putting together a checklist, seeking legal advice, establishing a business plan, and obtaining start-up funds. Other services include making a market analysis, determining the best way to advertise services and expertise, and expanding a business. At no cost, counselors will meet with the prospective businessperson individually, listen to ideas for starting up a business, and provide expert advice on how to succeed. Counselors are individuals who have had successful careers as owners of their own small business, or careers as company or corporate executives.

We cannot overemphasize the importance of seeking expert advice when setting up an individual business, whether as a career move, a part-time endeavor, or a retirement activity. According to the Small Business Administration there were 52,256 bankruptcies, 71,520 failures, and 803,127 terminations among approximately 22 million small businesses in 1994. An analysis of business failures showed that among companies creating up to four jobs, 6% were dissolved during the first 2 years, 19.6% after 4 years, 23.5% after 6 years, and 46.5% after 8 years. The prospective consultant probably does not have to be concerned about these figures as they represent all types of small businesses, ranging from at-home businesses to manufacturing, food service, construction companies, retailers, and technology-based organizations. The bottom line, however, is that every individual aspiring to become an individual entrepreneur must have a solid background in how to operate a new venture in a businesslike manner. Organizations such as SCORE are a valuable source of free information on the "do's" and "don'ts" when planning and organizing a new business venture. SCORE volunteers are organized into more than 400 local chapters throughout the United States. Information on the nearest office may be obtained by contacting the National SCORE Office, 409 3rd Street, SW, Washington, DC 20024 (toll-free number 800-634-0245).

The Business Card

One of the first steps before opening the doors of a new consultancy is to design a business card—along with a professional-looking letterhead for your stationery. Both items are essential for getting the attention of clients. The business card should have a logo printed in a color that contrasts well with the background. A medically oriented business might use a caduceus, an international consultancy a globe, or an environmental specialist a wading bird such as an egret or heron. This form of advertising is inexpensive and is essential for increasing the credibility of a firm. A cheap or unattractive business card is soon laid aside and forgotten.

We retell a classical example of a business card leading to unexpected and unsolicited business. John McDermott had been standing in line at a local supermarket when he heard a husband and wife voicing their frustration over a gasoline leak at their service station. They were required to close the station until all local and federal environmental and safety requirements could be met. The owners were overwhelmed at the "bureaucratic" list of items requiring approval for the safety inspection. John apologized for overhearing their conversation, handed them a business card, and explained that his company specialized in environmental clean-ups. He gave them an estimate at no cost and they soon asked for a contract. John's experience in the grocery store is only one of many examples of how the business card may lead to unsolicited and unexpected financial gain for the consultant.

How many times do we enter a restaurant or other place of business and see a jar from which business cards are drawn for a free meal or other item? We, at Rescon Associates, placed our card in a jar at an office supply store where a set of Samsonite luggage would be given to the winner. The winning card was ours, and whenever we pack for a trip, we are reminded of the value of a business card.

Business cards also are useful for jotting down reminders—to send a brochure, return a phone call, or remember other important items of conversation with individuals or potential clients. Over the years, we have amassed a sizable collection of business cards of all shapes and colors. Those that are simple and unattractive and do not call attention to the individual or nature of the business or consultancy, are soon discarded.

Index